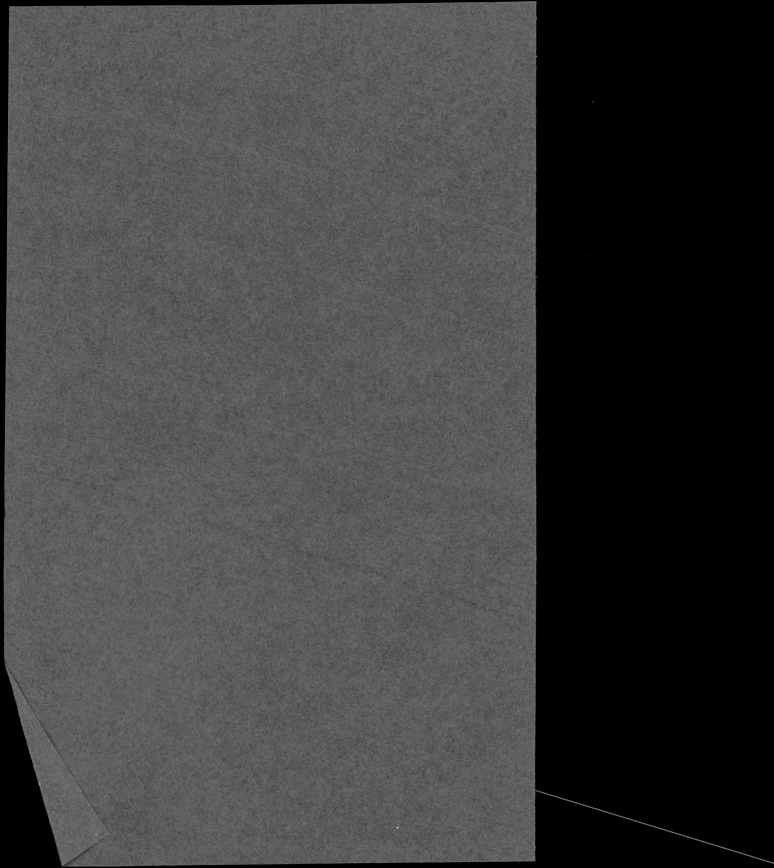

A WOMAN'S WORDS:
EMER AND FEMALE SPEECH IN THE ULSTER CYCLE

JOANNE FINDON

A Woman's Words: Emer and Female Speech in the Ulster Cycle

UNIVERSITY OF TORONTO PRESS
Toronto Buffalo London

© University of Toronto Press Incorporated 1997
Toronto Buffalo London
Printed in Canada

ISBN 0-8020-0865-8

Printed on acid-free paper

Canadian Cataloguing in Publication Data

Findon, Joanne, 1957–
A woman's words

Includes bibliographical references and index.
ISBN 0-8020-0865-8

1. Emer (Legendary character).   2. Epic literature,
Irish – History and criticism.   3. Tales, Medieval –
History and criticism.   4. Women in literature.
I. Title.

PB1397.C8F55 1997   891.6′231   C97-930008-8

University of Toronto Press acknowledges the financial assistance to its
publishing program of the Canada Council and the Ontario Arts Council.

This book has been published with the help of a grant from the Humanities
and Social Sciences Federation of Canada, using funds provided by the
Social Sciences and Humanities Research Council of Canada.

For Steve

Contents

Acknowledgments

Many people deserve thanks for their enthusiastic support of this project. I would like especially to thank Ann Dooley, without whose generous advice and constant assistance this study would never have been completed. I am also indebted to David Klausner, Mary Nyquist, David Townsend, Linda Hutcheon, Margaret Sinex, and the members of the Medieval Studies Work in Progress Circle at the Centre for Medieval Studies for their insightful comments and helpful suggestions.

I am also grateful to Harry Roe and Máirín Ní Dhonnchadha for their generous help with the translations of some difficult passages.

Finally, I am deeply indebted to my husband, Steve Riddle, for his constant support and encouragement.

An earlier version of chapter 3 first appeared as 'A Woman's Words: Emer versus Cú Chulainn in *Aided Óenfir Aífe*,' in *Ulidia: Proceedings of the First International Conference on the Ulster Cycle of Tales, Belfast and Emain Macha, 8–12 April, 1994* (Belfast: December Publications, 1994): 139–48.

Preface

The medieval Irish texts considered in this study are likely to be unfamiliar to many readers. Although a detailed summary of each text is given in the relevant chapters, those who prefer to have a complete translation at hand may wish to use Jeffrey Gantz's *Early Irish Myths and Sagas*, or Cross and Slover's *Ancient Irish Tales*. Thomas Kinsella's translation of the *Táin* also includes translations (often abbreviated) of some of the other Ulster Cycle tales, including *The Wooing of Emer* and *The Death of Aífe's Only Son*. While none of these collections provides definitive translations of the tales, they are certainly adequate for the non-specialist and have the advantage of being widely available in bookstores and libraries.

Throughout this study, citations in Irish are taken from the most recent editions of the texts. Translations of passages from the four main tales discussed here are my own. In the case of citations from other 'intertexts,' a translation by the editor will be cited if available and satisfactory; otherwise, I provide my own translation.

The Irish titles of texts referred to are translated and subsequently referred to by their English names. The one exception is the *Táin*, which is now so well known by that title that there seems no necessity to impose the rather long and awkward English equivalent upon the reader.

Abbreviations

CIH	*Corpus Iuris Hibernici*
CMCS	*Cambridge Medieval Celtic Studies*
DIAS	Dublin Institute for Advanced Studies
DIL	Dictionary of the Irish Language
LU	Lebor na Huidre
PRIA	Publications of the Royal Irish Academy
RIA	Royal Irish Academy
SEIL	*Studies in Early Irish Law*
ZCP	*Zeitschrift für celtische Philologie*

A WOMAN'S WORDS

Introduction

This study began as a quest for a method of reading female figures in medieval Irish prose texts which did not depend on the assumption that a submerged pre-Christian goddess lurked beneath their 'human' skins. I was particularly interested in finding a strategy for reading Emer, the wife of the great hero Cú Chulainn, a woman whose strength and verbal prowess on the one hand and lack of discernible supernatural traits on the other set her apart from many other female characters in the early Irish tradition. It soon became clear, however, that the issues raised by such a project extended far beyond the problems of Celtic Studies and into an area which concerns feminist critics of medieval and modern literature alike: how to read the representation of female characters in male-authored texts.

The explosion of scholarly work on medieval women in the past two decades provided a critical context for my inquiry. This increasingly extensive body of scholarship has opened up many new vistas, shattering old assumptions and highlighting new problems of interpretation. Yet still there are no easy answers, and the problems of female representation must be tackled text by text, author by author. Some strategies which work well for the analysis of modern works fail miserably when applied to medieval texts. And even among feminist critics there are disagreements about how we should read women created by male authors in light of the overwhelming structures and assumptions of patriarchal discourse. How might the student of medieval Irish texts negotiate this labyrinth of criticism and discover a strategy for reading a female protagonist of the Ulster Cycle tales?[1]

Women in Medieval Literature

Much of the recent work in medieval women's studies has tended to concentrate on English and Continental women from the late medieval period, although discussions of texts from the twelfth century are becoming more common. Clearly, there are good reasons for this focus on material from the twelfth century onward: there is relatively more information from this period about both the authors and their audiences, and the authors of texts are more likely to be named and identifiable. The works of Chrétien de Troyes and Chaucer, for instance, have received intensive study and critique from many different feminist perspectives.[2] The roster of late medieval authors even includes a few women, including Marie de France, Christine de Pizan, Hildegard of Bingen, and Margery Kempe. Such female authors present especially exciting and fruitful subjects for feminist critics, since they can be seen to encode a distinctively female view of their world.[3]

Some of the most intriguing work has focused on analysing the representation of women's speech in male-authored texts. Here, feminist scholars often disagree as to what extent the words of women actually embody a feminine perspective, since these words have literally been put into the women's mouths by their authors. Modern feminist theory has shown how a woman in a male-authored text tends to be constructed as absence, as Other, and as the ground upon which male concerns are constructed.[4] She tends to be depicted as the object rather than the subject of the narrative, reflecting the projected desires and fears of the male author and his audience rather than her own.[5] Perhaps most importantly, such a female character is usually denied the position of 'speaking subject' in the text, and when she does speak she often produces mere chatter instead of meaningful discourse.[6] If this is true, one must ask whether a woman's voice can ever be her own in such a text. Can a male author ever write a woman who is 'subject' of her own story? Even Chaucer, an author who has long enjoyed the approval of modern scholars for his ability to create 'lifelike' women, has come in for heavy criticism of late from critics who claim, with Elaine Tuttle Hansen, that in his texts

through the construction of notorious, ambiguous, 'lifelike' female characters like the Wife [of Bath], the problems and anxieties of (masculine) identity are strategically displaced onto Woman; and women are fixed in the text at least in opposition, silence, and difference.[7]

The reader of the male-authored text must therefore be aware of such problems.

Of course, certain genres are more overtly misogynistic in their representation of women's speech than others. In the Old French *fabliaux*, for instance, women's words are repeatedly condemned as excessive, deceitful, and manipulative; bad women are represented as garrulous while the good women are those who remain silent. Recent studies of female speech in Old French literature has highlighted the overwhelming presence of a misogynistic discourse which asserts or implies 'a fundamental belief that women are able manipulators of language and that their skill can only be construed as threatening to established order.'[8] This prejudice against female speech is supported by a vast corpus of non-literary texts, including the writings of many of the Church Fathers, dating from late Antiquity and through the Middle Ages.[9]

At the same time, other works represent female speech in more ambiguous ways, and allow for more subtly nuanced readings. In some of these, the perceptive reader can see in the words of women a critique of the contemporary social landscape, and even of its particularly male norms. In many cases such a critique seems deliberately embedded in the text by the author. Joan Ferrante, for instance, argues that the authors of some French courtly romances use realistic females as foils for male characters in order to question the male fantasies on which the romance genre is based.[10] Jeanie Watson's study of Enid's disobedient speech in the Middle Welsh tale *Gereint ac Enid* produces a similarly subversive reading, as does Patrick McConeghy's discussion of Hartmann von Aue's version of the same tale.[11] Even in the more overtly misogynistic depictions of women, an embedded resistance can often be discerned; that is, the women in these texts seem to challenge the very stereotypes that seek to constrain them. Burns argues in an examination of the *fabliaux* that the female voices in these texts

issue from a position lodged in between the stereotypical oppositions of phallic/ non-phallic, logos/silence, rational head/irrational head ... thereby calling into question the very logic used to structure portraits of femininity in the texts they inhabit.[12]

By challenging the expectations that cluster around the standard male/ female oppositions, women in these texts can emerge as ambiguous figures who express a subtle critique of the rigid assumptions of standard male discourse. While one could argue that such women are ultimately employed to encode an exploration of male anxieties, they at least allow for an opening up of the text to multiple readings by members of both sexes in the audience.

If the texts of the twelfth century onward – with their more verifiable social contexts and numerous named authors – pose problems for the reading of women, the earlier, largely anonymous texts, which were clearly reshaped by a series of writers, are even more problematic. The literature written in Old English, Old Norse, Middle Welsh, and Middle Irish presents a host of problems for modern readers, and for feminist critics in particular. Not only do these texts usually lack identifiable authors, but in many cases the social context in which they took shape remains remote and elusive. These texts present female characters who may have originally been created within the oral story-telling traditions of pre-literate cultures; at the very least, their stories were written down and reshaped by men within a Christian monastic setting. Perhaps most frustrating, in most cases no single author can be credited with molding the final forms of these texts. As a result, they may contain several layers, each of which was shaped to address the concerns of a particular cultural moment. While in some instances a case can be made for a text's composition by a woman, or for its composition for a largely female audience, these texts do not provide a *verifiably* female view of the world.

On the other hand, some would argue that the idea of a text's *author-(ity)* is a trap for feminist criticism, and that in fact an approach which posits what Roland Barthes called 'the death of the Author' is more appropriate.[13] This strategy views each text as a complex, multivalent construct which must be 'disentangled' rather than explained, and refuses to accept the notion that once its author has been identified the text is somehow automatically decoded.[14] Such an approach is liberating for the reader of early medieval texts, as it allows for multiple readings and a dissection of meaning which must remain provisional.

In recent years a number of scholars have begun to focus on the representation of women in these early texts. A good deal of work has now been done on women in Old English literature. A collection of essays entitled *New Readings on Women in Old English Literature* provides an introduction to feminist approaches in Old English, and includes both historical and literary perspectives.[15] Gillian Overing's *Language, Sign and Gender in Beowulf* is a particularly important study for its exploration of women's speech in that poem.[16] Jane Chance's illuminating analysis of female heroes sheds new light on the most common images of Anglo-Saxon women as either chaste and heroic, or married and passive.[17] Barrie Ruth Straus's ground-breaking application of speech act theory to 'The Wife's Lament' is another significant contribution.[18] A number of essays on the Welsh material have also appeared in the last decade, including Watson's study of Enid (noted above) and Roberta Valente's discussion of gender slippage in the Fourth Branch of the *Mabinogi*.[19] At the same time, Old Norse literature has finally begun to attract the attention it deserves. The numerous studies by Carol Clover and Jenny Jochens have opened up many new avenues of discussion,[20] and Judith Jesch's *Women in the Viking Age* is particularly adept in its subjection of the saga texts to literary analysis from a feminist perspective.[21] And in her latest book, Margaret Clunies Ross places gender issues in Old Norse myths within the context of northern medieval society.[22] While demonstrating how women remain in some sense trapped within the confines of their cultures, all of these studies also probe the ways in which these figures can push at the boundaries of the social norms which construct them.

But what of the Irish texts of the early Middle Ages? How are women represented in the vast corpus of medieval Irish literature? How and when do these female characters speak? Are they mere mouthpieces for a patriarchal discourse?

On the one hand, many medieval Irish tales seem striking for their portrayal of strong, active women who have much to say. This characteristic has long impressed modern readers. The Ulster Cycle narratives seem at first glance to be very male-centred texts, focused almost obsessively upon combat and slaughter. Yet they also contain a variety of female figures, both mortal and immortal, who play important roles in the tales. In the introduction to his translation of *Táin Bó Cúailgne* (*The Cattle Raid of Cooley*), Thomas Kinsella remarks, 'Probably the greatest achievement of the *Táin* and the Ulster cycle is the series of women, some in full scale and some in miniature, on whose strong and diverse personalities the action continually turns.'[23] Such an apparent interest in the representation of women is surprising given the aggressively heroic concerns of these narratives.

On the other hand, some of these same Irish texts ultimately appear to censure such female behaviour, thereby aligning themselves with the wider misogynistic discourse endemic in the European Middle Ages. The *Táin*, with its portrayal of the fiery queen Medb as a disastrous warleader, is only the most obvious example.[24] For Medb, as for other women, an active role proves to be a double-edged sword. The power to act is offset by the ultimate censure of her actions.

Yet in other works, women remain free to act and to speak their minds without suffering any adverse consequences. Emer is perhaps the most well-developed example of this type of female protagonist. Throughout the Ulster Cycle stories she acts and speaks in many different situations. Significantly, her heroic husband chooses her as his bride *because* she is so highly skilled with words. How do we read such a woman? And how might the medieval hearers or readers of these texts have 'read' her? Does she owe her independence to some archaic and half-forgotten conception of the pagan goddess, or to the lives of 'real women' in early medieval Ireland?

Is There a Woman in This Text?

Until recently, it has been common among many scholars of Celtic literature to assume that the strength and prominence of female characters in these texts must represent the residue of an earlier mythic discourse. This has led to a disproportionate emphasis on mythological analysis of various sorts, from the quest for reflections of identifiable pre-Christian deities in literary figures, to the search for traces of cultural paradigms in narrative patterns.[25] These ideas have been highly influential in the interpretation of medieval Celtic, and particularly Irish, narratives.[26] Yet in many cases they continue to privilege the mythic paradigms discernible in the narrative over the narrative itself.[27] Thus, the quest for survivals from a presumed past overshadows the possible concerns of the text's 'present' – that is, the time(s) in which it was composed and transmitted.[28] The result is a radical dehistoricizing of the text, its characters, and concerns. Women are read not as themselves but as archetypes in disguise, bearing the weight of a mythic past that can be glimpsed only dimly at best.

The most obvious casualty of this approach is Medb, the aggressive queen of Connaught, who is portrayed as instigating the *Táin* because of her desire to prove herself equal in possessions to her husband Ailill. A seminal article by Tomás Ó Máille, which argued for Medb's essentially mythical character as a sovereignty goddess, has had far-reaching consequences for the interpretation of all female characters in medieval Irish texts.[29] While Ó Máille's intention was to rescue Medb from the category of 'whore' into which other more literal-minded scholars had placed her, his article had much more serious effects. With one stroke, aggressive sexuality on the part of a woman was placed in a neat mythic framework. Medb acted this way because she was a reflex of something beyond herself, a pagan Celtic deity whose function was to mate with and thereby validate the male ruler of the land. Thus, Medb's otherwise shocking behaviour was categorized and explained away, brought within a framework which subjugated the woman – powerful though she might be – to the larger political interests of men. She could thus be defined within the male concerns of sovereignty. Although this new reading of Medb rehabilitated her in the eyes of scholars who otherwise found her behaviour distasteful, it also effectively foreclosed any discussion of her as a *literary* figure.[30]

This process left little room for the women in the texts who were *not* aggressively sexual and linked in some way with kings or other male rulers. Some critics have attempted to link other females with this myth, either by identifying them with the land (and thus with concepts of fertility) or by linking them with Otherworld forces (and thus with a whole range of pagan beliefs and deities). Roberta Valente lamented in 1986 that little had changed in the interpretive methods being used to analyze the roles of female characters in Celtic narrative since Ó Máille's article appeared in the late 1920s.[31] The easy categorization of female characters as goddesses has continued to produce simplistic analyses of complex issues. More importantly, this type of criticism tends to automatically assimilate female figures into the heroic male discourse at the same time as it appears to empower them – a degenerative process which has also been noted in connection with the valkyrie figures of Old Norse literature.[32] Divinity is not empowering for women; on the contrary, it works to erase their womanhood even as it forces them to 'represent the unrepresentable.'[33]

Related to the 'sovereignty goddess' stereotyping of women in Irish literature is the enduring idea that women in Celtic (and especially Irish) narratives are intimately connected with the land and with natural forces, and therefore represent 'nature' as opposed to the male realm of 'culture.' Under the influence of the writings of Claude Lévi-Strauss, the nature/culture dichotomy has become a common model in discussions of male and female roles, especially in traditional tales.[34] What is perceived (at least by western minds) as woman's near-universal subordination to men has been attributed to her association with natural forces.[35] Whether woman is viewed as completely aligned with nature, or merely as an intermediary between nature and culture (for instance, in the rearing of children), her 'otherness' on the periphery of civilization tends to be affirmed wherever this binary pair is in operation.

Whether or not the nature/culture model is valid for describing early Celtic society, Marie-Louise Sjoestedt applied it to Celtic narratives in her influential study *Gods and Heroes of the Celts*, concluding 'we have a male principle of society to which is opposed a female principle of nature, or rather ... social forces of male character opposed by natural forces of female character.'[36] This has proven to be a very influential statement, particularly among those already predisposed to viewing women as reflexes of pagan divinities. There has been a strong tendency to accept this as an appropriate model for looking at *all* medieval Celtic narrative. The strong identification of the sovereignty goddess with the land – an identification made explicit in many tales – has perhaps made this inevitable. Yet the feminization of the land in the sovereignty myth has led to the association of nearly *all* females with forces of nature, through a process of identification of woman as goddess and then of goddess with natural forces.[37] This is not to dismiss this association outright; indeed, in some instances the model can reasonably be extended to include women who otherwise exhibit no overt mythological connections. Máire Herbert has recently argued convincingly for Deirdre's association with nature as an uncontrollable force in *The Exile of the Sons of Uisliu* (*Longas mac nUislenn*).[38] However, the woman-nature association quickly becomes an interpretive strait-jacket when applied wholesale, and can lead to naïve, simplistic, and misogynist readings.

Indeed, the nature/culture dichotomy has proven highly problematic. Recent discussions by social anthropologists and feminist critics has exposed the ambiguities inherent in each of the terms 'nature' and 'culture.'[39] In many cases the boundary between the two realms is not easily drawn, and how it is interpreted can vary widely from culture to culture. In fact, as Carol MacCormack has pointed out, the specific nature/culture distinctions drawn by Lévi-Strauss arise out of a context of western thought descended from Rousseau and eighteenth-century concerns.[40] As a result, they may not apply to early medieval or traditional societies, where nature/culture associations appear to have been more fluid.[41]

It is not the goal of this study to discount the search for underlying mythic or cultural patterns as a valid method of studying medieval Celtic narrative. Nevertheless, such analysis is of limited use to the literary critic. Like the broader 'search for sources' which characterized medieval studies in general in the earlier part of this century, it can only posit an 'original' form which no longer exists and indeed may never have existed. As Paul Zumthor has pointed out, such a method, 'far from constituting a referent for historical discourse, ... reifie[s] a referential illusion.'[42] The quest for a mythic or primordial past can tell us little about what these texts meant to their medieval creators, readers, or hearers.

What is needed is a new awareness of medieval Irish narratives as *literary* constructs affected and shaped by a whole range of historical and cultural considerations. It is certainly true that the literary tradition of medieval Ireland demonstrates a remarkable consistency from the seventh through the twelfth centuries. Nevertheless, the secular Irish tales were recopied and reshaped by scribes who clearly did not view them as sacrosanct, but who had their own ideas about what should or should not be included in the versions they copied. In some cases, these scribes reshaped the texts in drastic ways, erasing older versions and replacing them with different ones, even adding extra leaves to the manuscript if necessary.[43] Sometimes they inserted passages of traditional lore which modern readers find bafflingly irrelevant, while in other cases they added glosses to help (apparently, even medieval) readers to understand the texts. All of these interventions suggest that the redactors and scribes who preserved the tales were conscious of their role in mediating between the texts and their audience.[44]

Fortunately, the long-standing neglect of medieval Irish literature as 'literature' is rapidly being reversed. Joseph Nagy and Tomás Ó Cathasaigh have both looked closely at the roles of characters, in the *The Colloquy of the Old Men* (*Acallam na Senórach*) and *The Story of Cano Son of Gartnan* (*Scéla Cano meic Gartnáin*) respectively.[45] Máire Herbert's recent study of the representation of Deirdre is particularly refreshing.[46] Roberta Valente and Jeanie Watson have drawn attention to the impact of gender roles on thematic structure.[47] Recently Kim McCone has suggested that the pre-Christian goddess-figure, the 'woman of sovereignty' who grants the kingship of the land to the spouse of her choosing, was co-opted by Christian revisers and allegorized to fit into the framework of a Christian world view.[48] Patricia Kelly has offered a new way of reading Medb, not as a debased sovereignty goddess but as a female deliberately constructed to contrast negatively with Deborah of the Old Testament, who managed to wield power successfully.[49] More recently, Ann Dooley's perceptive discussion of women in the *Táin* has suggested new ways of reading these figures even within the misogyny of that text.[50] Several valuable studies of issues pertaining to women and the law have signalled the importance of understanding social context for reading women in medieval Celtic tales.[51] However, to date there has been no formal critical discussion of the representation of female speech in medieval Irish narratives.

Given that these texts were written down within a cultural context which embraced both the heritage of the Latin-Christian world and the pre-Christian native tradition, it is worth pointing out that the medieval audience which heard or read these tales in the eleventh and twelfth centuries had been Christian for hundreds of years. While these people likely recognized mythic overtones in the female figures who appear in the narratives, they also most certainly had other images of women in mind – the women of the Old Testament, Mary, and the saints (especially St Brigit), as well as queens and other secular women.[52] It is thus important to try to re-situate these tales in some sort of broad historical context. When an eleventh- or twelfth-century listener heard the story of the *Táin*, did he or she see goddesses or 'real' women? What did the portrayal of Emer in tales composed in the ninth and tenth centuries, and reshaped in the tenth to the twelfth centuries, mean to women and men of medieval Ireland? While these questions are probably not answerable at this stage – and may indeed never be answered adequately – they are nevertheless valid questions for the literary critic to raise.

To begin to approach these problems, we will need at least a rudimentary understanding of the social and cultural context in which these tales were composed and transmitted. Any discussion of medieval Irish literature must take into account the overall coherence of a literary tradition which is surprisingly consistent throughout the seventh to the twelfth centuries, while at the same time acknowledging particular innovations in the texts. Consequently, both aspects will be considered in this study. Since most of the tales discussed here are found in the eleventh- or twelfth-century manuscript Lebor na Huidre, this time period will be the primary focus of our discussion of historical context, while further background concerning the tales' composition and transmission will be provided where necessary.

The Nature of the Tradition: Text, Intertext,[53] and Context

Writing and literacy came to Ireland very early, probably by the fourth century A.D.[54] Medieval Ireland produced the most extensive and diverse vernacular literature in all of Europe, as well as a substantial corpus of Latin texts. These works span a wide range of genres – everything from law texts, annals, genealogies, sermons, and biblical exegesis to poems, saints' lives, pseudo-history, and secular tales. These genres often overlap in their interests; some of the legal texts, for example, make use of secular stories to illustrate points of law. One important group of texts, the *dinnshenchas* or 'lore of places' (short tales or poems which explain the origins of place-names) often connect topographical sites with notable persons or events from the saints' lives or secular tales. Although much of this material must have originated in an oral society, it is clear that from an early date oral and written texts existed side by side. The advent of Christianity naturally brought with it the need for literacy, as well as an enthusiasm for copying and studying sacred texts.[55] Yet there is evidence that the medieval Irish *literati* were also remarkably conversant with a wide range of secular Latin literature, including the works of Isidore, Ovid, Vergil, and Sidonius, and that they often used classical texts as models even when writing in the vernacular.[56]

It is important to note that because of changes in the Irish language during the seventh to twelfth centuries, texts can often be dated on linguistic grounds to much earlier than their first appearance in manuscript form. Irish scribes continued to copy and recopy old texts throughout the medieval period, often retaining archaic spellings and grammatical constructions which offer clues as to the original date of the works. Thus, for example, a tale found in a twelfth-century manuscript may show clear signs of having been composed or reshaped in the eighth or tenth century. This conservative tendency of the scribes also accounts for the continuity of a literary tradition in which the eleventh- or twelfth-century reader or listener had access to texts from a variety of time periods, and would have been familiar with stories that had been circulating for hundreds of years.

Although some of this early Irish material clearly had its origins in a pre-Christian past, the whole of the surviving literature was written down by scribes educated in monasteries after the coming of Christianity. Thus, as the 'anti-nativist' scholars who stress the importance of outside influences point out, the entire corpus of medieval Irish literature, whatever its oral or pre-Christian roots, comes down to us mediated through a literate, Christian culture.[57] As a result, even texts which may appear archaic and 'pagan' are likely far removed from their original forms.

Yet the imprints of Christianity are not always as easily discerned as McCone and the other anti-nativists would have us believe. This is especially true when we consider the conflicting portraits of women in medieval Irish literature. On the one hand, some texts do betray a strong misogynistic flavour. For instance, *The Instructions of Cormac* (*Sanas Cormaic*), which purports to record the advice given by the famous king, Cormac mac Airt, describes in some detail the folly of choosing women as counsellors.[58] *The Wise Words of Fithal* (*Senbriathra Fithail*), another text of the genre of 'instructions to princes,' warns against marrying a variety of different women, including 'in cenaind n-gárechtig' ('the fair-haired boisterous one') and 'in míarlig míepertaig' ('the evil-counselling, evil-speaking one').[59] The disastrous consequences of listening to women's advice seems to be vividly illustrated in *The Second Battle of Mag Tuired* (*Cath Maige Tuired*), where the election of Bres as the ill-fated king of the Túatha Dé Danaan is engineered by women rather than men, as would be customary.[60] The version of the *Táin* found in the twelfth-century Book of Leinster likewise portrays Medb's aggressiveness in a very negative way. Her lover Fergus remarks that the expedition has failed because it was led by a woman:

Ra gattá 7 ra brattá in slúag sa indiu. Feib théit echrad láir rena serrgraig i crích n-aneóil gan chend cundraid ná comairle rempo, is amlaid testa in slúag sa indiu.

This host has been plundered and despoiled today. As when a mare goes before her band of foals into unknown territory, with none to lead or counsel them, so this host has perished today.[61]

The first three of the texts mentioned above likely took their present shapes some time in the eleventh or twelfth centuries, but were redacted from mainly ninth-century materials. They would thus likely have been in circulation at the time of the redaction of the Ulster Cycle tales discussed in this study. There is an unmistakable current of misogyny running through these texts, and the censure of women's speech in particular situates these works firmly within the larger misogynistic discourse of medieval Christian Europe.[62]

Yet other contemporary texts present positive images of women. The twelfth-century *Lore of Women* (*Banshenchas*) is an extensive list – unique in medieval Europe – of famous secular women in Irish literature and history. Despite the fact that this work dates from the same period as the Book of Leinster version of the *Táin* with its negative portrayal of Medb, there is very little censure of the women listed in it.[63] An ecclesiastical parallel is the list of the mothers of Irish saints, which celebrates the saints' maternal ancestry.[64] The Otherworld woman in the early voyage tale, *The Voyage of Conla* (*Echtrae Chonlai*), is also presented in a relatively positive light, and even – as Carney has argued – identified with the Christian Church in opposition to the 'paganism' of the druid in the tale.[65] In the late Old Irish story *The Wooing of Becfhola* (*Tochmarc Becfhola*), the heroine is depicted as going on a journey to seek out a mate for herself, and eventually ends up with a man who pleases her.[66] Emer and other women in the secular literature speak out repeatedly, often without being rebuked for their speech. And in one Irish version of the Adam and Eve story, even Eve herself is treated somewhat sympathetically by the author.[67]

Medieval Irish literature from the seventh to the twelfth centuries thus presents a conflicting set of views pertaining to women. The misogyny evident in some texts coexists with a considerable respect for women in others. Some narratives seem to betray the essentializing influence of the Mary/Eve dichotomy, while others seem to insist on portraying women as individuals. This apparent contradiction within the literary tradition can perhaps be better appreciated in the context of a society marked by a number of cultural and political tensions – between the pre-Christian heritage of myth on the one hand and Christian tradition on the other; between the production of fixed, written manuscripts and the ongoing influences of oral tradition; between the native Irish laws of marriage and the demands of canon law (particularly in the eleventh and twelfth centuries); and in the turmoil of inter-tribal conflict as native political models came increasingly under Continental influence.[68] It is important to remember that Ireland, like other medieval cultures, was not 'univocal and homogeneous' but instead 'heterogeneous and ambiguous.'[69]

Although relatively sparse in references to women, the legal and historical records seem to confirm these tensions. The native Irish marriage laws, originally composed in the seventh and eighth centuries, were preserved, recopied, and glossed throughout the Middle Ages.[70] Although no records of actual cases survive from the pre-Norman period, it is clear from later court documents from the Norman era that many of these marriage customs continued to be observed by at least the aristocratic families well after the Norman conquest in 1169. We can thus surmise that the status of women and the laws of marriage as presented in the law tracts remained fairly static throughout the seventh to twelfth centuries.[71] These native marriage laws present an inconsistent view of women's lives. On the one hand, according to the law tracts adult females in medieval Irish society enjoyed relatively high legal status, and had the right to divorce their husbands on a variety of grounds.[72] A woman's body was surprisingly well protected by law; if her husband beat her, she was entitled to receive fines and compensation for the injury, and could divorce him if the blows inflicted caused a permanent blemish.[73] This relative respect for women was partly due to the fact that an Irish woman's husband did not become her sole guardian when she married, nor was her property transferred into his hands; her kin-group contributed her bride-price, and retained an interest in her.[74]

On the other hand, women's lives were more restricted than men's. Their ability to own land was generally very limited. One could certainly point to some notable exceptions including Mór, queen of Mide, who along with her husband seized Dún Carraic, the traditional residence of the kings of Fir Tulach; after this the property was said to be held by every queen of Mide after her.[75] However, in general a woman could acquire only a life-interest in land, and then only if her father had no male heirs.[76] Women had no direct access to the justice system, and they seem to have been barred from official political leadership roles.[77] Moreover, women could not generally give testimony in legal disputes, their evidence being considered 'biased and dishonest.'[78] Even the liberal divorce laws seem to have proven less advantageous for women than for men, if evidence from Norman Ireland is any indication. In her valuable study of records from the period in which Gaelic law and Norman law coexisted (after 1169), Simms points out that in many cases the liberal Gaelic divorce laws were used by husbands to repudiate older wives in favour of younger ones; men often used Gaelic law to justify uncanonical marriages, and then later used canon law to justify annulments.[79] The persistence of native marriage laws which allowed several forms of marriage (and which could result in a man having more than one wife at a time) must inevitably have caused tensions within the family unit.

It is true that women of high status and considerable wealth are mentioned in the Annals, and are sometimes depicted as bestowing liberal endowments on churches or monastic foundations.[80] Yet it is also clear that aristocratic women were routinely used to cement political alliances. One famous example is that of Diarmait Mac Murchada's 1166 offer of his daughter Aífe in marriage along with the kingship of Leinster after his own death, to the Norman Richard fitz Gilbert (Strongbow). This offer was intended to win Norman aid against Mac Murchada's enemies at home, but resulted in the eventual Norman settlement of Ireland.[81] The recycling of aristocratic wives through a series of political unions has often been idealized by those seeking historical traces of the sovereignty goddess motif.[82] In fact, life for most of these women was likely anything but glamorous. What is evident, at least from eleventh and twelfth century records, is the primacy of political considerations among aristocratic families over any personal relationship between husbands and wives.[83]

Thus, the historical ambiguity in women's lives parallels the ambiguities within the literary tradition of the same period. Despite the undeniable overall continuity of the literary tradition throughout the Irish Middle Ages, the extended period of literary development, from composition in the seventh, eighth, and ninth centuries to the reshaping of texts in the tenth to the twelfth centuries, might be speculatively termed a 'transitional' phase. Not only was Irish society undergoing changes caused in part by the incursions of the Vikings, developments in church doctrine and hierarchy, and political upheavals in both England and Wales to the east, but its literary culture was also evolving as the practice of writing in the vernacular took hold. The transfer of oral tales to the written form and the composition of new texts of all kinds culminated in the production of the great manuscripts of the eleventh and twelfth centuries.[84]

A more comprehensive survey of the social, legal, religious, and literary context of medieval Ireland during the eleventh and twelfth centuries is beyond the scope of this present work. It is nevertheless prudent to keep in mind the relevant historical and legal materials mentioned above in an attempt to situate our tales within their context as much as possible. Especially important is the consideration of the *literary* context of the Ulster Cycle tales.

The Ulster Cycle

The *Cattle Raid of Cooley* (*Táin Bó Cúailgne*) is clearly the central text of the Ulster Cycle, but there are a number of other stories which involve many of the same characters. Some of these may have been originally independent tales which were drawn into the orbit of the *Táin* over time, and refashioned to connect with it in some way. Other stories likely evolved later, as additions to the main adventures of the Ulster heroes.

Because the Ulster Cycle tales are linked in many ways, there are numerous verbal echoes between them, and many refer to events in other tales. These linkages would have been crucial factors in the reception of these stories by medieval audiences, whether in oral or written form. That is to say, any reading or performance of one tale would have immediately evoked not only the other tales, but also variant versions of them, both oral and written. While a thorough examination of these links is beyond the scope of this study, it is important to note that the four tales discussed here refer to each other in various ways. *The Wooing of Emer* (*Tochmarc Emire*) tells of how Cú Chulainn begot his only son on a warrior-woman named Aífe; *The Death of Aífe's Only Son* (*Aided Óenfir*

Aífe) summarizes this episode and then tells of the consequences when father and son finally meet. *Bricriu's Feast* (*Fled Bricrend*) contains many verbal echoes of both *The Wooing of Emer* and *The Wasting Sickness of Cú Chulainn* (*Serglige Con Culainn*), especially in its descriptions of women. One episode of *The Wasting Sickness of Cú Chulainn* seems to refer to a character whose wife seeks to marry Cú Chulainn in *The Wooing of Emer*. Thus, these tales are linked by a web of intertextual references, some more significant than others, which all point to important interrelationships between the Ulster Cycle tales as a body of narrative.

Although there is still some debate concerning the dating of specific tales, most scholars agree that at least some of these texts originally took shape in written form between the eighth and ninth centuries.[85] The oldest stratum of the tradition appears to be represented by texts which now survive only in later manuscripts but which once formed part of the Cín Dromma Snechta, an important early codex (now lost, but referred to by numerous scribes as their source[86]) which may have dated from as early as the eighth century or as late as the tenth.[87] The texts in question are *The Conception of Cú Chulainn* (*Compert Con Culainn*) and a poem of prophecy entitled *The Words of Scáthach* (*Verba Scáthaige*) which, in a modified version, forms part of the tale *The Wooing of Emer*. *The Words of Scáthach* is judged to represent one of the oldest layers of the *Táin*, providing a somewhat obscure view of the saga's main events.[88] Although not among the texts directly traceable to the Cín Dromma Snechta, both *The Wooing of Emer* and *Bricriu's Feast* have also been dated to between the eighth and tenth centuries in their original forms,[89] while *The Death of Aífe's Only Son* and *The Wasting Sickness of Cú Chulainn* have been dated to the ninth or tenth century.[90]

During the Middle Irish period (roughly the ninth to the twelfth centuries) the tales were substantially reworked and embellished, and in some cases expanded.[91] The earliest surviving manuscript versions derive from this later period. Among these manuscripts the Lebor na Huidre (LU), copied sometime in the eleventh century, and revised sometime in the twelfth, is the oldest.[92] Three of the tales discussed in this study are found in the Lebor na Huidre. The other tale is found in the fourteenth-century section of another important manuscript, the Yellow Book of Lecan. This is a huge manuscript containing a variety of texts from all branches of Irish learning, and consisting of several sections written at different times. The fourteenth-century section, which forms the earliest nucleus of the book, was apparently written at Leacán, Co. Sligo by the famous scribe Gilla Ísa mac Fir Bhisigh.[93] The manuscript contains versions of many of the Ulster Cycle tales including the *Táin* and *Bricriu's Feast*, as well as a number of death tales, all of which were clearly composed much earlier.[94] More detailed discussions of the manuscript traditions of each of these texts can be found in the appendix.

The Irish had their own way of classifying their traditional tales according to general subject matter. Thus, the two surviving lists of these *scéla* (tales) divide the proper narrative repertoire of the *filid* (the professional poets) into categories like cattle-raids, feasts, wooings, abductions, elopements, voyages, battles, death tales, and the like.[95] These categories were, of course, necessarily culturally loaded and carried with them certain narrative expectations and conventions.[96] Despite Mac Cana's caution about the specifically *learned* interests of these tale lists, they still provide the modern critic with a glimpse of the generic assumptions among the medieval Irish *literati*.[97] Some of these expectations will be shown to be crucial to an understanding of the tales discussed in this study.

Audience

If the *literati* held certain assumptions about specific genres, surely the eleventh- or twelfth-century audiences which heard these tales recited or read on various occasions would have shared these assumptions. Although we have little specific information about the audience of medieval Irish literature, we are probably safe in assuming that the listeners included at least the upper classes who frequented the courts of chiefs and kings where tales were told. It is also likely that both men and women were present at these gatherings, especially at weddings or victory feasts or other important public occasions.[98] In fact, the tale lists themselves might be viewed as evidence of some level of audience demand for stories and of the related necessity of organizing these tales efficiently.

Thus we can probably assume that aristocrats of both sexes were familiar with a number of secular tales. We can be reasonably certain that the *Táin* (at least in some form) was well known, as were other Ulster Cycle stories. Considering the presence of many of these tales together in the manuscript LU, it is certain that the scribes of the eleventh and twelfth centuries were familiar with them.[99] Indeed, as recent scholarship has shown, the monastic *scriptoria* borrowed manuscripts from each other to recopy them for their own communities, a practice which suggests that these tales were well known in many areas of Ireland.[100]

It is also worth noting that the eleventh- or twelfth-century audience would have been a Christian one. Yet its Christian character would have coexisted with a number of archaic survivals in society, such as the stubbornly retained marriage customs discussed above. The very existence of books such as LU attests to a certain desire to preserve the tales of the past, even if the scribes also sometimes felt compelled to comment on the 'pagan' elements in them. While we will never be able to reconstruct completely the social milieu in which our tales were redacted as we now have them, there is ample evidence that they evolved in a society where competing voices and traditions – Christian and pre-Christian, Latin and vernacular, oral and written, innovative and archaic – constantly vied for the right to be heard.

Considering the early, obscure origins and apparently long textual history of the Ulster Cycle tales, the fact that the characterization of the major players varies little from tale to tale is astonishing. The consistency with which Emer is portrayed is perhaps particularly striking, considering that she never features as the protagonist in any of the tales, and in fact has only a 'walk-on part' in some of them. This remarkably coherent portrayal of a female character across a number of tales in a tradition allows for a sustained analysis of Emer as a literary figure.

Emer

By looking closely at the words of one female character in several connected tales, and by paying close attention to what is known of the literary, social, and historical context of these works, this study will seek to illuminate the role of Emer's speech. As the spouse of a hero instead of a king, Emer is perhaps more likely than some other female characters to reflect the behaviour and attitudes of an aristocratic Irish woman rather than the functions of the sovereignty goddess of pre-Christian myth. At the same time, she not only spends more time on the narrative stage than most other women, she also has a good deal to say. Her words play prominent and powerful roles both in generating the plots of the tales and in their construction of meaning. Most significant is the uniformly positive portrayal of Emer in these texts, a factor which sets her apart from many of her sisters in medieval English and Continental literature.

In focusing on Emer, this study will consider four tales in which she plays important roles. These tales form part of what we might term the 'heroic biography' of the extraordinary hero Cú Chulainn.[101] In the first two tales, *The Wooing of Emer* (*Tochmarc Emire*) and *Bricriu's Feast* (*Fled*

Bricrend), Emer seems to play the roles expected of an aristocratic medieval Irish woman within a patriarchal, heroic society, although she certainly tests the boundaries of these roles. In the other two tales, *The Death of Aife's Only Son* (*Aided Oenfír Aífe*) and *The Wasting Sickness of Cú Chulainn* (*Serglige Con Culainn*), Emer breaks out of these strictures to interrogate and oppose both her husband and the expectations of her culture. It is in these last two tales that the fissures in the heroic ethos of the traditional narratives are perhaps most clearly revealed. These two tales, in particular, seem to reflect the anxieties and pressures of Irish culture in the tenth to the twelfth centuries, rather than the preoccupations of ancient myth and archaic social structures.

Despite the positive portrayal of women in many Irish texts, this is not to be viewed even as an incipiently 'feminist' literature. Although there is reason to believe that in the early days of Irish Christianity women, like their male counterparts, took an active role in copying manuscripts and composing poems and tales, they seem to have been progressively excluded from these roles by the eleventh century.[102] Indeed, by the time of the flourishing of the bardic schools, there were apparently no female professional poets. The poet was even portrayed as the 'spouse' of his (male) patron' – a move which effectively appropriated the role of wife and thus symbolically excluded real women from active participation in official literary creation.[103] It is thus wise to heed the warnings of critics like Burns who caution us against hearing the voices of 'real women' speaking through these texts.[104]

Despite this, Emer is one of the most fully delineated female figures in medieval Irish literature, and perhaps comes as close to representing a female 'speaking subject' as any woman in the tradition. Her words are many and various. And although she does utter warnings and laments – the forms of speech which seem traditionally and consistently open to women – Emer speaks in many other contexts as well. She matches her future husband in an arcane riddling contest; she renames the landscape after his heroic deeds; she warns and advises both her husband and the other Ulster heroes and even the king, Conchobar; she boasts of her own beauty in a contest of women's words; she admonishes her husband when he is ill; she rebukes him for his affair with another woman and debates with her Otherworld rival. She even issues a spirited retort to the one misogynistic attempt to silence her voice. Emer's words cover a whole range of human discourse, not only those topics normally associated with women. Moreover, unlike the aggressive Medb, she is not censured for her forthright speech and behaviour.

Emer is thus a figure of great interest to feminist critics in general, and to feminist medievalists in particular. Although she shares many traits with her English and Continental sisters, she also differs from them in other respects. She is neither the idealized woman of courtly romance, nor the fast-talking shrew of the *fabliaux*. She eludes the dichotomy between 'heroic and chaste' on the one hand and 'passive and married' on the other, which plagues her Old English counterparts.[105] Her words, unlike those of her Scandinavian sisters in the Old Norse sagas, do not unleash disaster, but in fact seek to avert it.

The present work does not claim to be a definitive study of Emer as a literary figure. My goal is simply to present a literary analysis of the speech of this little-known female character in the hope that such a discussion will encourage further investigation into the representation of women in medieval Irish texts. Emer is an intriguing figure, a woman both enmeshed in the customs and structures of her fictional world and at the same time remarkably adept at speaking powerfully within and against those structures. More than a beautiful body or a shrill mouth, Emer is a complex and compelling character who is worthy of our attention.

1

The Wooing of Emer:
The Sweet Speech of Courtship

In the implied chronology of Cú Chulainn's heroic career, *The Wooing of Emer* (*Tochmarc Emire*) marks the introduction of Emer into the hero's life. This is a long and complicated narrative, which takes several detours into seemingly peripheral adventures. Yet it remains focused primarily on the hero's courtship of Emer and her assignment of the deeds he must perform to win her, his fulfilment of her requirements, and his eventual marriage to her. The tale introduces other important details as well, for it is here that the account of Cú Chulainn's training in arms abroad with the warrior-woman Scáthach is narrated in full, including his encounter with Scáthach's enemy Aífe and his mastering of the *gáe bolga*, the strange and deadly weapon which sets him apart from his peers. Both of these incidents are important for their connections with other Ulster Cycle tales.

Despite its centrality to the Ulster Cycle, *The Wooing of Emer* has been the subject of relatively little sustained analysis. Most scholars have focused their attention on the mythic and folkloric elements in the story. This is not surprising, since *The Wooing of Emer* contains a number of international folk motifs. Rudolph Thurneysen's early characterization of the tale as one filled with foreign saga motifs seems to have set the tone for the little scholarly comment that has followed.[1] Thus, in one of the earliest discussions, A.C.L. Brown draws attention to parallels between the lion that helps Cú Chulainn in *The Wooing of Emer* and the helpful lion in Chrétien de Troyes' *Ivain*.[2] Josef Baudiš explores some of the other international motifs in detail, including the hero's initiation in a hostile foreign land, the quest for a bride and the riddling contest that accompanies it, the father's opposition to the hero, and the father's ultimate death.[3] Although interesting in their own right, such discussions tend to reinforce the impression of a fragmented hodge-podge of a text composed of disparate elements thrown loosely together.

Alwyn and Brinley Rees also make reference to these folk motifs in the context of their mythological analysis of the tale. Drawing on a number of wooing stories from the Irish tradition and beyond, they argue for the essentially mythic nature of these tales in depicting a

victory of a principle from an upper realm over the sinister powers of a lower one, a victory won on the conditions set by those powers themselves. The prize is the emancipation from that lower realm of the opposite principle and the consummate union of the two.[4]

While this type of analysis presents a somewhat more coherent view of the wooing tale, it does little to illuminate the text as a literary construct.

In a more recent article, Brendan O Hehir cites *The Wooing of Emer* as a parallel to the later tale, *The Voyage of Art Son of Conn and the Courtship of Delbchaem Daughter of Morgan* (*Eachtra Airt Meic Cuind ocus Tochmarc Delbchaime Ingine Morgain*). Although he pays considerable attention to Emer and the other women in the story, his discussion focuses on the women as *goddesses* rather than as characters in a literary narrative.[5] Vincent Dunn includes *The Wooing of Emer* in his study of the connections between tales of cattle-raids and courtships in medieval literature. His analysis, which sees these as a paired set of initiation stories – the realistic 'syntagmatic' cattle-raid story and the more mythic 'paradigmatic' courtship story – is certainly illuminating.[6] Yet he too confines himself to a view of *The Wooing of Emer* which stresses its mythic rather than its literary qualities.[7]

Much has already been written about the mythic layers of the Ulster Cycle tales and it is not the purpose of this study to revisit these arguments.[8] It is certainly true that the father's opposition to the prospective son-in-law in wooing tales is often presented in mythological terms; but it is equally possible that such a motif also reflects the psychological reality of a father's unwillingness to let go of his daughter. It is not obvious that in the wooing stories 'understanding takes place at a level other than that of the literal and rational' and that 'the stories themselves militate against such rational scrutiny and attune us to perceptions of a different sort' as Dunn argues.[9] Reading the texts 'vertically' (that is, mythologically) as he suggests ignores crucial layers of meaning in the narrative.

The three works which come closest to sustained literary analysis of *The Wooing of Emer* are Raymond Cormier's study of Cú Chulainn and the French hero Yvain,[10] William Sayers's recent examination of eloquence in the tale,[11] and Doris Edel's *Helden auf Freiersfüssen*.[12] Cormier's article is a comparative reading of *The Wooing of Emer* which engages in some real literary analysis of the text.[13] Sayers's discussion is the most valuable of the three for the purposes of this study, for it is a detailed and insightful examination of the rhetorical concerns highlighted in the tale. Edel's book offers helpful discussions of the folk-tale, epic, and learned aspects of the tale, but is so lengthy that her many valuable observations tend to get lost in the verbiage.[14]

Yet none of these works takes account of the crucial role played by Emer and her speech in the narrative. Unlike the brides in many other traditional wooing tales, Emer is more than just the beautiful object of the young man's quest.[15] Instead she appears to be a model of female eloquence, a figure unusual for her skilful manipulation of language within traditional codes of speech and behaviour. She thus embodies different meanings than the standard framework of the wooing story allows, and emerges as a more active and complex figure than the traditional bride.

The Wooing of Emer introduces Emer as a character and establishes the traits which continue to characterize her in other tales in the tradition. Emer is portrayed as a strong woman, willing to adhere to the customs of her society up to a certain point, yet also prepared to break with those customs to marry the man of her choice. Her most important gifts are those of intellectual acuity and eloquence, and she possesses the courage and independence of mind to use both when necessary. She is the only possible match for Cú Chulainn – his female counterpart and foil, extraordinary as he is extraordinary.

Women and their voices fill *The Wooing of Emer* from beginning to end, beginning with Emer's challenging stance towards the hero in the wooing dialogue and ending with her renaming of the landscape through which she escapes to her new life. Yet women's words are not simply 'chatter' in this tale. In *The Wooing of Emer* women's words – and especially those of Emer – have *power*. They are speech *acts* which affect other people and ultimately reshape the world.[16] The effects of these speech acts on *men* are particularly significant. Although *The Wooing of Emer* continues a pattern in medieval Irish literature in which men and women tend to establish relationships on an agonistic level before they find ways to cooperate, the tale also demonstrates that harmonious male-female relationships can indeed be forged through judicious speech.[17] Emer and

Cú Chulainn begin by challenging and testing each other but they ultimately establish a meshing of feminine and heroic language.

Since *The Wooing of Emer* is not well known, a detailed summary is necessary before we proceed to an analysis of the tale.

Summary of *The Wooing of Emer*

The story opens in the court of Conchobar at Emain Macha, the epitome of ancient Irish heroic society. Here Cú Chulainn surpasses all other warriors at feats and is admired by the women. The Ulstermen decide that he must have a wife, for they fear he will lure away their own wives and daughters. A search is conducted for a year in all the five provinces of Ireland but no suitable woman is found. At last, Cú Chulainn journeys alone to Luglochta Loga, where he knows a girl named Emer.

He approaches her father's fort, where Emer is outside teaching needlework to the daughters of the neighbouring landowners. She and Cú Chulainn converse in riddles so that the young women listening will not understand them. Emer indicates her willingness to marry the young hero but points out that Cú Chulainn must abduct her since her father will oppose the match. Moreover, she specifies a number of feats that he must perform in order to win her. He promises to fulfil her demands and she agrees to marry him. He leaves and returns to Emain Macha.

The landowners' daughters report the strange conversation to their fathers, who in turn tell Forgall Monach, Emer's father. Determined to foil the couple's plans, Forgall travels to Emain Macha in disguise and persuades Cú Chulainn to go abroad to a man named Domnall for further training. Cú Chulainn agrees, but visits Emer secretly before he departs. She warns him that the journey is a plot by her father to expose him to danger and death. He agrees to be careful and they promise to remain true to one another while they are separated. Cú Chulainn departs, accompanied by several other heroes.

He stays with Domnall for some time learning heroic feats. But Domnall urges the young hero to go to Scáthach, who lives further east, for the best training. Meanwhile, Domnall's ugly daughter Dornolla falls in love with Cú Chulainn but he spurns her advances. She swears revenge and conjures up visions to hinder him. When it comes time to depart for Scáthach's realm, she raises a vision of Emain Macha that prevents the hero's companions from going past it, thus compelling Cú Chulainn to journey on alone.

Cú Chulainn travels across a hostile land, not knowing which direction he should take to Scáthach's domain. But he is guided by a series of helpers – a beast like a lion which carries him to an island of youths, a nameless former foster-sister who offers him food and drink but whose company he then rejects, and finally the youth Eochu Bairche, who shows him the path to Scáthach's dwelling and gives him the means to avoid the dangers on the way. At last Cú Chulainn reaches the island on which Scáthach dwells. When he arrives at her fort he strikes the door violently with the staff of his spear. Scáthach sends her daughter Uathach to see who is there, and the daughter falls immediately and passionately in love with the young hero. She serves him food and drink, and apparently makes advances towards him, for he breaks her finger and her scream rouses Scáthach's champion. Cú Chulainn attacks and defeats the champion, then replaces him as guardian of the fort. Uathach then tells Cú Chulainn how to approach her mother.

Cú Chulainn follows Uathach's advice and surprises Scáthach, laying his sword on her breast and demanding that she teach him feats, that she give him her daughter without payment of dowry (as would be customary), and that she prophesy his future. Scáthach agrees to his demands and Cú Chulainn and Uathach form a temporary union.

The text then turns briefly to Ireland, where Emer's father has betrothed her to a young king. But when the wedding day arrives, Emer declares that she has promised herself to Cú Chulainn and is under his protection. The young king is afraid to challenge Cú Chulainn and leaves. The story returns to the realm of Scáthach, who is teaching Cú Chulainn feats of arms. She is also at war with another warrior woman, Aífe. When the two hosts assemble to fight, Scáthach gives Cú Chulainn a strong sleeping draught to prevent him from coming to the battle because she fears he will be killed. However, Cú Chulainn wakes after only a short time and comes to the battlefield. He joins the two sons of Scáthach in combat against the three sons of Aífe, and defeats the latter single-handedly. When Aífe then challenges Scáthach to single combat, Cú Chulainn asks Scáthach what Aífe loves the most. She tells him that Aífe loves her horses, her chariot, and her charioteer the most. Cú Chulainn then fights in Scáthach's place and uses this knowledge to trick Aífe when he meets her in single combat. He defeats her and she begs for her life. He makes three demands of her, one of which is that she will bear him a son. She agrees, spends the night with him, and tells him she will bear a son. Cú Chulainn lays injunctions on the son, leaves a ring and a name for him, and returns to Scáthach.

On his way back to Scáthach's people, Cú Chulainn encounters the mother of the last three warriors he killed. She tries to kill him but he kills her instead. He returns to Scáthach and completes his training with her. She then prophesies his future to him and the role he will play in the Táin. The hero then sets off for Ireland, and an apparently uneventful journey brings him to his ship and companions. They travel across the water to the land of Ruad, King of the Isles (probably the Orkneys), where the Ulstermen are collecting tribute. But the Fomorians are apparently also collecting tribute, in the person of the king's daughter, Derbforgall. Cú Chulainn goes to the beach where she is waiting and defeats the Fomorians when they arrive. Derbforgall identifies her saviour to her father, who offers her to Cú Chulainn. The hero refuses but makes a tryst with her to meet in Ireland in a year.

Cú Chulainn returns to Ireland and travels to Forgall's fort. However, it is so well guarded that he cannot reach Emer. He tries to gain entrance for a year, but does not succeed. Then he and his charioteer go to keep the tryst with Derbforgall. They see two birds on the sea and Cú Chulainn shoots at them, bringing one of them down. The birds are then transformed into two beautiful women, Derbforgall and her handmaid. Cú Chulainn sucks the stone out of Derforgall's arm, and then declares he cannot marry her because he has drunk her blood, and bestows her on his foster-son Lugaid instead.

Cú Chulainn then tries again to enter the fort of Forgall. This time he travels to the fort in the scythe-chariot, then leaps across the three ramparts, seizes Emer and her foster-sister, kills the warriors there but spares Emer's three brothers (as she has stipulated), then leaps back out of the fort with the women and their weight in gold and silver. Forgall leaps from the fort and dies. Cú Chulainn is pursued by the men of Forgall. At each point where he turns and kills some of his pursuers, Emer remarks on his prowess and together they rename the landscape after his deeds. At last they reach Emain Macha safely and Emer is presented to the company.

However, the troublemaker Bricriu reminds them all that Conchobar as king has the *ius primae noctis*, the right to sleep with Emer the first night. Cú Chulainn is furious. The Ulstermen send him out again to the wilderness to work off his anger. When he returns, they formulate a compromise: Emer will sleep with the king, but with others in the bed with them to make sure that Cú Chulainn's honour is not violated. The hero agrees to that. Cú Chulainn and Emer are wed and live together for the rest of their lives.

Clearly, this is a lengthy and complex narrative. In order to explore the role of Emer's words, we need first to place the tale in its literary and legal context.

Context: Wooing Tales

Bridal quest tales are common in all cultures. *The Wooing of Emer* is one among several such tales known to have been familiar in medieval Ireland, and would undoubtedly have been read or heard by an eleventh- or twelfth-century audience with these other tales in mind.

There are two surviving lists in medieval Irish sources which purport to catalogue the repertoire of a story-teller. These catalogues list a number of different wooing tales (*tochmarca*), among them *The Wooing of Emer*.[18] Most of these tales have certain patterns in common: the quest for a bride is opposed at some stage by a parent or rival; the hero must accomplish a series of difficult or dangerous tasks before winning his bride; his journey usually involves a separation from his familiar surroundings and often a passage through a hostile realm; he receives help in his quest, often from the bride herself; and he eventually overcomes all obstacles and claims his bride.

The *tochmarca* of the tale lists include both mythical and more realistic narratives.[19] Both types are important as intertexts for *The Wooing of Emer*. Perhaps the most well-known mythical wooing tale is *The Wooing of Étaín* (*Tochmarc Étaíne*), a story in which mortals and Otherworld figures interact freely and compete for the right to wed a woman who passes through a number of incarnations in several different lifetimes.[20] Less overtly supernatural tales include *The Wooing of Ailbe* (*Tochmarc Ailbe*),[21] *The Cattle Raid of Froech* (*Táin Bó Fraích*),[22] and *The Voyage of Art Son of Conn and the Wooing of Delbchaem daughter of Morgan* (*Eachtra Airt Meic Cuind ocus Tochmarc Delbchaime Ingine Morgain*).[23] Before considering *The Wooing of Emer* in detail, it will be useful to sketch the outlines of these other narratives in order to establish the tale's literary context.

The Wooing of Étaín is a complicated story consisting of three different but connected narratives, all of them involving a woman named Étaín.

Summary of *The Wooing of Étaín*

The first of these (Étaín 1) is the most overtly mythical, for it involves the Dagda, king of the supernatural race, the Túatha Dé Danann. In this tale Mider, foster-father of Oengus the son of the Dagda, seeks to wed Étaín, the fairest woman in Ireland. Oengus goes to woo the girl on Mider's behalf. Her father at first refuses to negotiate, and then agrees when Oengus promises to pay the girl's weight in gold and silver and to perform a series of monumental tasks – clearing forests for grazing land and dividing the course of twelve rivers. He accomplishes all of this and Étaín is given to Mider in marriage. But Mider has a wife already, a powerful worker of magic named Fúamnach. Although she appears to welcome the couple home, she soon turns Étaín into a puddle of water, then into a worm, and then a fly. In this last shape Étain is vulnerable to the winds which Fúamnach raises to blow her all over Ireland. At last, she falls exhausted into the drinking cup of a mortal woman in Ulster; the woman conceives and Étaín is born again as a beautiful girl of the same name.

The second narrative (Étaín 2) concerns Eochaid Airem, king of all Ireland, whose people forbid him to hold a special feast because he has no wife. A search is conducted for a virgin woman who is Eochaid's equal in every way. Étaín meets these qualifications and weds the king. However, his brother Ailill falls in love with her and wastes away from love-sickness. Étaín nurses him while her husband is away and he confesses his love for her. She agrees to a night-time tryst outside the house on a hilltop. Ailill falls asleep and misses the tryst, but Étaín encounters a man who looks like him. The same thing happens for three nights, until finally Étaín confronts the man and he confesses that he is Mider, her husband in a previous life. She refuses to come with him but says that if her present husband Eochaid permits her to go with him she will go.

The third narrative (Étaín 3) takes up where the second leaves off. One morning Eochaid Airem awakes to find a strange young man in his fortress. The young man challenges him to a game of *fidchell*, a board game similar to chess.[24] They play a series of games with ever-increasing stakes. When Eochaid wins a second time he demands that Mider perform several extraordinary tasks in one night, among them clearing a forest and building a causeway. Mider accomplishes the tasks and returns the next day demanding to play *fidchell* again for unspecified stakes. This time Mider wins, and asks for a kiss from Étaín. Eochaid reluctantly agrees but asks him to return in a month. When Mider returns the fortress is heavily guarded. Mider reminds Eochaid of his promise and reminds Étaín of her agreement to leave with him. Eochaid allows Mider to put his arms around her and when he does, both of them are transformed into swans and fly away. Eochaid searches for Étaín all the next year, digging up many *síd*-mounds (the dwellings of immortal beings) in the process. When he reaches Mider's *síd*, Mider agrees to return Étaín to him. He brings her to the king along with fifty other identical women, among whom Eochaid must choose. Eochaid chooses one woman, but eventually learns that he has chosen his daughter instead of his former wife. By this time the daughter is pregnant by him, and when the baby girl is born Eochaid gives orders that she be killed. She is rescued, reared by a cowherd and his wife, and eventually marries king Eterscel.

Although this is a complicated story, several key features emerge. All three narratives stress the difficulties that must be overcome before Étaín and any given suitor can be united. In Étaín 1 and Étaín 2, Mider (or Oengus on his behalf) must significantly reshape the landscape of Ireland. In Étaín 1, the pattern of two rival men fighting over one woman is temporarily inverted once the bride is won, when Étaín herself faces a rival in the form of Mider's first wife Fúamnach. The mythic layers of the story are particularly evident not only in Étaín's remarkable ability to retain her identity throughout a series of successive lives, but also in Mider's obvious immortality.

Yet throughout all of this Étaín herself has little to say. Even the rival first wife Fúamnach (in Étaín 1) is able to speak and explain herself, but in this first story Étaín is the silent object of desire, submitting herself first to the barter and exchange of men and then to the enchantments of Fúamnach. In Étaín 2 she does find a voice, refusing to sleep with Ailill in his brother's own house (although she agrees to meet him outside) and declining to return with Mider unless Eochaid sells her to him. Yet on the whole she is strangely passive in the face of her numerous adventures. Her suitors fight and win her, and she abides by the rules of their games. Given the apparent mythic content of these tales, and Étain's immortality, it is odd that she displays so little affinity with the other typically strong-willed goddess figures whose aggressive behaviour has been consistently explained mythologically by scholars.

The Wooing of Étaín is an important intertext for *The Wooing of Emer* for its depiction of the difficulties inherent in winning the perfect bride. Yet it is not necessarily typical of the medieval Irish tradition. Several other tales present varying portraits of the men and women involved in the wooing process.

The Cattle Raid of Froech, for instance, presents a much more active heroine in the person of Findabair, daughter of Ailill and Medb.[25]

Summary of *The Cattle Raid of Froech*

The story recounts the wooing of Findabair by Froech, son of a mortal father and an Otherworld mother. When he hears that Findabair has fallen in love with him he travels to the court of Ailill and Medb, bringing wondrous gifts. He is welcomed at the court, and after playing *fidchell* for three days he manages to meet Findabair alone by the river. He asks her to elope with him. She refuses but gives him a thumb-ring given to her by her father as a token of her love, and persuades him to ask for her formally. But when Froech asks Ailill to give Findabair to him, the bride-price that he stipulates is so high that Froech rejects it.

Fearing that Froech will now abduct the girl, Ailill and Medb plot to kill him. They persuade Froech to go swimming in a pool known to contain a water-monster. Once he is in the water, Ailill searches Froech's clothing and finds the thumb-ring. He throws it into the water but a salmon swallows it. Froech sees all this and catches and hides the salmon. Eventually he is attacked by the monster and calls for his sword. Findabair herself seizes the sword and jumps into the water with it. Seeing this, Ailill casts his spear at Findabair; Froech catches the spear and throws it back at him. Froech then kills the water-monster and emerges from the pool. He is taken to the Otherworld by a company of women from his mother's *síd* to be healed of his wounds.

Medb and Ailill regret their treatment of him, but Ailill determines to punish Findabair for her betrayal. Ailill demands the thumb-ring from her and threatens to have her killed if she cannot produce it. She cannot immediately produce the ring but swears that if she can she will no longer be under her father's power. Meanwhile Froech has retrieved the salmon and sent it to her to cook. The fish is brought to Ailill and Medb with the ring sitting on top. Froech explains what has happened, altering the story to omit Findabair's gift of the ring to him. They make peace, Findabair and Froech are betrothed, and Froech agrees to give his cows for the Táin. (The remainder of the story does not concern us.)[26]

This story is clearly set in a mortal world of marriage negotiations and bride-prices. Unlike the passive Findabair of the *Táin*, the daughter of Medb and Ailill appears here as an independent and decisive young woman, determined to marry the man she loves and yet equally unwilling to have her worth devalued. Like many other heroines in wooing tales, she helps her lover in his suit – in this case going so far as to openly defy her father to save Froech's life. The description of her view of Froech as the most beautiful young man she has ever seen provides a brief but vivid glimpse of female subjectivity.[27] Findabair has a strong sense of self-worth and is ready to speak her mind, traits that are highlighted in her refusal to elope with Froech:

'Ceist, in n-élafe limm?' olse.
'Ni élub ém', olsi, 'úair im ingen ríg ocus rígnae. Ni fil dit daidbri-siu nachimm éta-sa óm muntir, ocus bid é mo thogu-sa dano dul cucut-su. Is tú ro charus, ocus beir-siu latt in n-ordnaisc se,' ol ind ingen, 'ocus bíd etronn do chomarthu.'

'I wonder will you elope with me?' said he.
'I will not, indeed,' said she, 'for I am the daughter of a king and queen. You are not so poor that you cannot get me from my people, and it will be my choice to go to you. It is you I have loved. And take this thumb-ring,' said the girl, 'and let it be as a token between us.'[28]

When her father threatens to kill her if the lost ring is not found, she makes clear her rejection of his control over her life:

'Tongu do día tonges mo thúath, dia fogbathar nicon béo-sa fot chumachtu-su bes íre, diandom roib forsa rol mo greis.'

'I swear by the god by whom my people swear, if it [the ring] be found, I shall not be in your power any longer if I have anyone under whose protection I may put myself.'[29]

Obviously, this section of *The Cattle Raid of Froech* depicts the wooing of a bride in a much different light from *The Wooing of Étaín*. This text shows an active female with her own desires, determined to marry the man of her choice and yet hemmed in by custom, the power of her parents, and particularly the jealousy of her father. Through their initiative and cooperation, she and her lover manage to effect compromise and change.

The slightly later tale, *The Wooing of Ailbe*, focuses on the verbal and intellectual skills of Ailbe, one of the daughters of Cormac.[30] King Cormac gives his consent to Finn's search for a wife, and Finn tests Cormac's daughters by asking a series of questions. Ailbe, who has already proven her intelligence in a debate with her father earlier in the tale, answers them correctly. Ailbe's attitude is very confident throughout the dialogue with her older suitor. Like Emer, she knows her own intellectual capabilities and is able to use them to her advantage in her verbal sparring with Finn. Ailbe's eloquence is discussed in more detail below.

The Wooing of Ailbe deviates from two of the patterns observed in the other wooing tales. First, the wooing does not involve a series of tests for the hero; instead, the woman herself is tested, first by the druid Citruad, then by her father Cormac, and finally by Finn himself. This testing is verbal and intellectual rather than physical. Secondly, neither the hero nor Ailbe herself must be geographically separated from home in order to take part in the wooing process.

The Voyage of Art Son of Conn and the Wooing of Delbchaem Daughter of Morgan (*Eachtra Airt Meic Cuind ocus Tochmarc Delbchaime Ingine Morgain*) is an ostensibly later example of the wooing tale. Although it is listed in the 'B' list of prime tales, it survives in only one extant version, in the fifteenth-century Book of Fermoy. Furthermore, since the language of this version is Early Modern Irish, scholars have questioned the early existence of the tale. However, it contains many elements which link it with older traditions. In one of the few published articles devoted to the tale, Brendan O Hehir contends that *The Voyage of Art Son of Conn* represents a later Christian reworking of 'a genuinely old theme – more a paradigm than a tale.'[31]

Summary of *The Voyage of Art Son of Conn and the Wooing of Delbchaem Daughter of Morgan*

Conn Cétchathach rules Tara prosperously until his wife Eithne Taebhfada dies, after which he is too despondent to rule properly. Meanwhile, in the Otherworld, Bécuma Cneisgel, wife of Labraid Luathlám-ar-Claideb, is found guilty of adultery and banished to Ireland for her sin. She arrives there seeking Art son of Conn, with whom she has fallen in love sight unseen, but encounters Conn instead. She decides to live with Conn since he has no wife, but makes him agree to banish Art from Tara for a year.

During that year there is a failure of corn and milk in the land, and the druids determine that Conn's wife is the cause. They decree that the land can only be restored by the sacrifice of the son of a sinless couple. Conn sets out to find such a child, leaving Art in the kingship in his place. After travelling to a strange island he finds a boy whose parents have only slept together once, at his conception. The boy agrees to return to Ireland with Conn. Before the boy is killed a mysterious woman with a cow appears to challenge the wisdom of the druids. She outsmarts them and advises Conn to rid himself of the druids and banish Bécuma. The woman then takes the boy and leaves.

Bécuma challenges Art to play *fidchell* for a wager, which she loses. Art demands that she bring him the warrior's rod that belonged to Cú Roí, and she goes off on a quest to find it. Aided by an Otherworld foster-sister, she gains the rod and returns with it. She and Art play again, and this time Bécuma wins. She demands that he bring back from an island a woman named Delbchaem, daughter of Morgan.

Art sets out and comes to an island ruled by Créide Fírálaind, who instructs him as to how to obtain Delbchaem from her dangerous parents. Delbchaem's monstrous mother knows that she will die if her daughter marries. Art engages her in battle and cuts off her head; Morgan arrives and Art kills him as well. Art and Delbchaem return to Ireland, and on Delbchaem's instructions he banishes Bécuma from Tara, and Delbchaem takes her place there.

O Hehir points out that there are really two wooing tales cobbled together here: first, the courtship of the Otherworld woman Bécuma (which, I would argue, is actually *Bécuma*'s courtship of *Conn*, since she is the one who takes the initiative) and later, Art's courtship of Delbchaem, a supernatural woman who lives on an island and must be won from her dangerous Otherworld parents. The story is rather confused, since it attempts to knit together sub-plots of both Christian and pre-Christian origin. However, several of the motifs recurrant in other wooing tales survive here: the opposition of a parent or rival to the bridal quest, the hero's journey through a hostile realm, and his eventual success.

However, like *The Cattle Raid of Froech* and *The Wooing of Ailbe*, *The Voyage of Art Son of Conn* also depicts strong female characters who make their desires known to the men around them and sometimes even take the initiative in love. In the first portion of the tale, Bécuma initiates relationships with both Conn and his son Art – a fact that is negatively portrayed in the text.[32] Bécuma's apparent 'double' in the tale, Delbchaem, whom she sends Art to woo, is more the typical guarded bride. She resides in a remote fortress on an island, protected by supernatural parents.

Like most heroes, Art receives help and guidance in his quest for Delbchaem. In Art's case the help comes from another apparently supernatural woman who lives on a strange island, Créide Fírálaind. She prepares him for the fearful obstacles that lie in his path to Delbchaem and gives him instruction on how to overcome them. Delbchaem is guarded not by a jealous father but by a monstrous mother, Coinchend Cendfada:

... nert cet indti a lathair chatha no comhlaind ... Et do gellsat na draighthi dísi cibe uair dogentai tochmharc a hingine co fuidhedh sí bas annsin. Conadh aire sin do marbad sí gac[h] fear dothigeadh do thochmharc a hingine ... Ocus is í roindill na heich neimhe 7 an droichit oighrita 7 an fidh dorcha cona conaibh cuilind ...

... and she had the strength of a hundred in battle or conflict ... And the Druids had foretold her that if ever her daughter should be wooed, in that same hour she would die. Therefore, she put to death everyone that came to woo her daughter ... And it was she that had contrived the venomous steeds, and the icy bridge, and the dark forest with the Coincuilind ...[33]

Delbchaem herself is not as vocal as Emer, Findabair and Ailbe, or Bécuma; yet she does bear a remarkable resemblance to Emer in her rather formulaic description:

Et ba halaind an ingin sin, eter cruth 7 chéill 7 gais 7 gres 7 genus 7 ordarcus.

Fair was the maiden both in shape and intelligence, in wisdom and embroidery, in chastity and nobility.[34]

It is interesting to note that Delbchaem's attributes do *not* include the gifts of voice and sweet speech, the two talents which so mark Emer's character in *The Wooing of Emer*.

This brief survey of intertexts demonstrates that *The Wooing of Emer* belongs to a network of tales about heroes wooing brides, and highlights some of the patterns common to most courtship narratives. It is clear that none of the prospective brides in *The Cattle Raid of Froech*, *The Wooing of Ailbe*, or even in *The Voyage of Art Son of Conn* are as passive and silent as Étaín. All of these women, to varying degrees, insist on pursuing relationships with the men of their choice. In this respect, Emer's portrayal in *The Wooing of Emer* appears to fit into the general tradition.

However, our tale differs from these others in several ways. First, in *The Wooing of Emer* it is the woman who sets the tasks for the suitor she has chosen, while in other tales the tasks tend to be imposed by an obstructive parent or a rival. Second, Emer is not only more vocal than the brides in these other tales, but her speech actually shapes the narrative itself. For all her talk, Ailbe's words have limited effect on a correspondingly more limited narrative. Third, as Edel has noted, *The Wooing of Emer* depicts at least the first portion of the courtship scene from the perspective of the woman, not of the hero.[35] That is, we see the hero's appearance and arrival through the eyes of Emer's sister Fíal, who in turn describes him in great detail to her sister. Contrary to what we would expect, we do not see the women from the point of view of the hero and his charioteer; in fact, although Emer's beauty is cited as one of the reasons Cú Chulainn woos her, she is never described physically in any detail. Although she is clearly the object of the hero's quest, she is not 'objectified' in the same way that many heroines of courtly romance are objectified. All of these characteristics make *The Wooing of Emer* of particular interest, and reinforce the impression of Emer's overriding structural and thematic importance in the narrative.

Before we move into a discussion of Emer's speech, one additional piece of the contextual framework needs to be put in place: that of the legal background in which the tale was composed and received.

Context: Law

A vast amount of legal material survives from medieval Ireland. As noted earlier, many of these texts are in Old Irish and were first written down in the seventh and eighth centuries; they continued to be recopied and glossed, and survive in often incomplete form in manuscripts from the fourteenth to the sixteenth centuries.[36] A careful reading of the secular literature suggests that these early laws were also influential in the narrative tradition. The Ulster Cycle tales contain many references to legal principles, and reading these texts with one eye on the laws can prove illuminating.

Medieval Irish law recognized a range of marital unions, from the most formal arranged marriages between kin-groups to casual liaisons, abductions, and rapes.[37] The legal texts describe a hierarchy of unions. The highest form of marriage was the 'union of joint property' (*lánamnas comthinchuir*) and seems to have been normally contracted between people of the same social class, since both partners and their families were required to contribute equal goods to the marriage.[38] Marriage by abduction is recognized in the laws, but it is the sixth form of union down the list and clearly a much inferior form of marriage. Indeed, we saw in the discussion of *The Cattle Raid of Froech* that Findabair refuses to let the hero abduct her, stating that it is beneath her as the daughter of a king.

In light of these marriage laws, *The Wooing of Emer* presents an intriguing picture. On the one hand, Emer's inquiry as to whether or not Cú Chulainn already has a wife suggests that a 'union of joint property' in which she would be the first or chief wife (*cétmuinter*) is the only kind of marriage acceptable to her as a woman of high status. Furthermore, she is careful to describe the strong men who will protect her from being abducted, and the strength and cunning of her own father Forgall. She also mentions an injunction upon her not to marry before her older sister Fíal. All of these factors imply a conformity to law and custom. On the other hand, Emer gives the hero explicit instructions near the end of their conversation as to exactly how she may be carried off. These demands not only provide the hero with difficult tasks to perform in order to win his bride, but also implicitly grant him permission to abduct her. In so instructing him, Emer implies that her earlier warnings and the mention of her sister were really intended to goad the hero into action.[39]

Faced with this apparent contradiction between legal norms and the tale itself, Alwyn and Brinley Rees can only exclaim:

How different are the marriages of mythology! Just as the hero's birth has an outward resemblance to the most disgraceful births in human society, so does his marriage have more in common with abductions and elopements than with the socially approved forms of marriage.[40]

Without denying the possible connections between Cú Chulainn and mythic heroes, this seems an overstatement of the case. Not all abductions in medieval Irish literature fit the 'mythological' patterns described in the Rees's analysis. The tales of Deirdre and Gráinne, for example, depict determined women *forcing* the men they love to abduct them, with very different consequences from those in The Wooing of Emer. While in The Wooing of Emer both Emer and Cú Chulainn are presented as extraordinary human beings – and thus people of whom extraordinary behaviour might be expected – they are consistently represented as *mortals*. Since Emer lives on the frontier of Ireland (and clearly not within the five provinces scoured for potential brides by the Ulstermen) she is perhaps not as subject to legal restrictions and social custom as other women.[41] On the other hand, the fact that Conchobar himself pays her *tinnscra* (bride-price) when the couple are eventually wed both highlights the unusual nature of their union and, at the same time, brings the marriage back within the parameters of law and custom. In paying Emer's bride-price, the Ulster king is acting in the place of her dead father and in the process legitimizing the union, probably as a 'union of joint property.' With this act Emer's movement from the frontier of Ireland to its cultural centre is completed.

Emer's 'abduction' thus need not be viewed solely from a mythological standpoint. Her story may in fact be a paradigm of social integration, wherein the unique hero who can only find a mate outside the established centres of his own civilization is able to rejoin his society once he unites with an equally unique woman. Moreover, it is important to recognize that the abduction motif is widespread in wooing tales of many kinds, both those deemed 'mythical' and those not.

Thus, Emer's behaviour toward Cú Chulainn both conforms to the framework of law and custom in some ways, and violates it in others. With this context in mind, we can now turn to an examination of her speech.

Women's Words

Words are crucial in the construction of this narrative; the 'speech acts' performed by the major players in the drama serve to construct both the plot of the tale and its meaning. The words of women perform a variety of functions within the fictional world of *The Wooing of Emer*. They thus transcend the strictures on women's speech noted in many medieval texts, where women often seem restricted to complaining about or lamenting events which they are powerless to control or change.[42] Speech act theory illuminates the ways in which the words of women have tangible effects on the fictional world of the narrative.

The primary speech act in the tale is the verbal contract which Cú Chulainn and Emer make with each other, the act of *promising* to marry – an 'illocutionary act' which drives the plot of the narrative.[43] But there are many other instances in the text where Emer's words affect the perceptions and actions of the characters. Through a number of illocutionary acts, Emer manages to reshape the world around her and with it her future life. In doing this she also shapes the narrative itself. Her speech is in fact the machinery that drives the tale.

Emer is the ultimate female wordsmith. Her words in the initial wooing conversation with Cú Chulainn serve both to confirm her as the ideal mate (both in the hero's eyes and in the eyes of the audience) and to launch the hero on his quest. Emer both offers herself as prize and lays out the difficult conditions for winning that prize; as Sayers has observed, her self-description constitutes 'a theatrical staging of herself as spectacle.'[44] This deliberate self-staging is also a 'perlocutionary act' – an act which achieves certain intended effects on the hero beyond that of simply describing herself to him.[45] By subtly shaping the conversation to put pressure on Cú Chulainn, Emer comes just close enough to impugning his honour to goad him into action to prove himself. It is she who sets the standard to which the hero must conform.

It is important to note, as Baudiš did long ago, that contrary to most wooing tales that involve riddling dialogues, *The Wooing of Emer* presents a hero who wishes to marry the woman because she is able to *understand* his riddles and to use them herself, not because she fails to solve her suitor's riddles or because he solves hers.[46] This implies that both man and woman are equally well educated in arcane speech and are evenly matched in intellect and eloquence.

The first and most dramatic demonstration of the role of words occurs in the courtship scene. The dialogue is a complex series of questions and responses by both Emer and Cú Chulainn, in which each question and answer advances the dynamics of interaction between the two young people. The conversation has many stages, including greetings, Emer's questions and Cú Chulainn's responses to them (including the explanation of the route he has taken to arrive at her home), Emer's enumeration of her virtues and her description of her father and of the strong men who guard her, her stated doubts about Cú Chulainn's prowess and his boastful response, the hero's offer of marriage and Emer's counter-offer of her older sister, Emer's enumeration of conditions to be met before marriage, and the couple's agreement to marry.

The arcane riddling speech employed by the couple serves to establish their equality in mental and verbal dexterity. Each stages him- or herself through speech, testing the other while at the same time promoting the self. An important aspect of Emer's eloquence is the ability to convey information within a densely coded, ritualized form of speech which alludes to mythological and historical lore. As Sayers has observed, 'intellectual ability is not enough for riddle-solving. It must be harnessed to work within the prevailing linguistic and cultural codes.'[47]

Emer and Cú Chulainn's learned dialogue belongs to a tradition within Irish literature, and thus has intertextual links with other texts. In her discussion of the dialogue, Doris Edel mentions *The Wooing of Ailbe*, the tale referred to earlier. Another pertinent intertext is the arcane dialogue between Ailill, Medb, and Fergus in the *Táin*. Finally, *The Kin-slaying of Rónán* (*Fingal Rónáin*) provides an example of a verbal test called verse-capping. It will be useful to look briefly at these intertexts.

The Wooing of Ailbe is the later wooing tale mentioned above, in which the hero Finn tests the daughters of Cormac with a series of questions. Only Ailbe is able to answer them all, and consequently becomes his wife. As Edel points out in her discussion of this tale, Finn's questions and Ailbe's answers are not couched in the same arcane language as those of Cú Chulainn and Emer; they are, rather, 'gnomic' utterances – statements of general wisdom or meaning which seem to be found the world over.[48] So, for instance, the first question Finn asks Ailbe is 'Cia lind as lethi cac rian?' ('Which lake is wider than any sea?'). Ailbe correctly answers, 'Leithi drucht' ('Dew is wider').[49]

Yet despite the different nature of these questions and answers, this courting dialogue does incorporate allusions to male-female relationships and the potential joys and problems inherent in them. In fact, the courtship register is present beneath the surface of the entire riddling dialogue. A few examples will illustrate this:

'Cid [as] milsi mid?' ol Find. – 'Tairisi comrad' air in ingen'...[50]
'Cid as briscim cuirir?' ar Find. – 'Accned mna ididhi' ar in ingen.
'Cid as trumu[51] crithir?' ol Find. – 'Ciall mna bis itir dis' ol in ingen.

'What is sweeter than mead?' said Finn. 'Trustworthy conversation [words of courtship],'[52] said the maiden.
'What is more brittle than a nut?' said Finn.
'The nature of a flighty woman,' said the maiden.
'What is lighter than a spark?' said Finn.
'The mind of a woman between two men,' said the maiden.[53]

Although Ailbe is the only one tested with questions before the marriage, and although she and Finn do not test *each other* as Emer and Cú Chulainn do in *The Wooing of Emer*, Ailbe is certainly Finn's equal in intellect and eloquence. In fact, the text adds an illuminating scene after the marriage in which Finn tries to 'instruct' Ailbe only to find, to his chagrin, that she can match him word for word.[54]

The verbal sparring in the *Táin* between Ailill, Medb, and Fergus also highlights the agonistic elements implicit in this type of speech. This conversation occurs after Ailill has obtained proof that Medb has been sleeping with Fergus. Ailill has sent a servant to steal Fergus's sword during Fergus's lovemaking with Medb in the woods. Later, when they are all back at the camp, Ailill invites Fergus to play *fidchell*. The verbal combat thus occurs in the context of a battle on the game board. It is also set against the background of armies gathering for the great conflict of the Táin itself. The scene is thus highly charged, setting the emotions of jealousy and rivalry within the immediate love triangle against larger forces of conflict.

When Fergus enters Ailill's tent the latter starts to laugh at his rival.
Fergus responds:

Fó fer fristibther
manib scéo mera[s]
mórgníme merthar
ar biur mo chlaidib
Macha mind
mos-dísem celga
de Galión gáir
maniped búaid mná
mis-rairlastar ...

Well for the man who is smiled at,
if it is not enmity which perturbs [him]
fateful deeds by which he is distracted.
By the point of my sword,
the halidom of Macha,
quickly would we avenge the treacheries
with a shout of the Gaileóin,
if a woman's feat
had not misled them [i.e., the Galeóin].'[55]

Ailill persuades Fergus to play *fidchell* with him:

Imbir fidchill scéo búanbach
ar bélaib ríg scéo rígnai
cluichi ara-fuiretar
fo mórslúagu duilecha
nibe cauma frit
cia toichell berae
ar is diar n-antaib
cungnas ar rígnaib ingenaib
am móreóla
bés ni gába cétchinta for mnaib ...

Play *fidchell* and *búanbach*
before king and queen,
games which are prepared
among greedy great hosts.

It will not be the same to you
what stake you win,
for ...
I am very experienced in
companionship concerning queens and daughters.
Perhaps one should not put the aforementioned faults on the women.'[56]

Medb intervenes to defend herself from Ailill's charge that she, as a woman, cannot act responsibly or exercise good judgment:

Léic de becbríathra[ib] aithig
ní deoraid rún roben
scéo attúar admaib
macraid mín i nÉri chuirm
nita cailtech esbrethach
fritoing di thúatha
nitat neóit étig
ar buaib scéo foicherthar
di gnúis glanfidir Fergus.

Refrain from the petty words of a churl.
[?]A noble lady is not the secret of a stranger.[?] She secures fierceness from
dexterous ones through her gentle offspring at the ale feast in Ireland.
I am not stingy, prone to unjust judgement.
Two tribes renounce it:
they are not stingy, unseemly
concerning the cows about which battle is waged.
By his presence Fergus will be cleared.[57]

Although the language of these verses is not as densely coded as Emer and Cú Chulainn's learned conversation, it certainly contains a strong sexual subtext. The dialogue cleverly weaves sexual innuendo into a discussion of political power. Yet as Olsen observes, there are no winners in this debate: 'Fergus has lost his sword, Medb has had to endure antifeminist slander from both her husband and her lover, and Ailill, instead of redressing his status as cuckold, emerges as a petty and irresponsible king.'[58]

A similar verbal battle occurs in *The Kin-slaying of Rónán* when the daughter of Echaid and Mael Fothartaig (who is Rónán's son) engage in a contest of verse-capping which ultimately costs Mael Fothartaig his life.

This situation is especially dangerous, for in *The Kin-slaying of Rónán* the young woman has been attempting to seduce her husband's handsome son for some time. The son, Mael Fothartaig, has repeatedly rejected her, and in revenge she has accused *him* of soliciting *her*. Reluctant to believe such a thing of his son, Rónán at last agrees to an ordeal by verse-capping. The conflict reaches its climax one day when Mael Fothartaig comes in from the cold:

> Buí in drúth Mael Fothartaig .i. Mac Glass, oc clessaib for lár in taige. Is and as-bert, ar rop úar in laa
>> Is úar fri cloï ngaeithe
>> do neoch in-gair Bú Aífe
> Cluinti seo, a Rónáin, or si-si. Gaib sin do-ridisi, or sí.
>> Is úar fri cloï ngaíthe
>> do neoch in-gair Bú Aífe.
>>> Iss ed ingaire mada, or si-se
>>> cen bú, cen nech no chara.
> (.i. sech ní ránac-sa, ní thucais-siu na bú lat.)
> Is fír són a fecht-sa, ol Rónán.

> Mael Fothartaig's fool, Mac Glass, was juggling on the floor of the house. Then he [Mael Fothartaig][59] said, for it was a cold day,
>> 'It is cold against the whirlwind
>> for one who herds the Cows of Aífe.'
> 'Listen to this, Rónán,' she [the daughter of Echaid] said. 'Sing it again,' she said.
>> 'It is cold against the whirlwind
>> for one who herds the Cows of Aífe.'
> 'It is useless herding,' said she,
>> 'without cows, without anyone who loves.'
> (that is, not only did I not come, you could not bring the cows with you).
> 'It is true on this occasion,' said Rónán.[60]

Rónán reluctantly accepts the apparent verdict of this ordeal and orders that his son be killed. *The Kin-slaying of Rónán* is a tragic tale which demonstrates all too clearly the power of words, particularly those between men and women. Words are fraught with social danger, and the wise person must be vigilant against using speech imprudently.

While the verbal battles in these passages occur in somewhat different situations from that of the wooing of Emer by Cú Chulainn, the cloaking of speech, the frequent sexual imagery, and the combative nature of the dialogues all provide links between the texts. It is sufficient to observe that the wooing dialogue between Emer and Cú Chulainn does not exist in a literary vacuum. On the contrary, it stands within a tradition of combative and arcane speech, particularly between men and women, and particularly in highly charged situations involving sexual relationships.

The Sweet Speech of Courtship

The greetings of Emer and Cú Chulainn to each other demonstrate their skill at arcane speech; their words are so strange that a glossator must intervene to interpret their phrases for the text's audience. Cú Chulainn approaches and greets Emer. Emer then responds in very decorous language:

'Bennachais dóib.'[61] Tócbaid Emer a gnúis cáimchruthaig i n-ardai 7 dobeir aichni for Coin Culainn conid ann asbert: 'Dess imríadam dúib,' ol sí, .i. Día do réidiugud dúib. 'Slán imroisc dúibsi,' ol éseom, .i. rop slán sibsi ó chach aisc.

'I greet you.' Emer raises up her beautifully shaped face and recognizes Cú Chulainn so that she then says: 'We ride around the right [side] of you,'[62] she said, that is, may God make it [the road] smooth for you. 'Freedom from distorted sight to you' he said, that is, may you be safe from every reproach.[63]

Emer's use of the image of driving a chariot does not necessarily place her in a normally male role, for a number of women in medieval Irish literature are depicted as driving chariots.[64] It does perhaps signal the relatively active role she will play in this relationship, and may also serve to foreshadow the warrior-women who will be so important in Cú Chulainn's training in the latter part of the tale.

After this initial greeting Emer asks Cú Chulainn a series of questions: 'Can doluidid si? Cía hairm i febair? Cé bu for fess ann? Cisí conar dolod?' ('Whence have you come? Where did you stay? What was your feast[65] there? Which way did you come?').[66] The hero responds to these questions in riddles. Emer clearly understands the meaning of his riddles, for when he in turn questions her she responds in the same type of arcane language (glossed again for the audience). When Cú Chulainn asks her to describe herself, her words are highly revealing:

'Temair ban, báine ingen, inching gensa,'.i. amal atá Temair ós cach thulaig, sic atúsa ós cach mnaí in gensa. 'Gass nád forfóemthar. Dercaid nad décsenach,' .i. nom décthar ó chách ar mo chaími 7 ní décaimse nech. 'Doirb i ndobur, ainder imnáir,' .i. in tan décthar in doirb, is i n-íchtur uisci téit. 'Tethra tethra dá lúa. Lúachair nád imthegar,' .i. ara caími. 'Ingen ríg, riches garta,' .i. enich. 'Conar nád forémthar ... Arcotaim trénfir tíarmóirset,' .i. atá lium trénfir dogénat m'íarmóracht, 'cid bé nom béra dar a terthogu cen forus mo chaingne cucu 7 co Forgall.'

'Tara of women, whiteness of maidens, champion of chastity,' that is, as Tara is above every hill, thus I am above women in chastity. 'A sprig not taken.[67] The one who looks but does not gaze,' that is, I am looked upon by all for my beauty and I do not look upon anyone.[68] 'A worm in water, a very bashful woman,' that is, when looked upon the worm goes to the lower part of the water. 'A sealord of Tethra (?) of the two Luas (?).[69] Rushes that are not traversed/broken,'[70] that is because of their beauty. 'Daughter of a king, a flame of hospitality,' that is, of honour. 'A road that is not to be taken ...[71] I have strong men who would pursue me,' that is, I have strong men who will follow me, 'if someone carries me off against their desire without a well-founded account of my doings to them and to Forgall.'[72]

As Sayers points out, Emer's coded responses here contain more poetic than mythological or topographical elements. He observes, 'Emer has illustrated a different, though still conventional speech art, one more in the sphere of the poet than of the archivist of toponymy or legendary history.'[73] The poetic nature of her speech here is highlighted by her use of binding alliteration.[74] However, her initial naming of herself as *Temair ban* (Tara of women), as well as her later allusions to *dinnshenchas* (lore of places) traditions in her darkly-worded marriage demands, demonstrates that her repertoire is not restricted to poetic diction alone.[75] 'Tethra tethra' is also a learned reference, and one that echoes Cú Chulainn's own description of his arrival at her home a few paragraphs earlier.

Emer employs a mixture of natural and cultural images to characterize herself to her suitor. On the one hand she compares herself to a *gass* (sprig), a *doirb* (worm), and to *lúachair* (rushes), all of which are drawn from the natural world. On the other hand, the majority of her images are cultural ones. Her initial metaphor for herself is that of Tara, an important centre of culture in medieval Irish tradition. Emer also calls herself an *ingen ríg* (daughter of a king), and a *conar* (road). The image *riches garta*, variously translated as 'a flame of hospitality' or 'a flame of glory' combines natural and cultural elements.[76]

Emer's repeated emphasis on her discretion or chastity (*genas*) has been understood by critics as a positive statement of wholeness and self-respect rather than a negative one of restriction or restraint. Philip O'Leary has observed that 'the pride in her chastity was rooted in a woman's sense of her personal integrity and independence, and not merely in her acceptance of her duty to satisfy her husband's demand for legitimate progeny.'[77] According to this reading, by presenting herself as a model of chastity Emer not only challenges her suitor but also assures him of her worth. She enhances her aura of potency and portrays herself as a valuable prize.

Emer's emphasis on chastity or restraint is especially clear in her phrase *dercaid nad décsenach*, (the one who looks but does not gaze) and the *doirb i ndobur* (a worm in water) who descends to the bottom out of shyness. This recalls her behaviour earlier, when Emer, hearing the approach of the chariot, does not look up but asks one of her companions to see who is coming. Her older sister Fíal (who, we later learn, has already slept with a man and is thus not a suitable mate for Cú Chulainn) is the one who describes the hero and his chariot in detail as he approaches. It is only when he arrives and greets Emer that she raises her eyes and looks upon him.[78] It is possible that we have here a reference to some standard of female behaviour in regard to 'gazing.' Emer's control over her gaze, and her self-description as one who is looked upon but does not look in return, adds to the impression of her self-containment.[79]

This emphasis on discretion, chastity, and self-containment does raise the possibility of clerical influence on the reshaping of female imagery here. The suggestion that Emer's sister Fíal is an unsuitable mate for the hero because she has slept with another man only adds to the impression that the inviolate status of the woman is being exalted in this section of the tale. Thus, it would be unwise to accept too readily the idea that Emer's self-contained imagery is based on some native Irish concept of woman's self worth; it may be a matter of clerical propaganda. This is all the more likely if, as Mac Cana and the Rees brothers have suggested, wooing tales were read or told at weddings.[80] In the context of such a social occasion, Emer's virginal state could be construed as an exemplum for behaviour in real life.

Yet despite this imagery of sexual restraint, Emer is far from the passive female prize. Throughout the dialogue, Emer maintains control over both the conversation and the hero's responses. While she appears confident and self-assured in her responses to questions about her own identity and reputation, Cú Chulainn on the other hand is easily goaded by her remarks about his prowess. After boasting of his strength, Emer counters with what Sayers calls a 'deflating, ironically maternal observation':[81]

'At maithi na comrama móethmacáim', ol in ingen, 'acht nád ránac co nert n-erred béos.'

'Those are good triumphs of a tender youth,' said the maiden, 'but you have not yet attained the strength of a champion.'[82]

Although Emer's remark falls into Searle's category of 'representatives' – speech acts which represent or describe a state of affairs – it is clearly also a perlocutionary act, subtly crafted to goad the hero into giving a closer account of his upbringing.[83] Cú Chulainn responds with a lengthy explanation of his fosterage with all the great men of Ulster – an explanation that is meant to establish that the hero is, like Emer's father and his own father Lug before him, samíldanach (skilled in many arts).

At the end of this section the hero counters with the question, 'Cindus rot altsu i Luchtlogaib Loga?' ('How were you reared in the Gardens of Lug?') Emer's response is briefer and more abstract than the hero's:

'Rom altsa ém,' ol sí, 'la feba Féne, i costud forchaíne, i fogart genusa, i comgraim rígnae, i n-écosc sochraid. Conid chucum bágthair cach ndelb sóer sochraid etir íallaib ban búaignige.'

'I was reared indeed,' she said, 'with the qualities of old Irish stock in restraining great beauty, in the honour of chastity, in queenly bearing, in beautiful appearance. So that one evaluates every noble, beautiful appearance among the glorious troops of women using me as a model.'[84]

Emer presents herself here as complete and whole, with nothing lacking. In this she stands in marked contrast to the hero, who, despite his illustrious upbringing, has yet to prove himself and realize his full heroic potential. She has become what she will be; he is still in a state of becoming.

It is also significant that Emer is not described physically in this text by the hero or anyone else; the only descriptions we find are those in which she describes *herself*. Both in her initial riddling speech and in the passage just cited, Emer presents a self-portrait which *she* creates and controls. Thus, although she is certainly the object of the hero's quest she is the arbiter of the ways in which she as object will be perceived, both by the hero within the text and by the audience outside the text.

After Emer's brief account of her upbringing, Cú Chulainn proposes that they should marry:

'Cindus dano,'ol Cú Chulainn, 'nachar chomtig dún dib línaib comríachtain? Ar ní fúarus sa cosse ben follongad ind airis dála imacallaim fon samail seo frim.'

'How then,' said Cú Chulainn, 'should it not be fitting for us both to come together? For I have not found until now a woman who kept up the subject as regards a conversation with me in this way.'[85]

This is a significant juncture in the dialogue. The hero clearly states that it is Emer's eloquence and quick wit, and her ability to carry on an extended, arcane conversation with him, which have convinced him that she is the right choice as a mate. She is his equal in verbal skill and mental acuity, and clearly he is seeking such a wife.

Emer confirms this assessment of her with her response. She asks if he has a wife already, and (as Sayers suggests, perhaps mischievously) offers him her older sister Fíal instead. These two perlocutionary acts are intended to achieve effects beyond those of the illocutionary act of questioning; that is, Emer is not simply seeking responses to her question and counter-offer, but in fact wishes to provoke an emotional response in Cú Chulainn. In this she succeeds, for the hero responds 'Ní hí ém ro charussa' ('It is not she with whom I have fallen in love'), and then goes on to express his sexual desire for Emer.[86] He adds a further reason for his rejection of Fíal – she has allegedly slept with another man. The text thus makes it clear that both Emer and Cú Chulainn demand the highest form of marriage, a 'union of joint property,' in which the couple contributed equally to the marriage and the wife enjoyed the status of *cétmuinter*, or 'chief wife' (who was apparently expected to be a virgin at marriage).[87]

In the final section of their conversation, Cú Chulainn admires Emer's figure in metaphorical language, using natural imagery and repeating the phrase, 'Caín in mag so mag alchuing' ('Fair is that plain, the plain of the noble yoke') three times.[88] Emer takes up the image of the plain, and repeats it. After each repetition of Cú Chulainn's phrase, Emer details – in equally metaphorical language – the three difficult feats that he must accomplish in order to win her. In the first of these three demands Emer combines poetic diction with learned references to place-name lore that call to mind the hero's own descriptions of his itinerary earlier:

'Ní rúalae nech in mag sa,' ol Emer, 'nád ruband comainm n-arcait for cach áth ó Áth Scéne Menn for Ollbini cosin mBanchuing n-arcait ara mbruinnend Brea diantos Fedelm.'

'No one approaches this plain,' said Emer, 'who does not slay a hundred on each ford from the Ford of Scenmenn[89] at Ollbine to the woman-yoke of silver where the quick froth [?] of Fedelm makes Brea leap.'[90]

This statement and those which follow are 'directives' – illocutionary acts designed to provoke action in the hearer, in this case *daring* him to do something.[91] Here again Emer seeks to shape both the life of the hero and the course of future events. She demonstrates that she too is well versed in traditional lore, and at the same time links her demands with Cú Chulainn's earlier itinerary.

The hero agrees to meet all of Emer's demands as specified. The two of them then make a verbal contract to marry:

'Asberthar, dogéntar,' ol Cú Chulainn.
'Forregthar, forimregthar, gébthar, arfóemtar,' ol Emer.

'It is said, it will be done,' said Cú Chulainn.
'It is bound, it is contracted on me, it will be taken, it will be accepted,' said Emer.[92]

This is the major speech act which governs the remainder of the narrative. As a promise, it falls into the category of 'commissives,' and the legalistic language used here adds weight to it as a verbal contract.[93] There is an important intersection of words and deeds in Cú Chulainn's pledge. He agrees to *act* according to Emer's demands. Emer, on the other hand, makes no pledge of real action. Instead, she merely accepts the hero's promise to fulfil her demands. She is the one who shapes with her words the parameters of the hero's future deeds. From this point on he will perform the physical acts required by her, and she will await his return.

However, this dichotomy between Emer's words and Cú Chulainn's deeds does not necessarily imply passivity on her part. In the subsequent narrative, during the account of the hero's training at arms, the story returns briefly to the scene in Ireland where Emer's father has arranged an alternate marriage for her. Her response to this situation reaffirms her skill in using words to her advantage:

In tan íarom dobretha Emer co Lugaid dochum in inaid i mbaí i suidiu fora láim di, gaibidsi a dá ngrúaid 7 dosbeir for fír a enig 7 a anmae, 7 addámair dó ba Cú Chulainn carastar 7 is fora gress baí, 7 ba coll enig cíab é dosbéradsi. Ní forlámair íarom intí Lugaid feiss la hEmir ar oman Con Culainn 7 imdasoí afrithisi dia thig.

Then when Emer was brought to Lugaid, to the place where he was sitting, she seized his two cheeks and laid it on the truth of his honour and of his soul, and confessed to him that it was Cú Chulainn that she loved, and that she was under his protection, and it would be a loss of honour if he should take her. Lugaid did not dare then to sleep with Emer for fear of Cú Chulainn and he returned to his house.[94]

Emer's words here clearly have unusual force, and are accompanied by the gesture of seizing the man's cheeks – a move very reminiscent of the gestures of Deirdre and Gráinne when forcing their respective lovers to elope with them.[95] Although her words thus may have ritualized overtones, nevertheless her statement that she is under Cú Chulainn's protection is in itself a potent disincentive to Lugaid to pursue their relationship. This brief incident serves a double purpose in the narrative: it reminds the audience of Emer's importance, thereby reinforcing the thematic links between the wooing and training-at-arms sections; and it reaffirms Emer's ability to use illocutionary acts to shape her life and the lives of those who interact with her.[96]

Although Emer's are the most important words in the tale's narrative structure, the words of other women play a significant role during Cú Chulainn's sojourn in the land of Scáthach. In two separate but strikingly similar incidents, Cú Chulainn is given specific advice on how to proceed in order to gain what he seeks. In the first of these, Scáthach's daughter Uathach advises him on how to approach her mother:

Dobert íarom in ingen comairli do Choin Chulainn dia tres laí, má bu do dénum láechdachta doluid, ara téised dochum Scáthaige co magin i mbaí oc forcetal a dá mac .i. Cúar 7 Cett, arin corad ích n-erred de isin iburdoss mór i mbaísi fóen and. Conid fuirmed etir a dá chích cona chlaidiub co tartad a thrí hindroisc dó .i. a forcetal cen díchell 7 a hernaidmsi co n-ícc tindscrae 7 epert fris nech aridmbaí, ar ba fáithsi.

Then the maiden gave counsel to Cú Chulainn on the third day, that if he had come to do heroic deeds, he should go to Scáthach to the spot where she was teaching her two sons, that is Cúar and Cett, to leap the salmon-leap in the great bush of yew-trees in which she was reclining. And that he should place his sword between her two breasts until his three wishes were granted to him: that is, teaching him without neglect, and his betrothal without payment of bride-price,[97] and telling him what would befall him, for she was a prophetess.[98]

Cú Chulainn follows her advice and does indeed obtain all of his de-mands from Scáthach. His success at finding Scáthach and gaining access to her stronghold is clearly of no consequence if he cannot obtain what he really wants from her – training at arms. To obtain this he needs the advice of a female, in this case one close enough to Scáthach to know how to approach her. Uathach the daughter is best placed for this since she is both well-disposed towards the hero through her desire for him, and close enough to her mother to know that force is the only way of ap-proaching her.

Later on in the tale, when Cú Chulainn asks Scáthach what her enemy Aífe loves most and then uses the information she gives him to trick Aífe, it is clear that he has learned from the earlier incident. His violent approach to Aífe and her response follow the same pattern as the con-frontation with Scáthach.[99]

Scáthach's prophecy of Cú Chulainn's future deeds is another signifi-cant example of women's speech in the text. It functions as a complement to Emer's conversation with the hero at the beginning. Just as Emer's words have shaped the hero's journey abroad, so Scáthach's prophetic words lay out the shape of his future life, particularly as the hero of the Táin.[100] Although the poem of prophecy is allusive and often vague, as befits a prophetic utterance, it clearly refers to many of the incidents featured in the various tales that make up Cú Chulainn's heroic career. Thus, while Emer and Scáthach play different roles in shaping the hero's destiny – Emer through her veiled taunts and demands spurs the hero to action, while Scáthach through her foreknowledge merely tells what is fated to happen – they both construct the hero's career in advance both for him (on a narrative level) and for the audience (on a metatextual level).

The final women's words in The Wooing of Emer again belong to Emer. After Cú Chulainn's return to Ireland he spends a year trying without success to gain access to Forgall's fort, meets Derbforgall the daughter of Rúad and rejects her, and then tries once again to storm the fortress, this time with the help of his scythe-chariot.[101] He finally succeeds in gaining access and abducts Emer and her foster-sister with their weight in gold and silver. While he and the two women are fleeing their pursuers, and Cú Chulainn is fighting Forgall's men, Emer comments on his deeds. Her remarks constitute the basis of new names for the places in question:

Tíagait asside co Glondath. Marbais Cú Chulainn cét fer díb and. 'Is mór in glond dorignis,' ol Emer, 'in cét fer n-armach n-inchomlainn do marbad.' 'Bid Glondáth a ainm co bráth,' ol Cú Chulainn. Doroich Cú Chulainn co Crúfóit. Ráe Bán a hainm ar tús co tici sin. Bentaiseom bráthbéimenn mára forsna slúagaib isind inud sin, coro maidset na srotha fola tairsiu for cach leith. 'Is fót cró in tilach so lat indiu, a Chú Chulainn,' ol in ingen. Conid de sin dogarar Crúfóit di .i. fót cró.

They went forth to Glondath. Cú Chulainn killed a hundred men of them there. 'Great is the deed which you have done,' said Emer, 'killing the hundred armed warlike men.' 'Glondath [Ford of deeds?] will be its name forever,' said Cú Chulainn. Cú Chulainn reached Crúfóit. Ráe Bán [White Expanse?] was its name at first until he came to it. He dealt great destructive blows on the hosts in that place, so that the floods of blood burst forth across it on every side. 'The height is a sod of blood because of you today, Cú Chulainn,' said the maiden. So that from that it is called Crúfóit, that is, sod of blood.[102]

This passage details Emer's role in renaming the landscape through which she and her husband-to-be escape from her father and his people. It is important to note that although the deeds are performed by Cú Chulainn, it is Emer's *articulation* of those deeds which gives rise to the renaming of landmarks. Emer's naming of the landscape also forms a thematic link with Cú Chulainn's recounting of his itinerary to her at the beginning of their wooing dialogue earlier in the tale. Emer and Cú Chulainn, who have both forged metaphorical links between themselves and place-name lore in their earlier dialogue, now have an opportunity to leave their own personal imprint on the land as they embark on their new life together.

Woman as Culture?

Emer's association with powerful and arcane speech seems to link her with the realm of culture, civilization, and reason. She appears to be rooted in human society, with its customs and laws and special modes of diction, rather than in the external realms of nature or the Otherworld.

In *The Wooing of Emer* she is presented as a paragon of civilized womanhood. Cú Chulainn chooses her above all other women because she is the only one who is 'chomadais dó ar aís 7 cruth 7 cenél di ingenaib Érenn ...' ('his equal in age and form and race, of the maidens of Ireland ...').[103] Besides this, she possesses the 'six gifts': the gifts of beauty, voice, sweet speech, needlework, wisdom, and chastity. This list of attributes immediately marks Emer as a locus of civilized arts; she is adept at conversation and possibly at singing; she can create the beautiful embroidery that seems to have been the mark of aristocratic dress,[104] and she possesses the mental acuity which will enable her to function in aristocratic society.[105] This catalogue of talents is presented almost as a *sine qua non* of ideal womanhood. It is perhaps even possible to view this list as a standard of education for aristocratic women. Significantly, it presents woman not as a merely ornamental creature but also as a being of character and intellect, one who need not be silent.

Emer's own self-description contains imagery which alludes to these connections with culture. The first image she uses to describe herself is *Temair ban* (Tara of women).[106] Although the primary meaning of *temair* is 'any high place, eminence, hill,'[107] it is also the place-name 'Tara,' a designation loaded with cultural connotations.[108] Tara is portrayed as the centre of Irish society in many medieval texts. Throughout generations of dynastic struggles, Tara was the ultimate political prize to be fought for and won as a seat of kingship.[109] It is to Tara that the god Lug seeks admission on the basis of his many civilized skills in *The Second Battle of Mag Tuired*.[110] It may be particularly noteworthy that one explanation for Tara's name in the *dinnshenchas* derives it from *múr* (rampart) of Tea, the daughter of Lugaid son of Ith, who is said to have made the first *soerchuir* (free convenants) in Ireland during the reign of her husband the king, and who brought peace and friendship to Ireland.[111] The making of covenants is clearly a civilizing action, pertaining to the realm of human culture. Thus, Emer's identification of herself with Tara at the beginning of her conversation with her suitor resonates with a whole range of traditional cultural associations.

Although she makes clear her interest in the young hero, Emer also establishes herself within the confines of law and custom. She makes a point of describing the strong men who protect her from abductors, and makes it clear that she will not be easily won. She repeatedly emphasizes her chastity, thus situating herself within the expected norms for aristocratic young women. In her question 'In fil banchéile lat?' ('Have you a wife already?') she implies that she will only consent to be the hero's *cétmuinter* (first or chief wife). Thus although she agrees to let Cú Chulainn carry her off against her father's wishes, she first determines his suitability as a husband and makes it clear that certain customs must be observed. In this she stands in marked contrast to the other women depicted in this text, who enter easily into sexual relationships with the hero. All of these details further enhance Emer's identification with civilized society.

In this tale the words of women in general, and those of Emer in particular, perform many different functions in the narrative. They thus transcend what has come to be considered the normal parameters of women's speech in medieval literature and enter the arenas of arcane discourse, legal contracts, advice, prophecy, and place-naming. Through a series of illocutionary acts, women shape the world around them and particularly the life of the hero.

Obviously, on the most basic narrative level, Emer provides the plot of the tale. She is the object of the hero's desire, the prize to be won. This feature is common to all of the medieval Irish *tochmarca* and indeed to wooing tales the world over. Unlike many other potential brides, however, Emer also generates the internal workings of the plot of her tale. It is she and not her father who stipulates the tasks the hero must complete before she will wed him. Emer constructs both the hero's future and the narrative itself through her illocutionary acts.

Emer also operates on other levels in this narrative. On the symbolic level she represents culture and stability. As a woman rooted in the manners and customs of aristocratic Irish society she represents the cultured civilization which is Cú Chulainn's true home. Her depiction as a model of female eloquence reinforces this impression. If, as Sjoestedt argues, Cú Chulainn is the 'hero within the tribe,' Emer embodies this connection to clan and culture.[112] To unite with Emer is to confirm his place as a mortal hero rooted in his society.

Emer may also reflect, to some extent, real aristocratic women in medieval Ireland. Although she is extraordinary – after all, she is an *ideal* – she is nevertheless a figure with whom upper-class Irish women could likely identify. While our inadequate knowledge of women's lives in Ireland before the Norman invasion of 1169 makes it unwise to draw strict parallels between real and fictional women, I would suggest that the text may have been shaped and embellished with actual women in mind. The historical and legal sources which survive tell us little about the daily lives of real women in eleventh- and twelfth-century Ireland, but they do suggest that at least aristocratic women enjoyed somewhat greater freedoms and legal rights than their counterparts in continental Europe.[113] They also indicate that women routinely formed part of the audiences which heard these secular tales read or told.

Because her presence hovers over the entire tale, Emer emerges as the standard of womanhood by which all other females in the tale are judged, by the audience as well as by the hero. For various reasons, all the other women Cú Chulainn meets along the way are found wanting in comparison with her. Emer is presented as Cú Chulainn's equal, and her ability to create a relationship of joint action and cooperation with him becomes a paradigm for the ideal aristocratic Irish woman. These considerations are perhaps all the more pertinent if, as Mac Cana and others have suggested, wooing tales were actually recited or read at weddings in medieval Ireland.

Yet in embodying the ideal qualities of aristocratic womanhood, does Emer herself become enmeshed in the patriarchal framework which defines her? Is all of her speech merely patriarchal discourse in a woman's mouth? The text itself would seem to resist such a reading. Although Emer does adhere in large part to the expected norms of her heroic society, her skilful control of the hero in the wooing dialogue, her self-definition through her own descriptions, and the crucial role of her words in setting desired events in motion, all suggest that some degree of autonomy is possible for a female figure – even within the confines of a wooing tale.

The Wooing of Emer clearly establishes the character of Emer in the network of Ulster Cycle tales to which it belongs. Emer is intelligent, eloquent, and self-assured; she has a highly developed sense of self-worth and conducts herself with dignity and charm. She is adept at using words to shape her world. She is, furthermore, firmly linked to culture and civilization. These traits continue to characterize her throughout the other tales in which she plays important roles.

2

Bricriu's Feast:
Women's Words as Weapons

Bricriu's Feast (*Fled Bricrend*) is another tale central to the Ulster Cycle. This narrative concerns the contention between Ulster's three greatest heroes over which of them is worthy to receive the finest cut of meat (the *curadmir*, or champion's portion) at a feast given by the notorious trickster Bricriu. Despite its heroic agenda, and its delightful scenes of slapstick humour, this tale – like the others discussed in this study – has received relatively little scholarly attention. Indeed, *Bricriu's Feast* is known mainly as a possible source for the 'beheading game' motif which provides the plot structure of the Middle English tale *Sir Gawain and the Green Knight*. Yet although it is the beheading episode which ultimately provides the solution to the conflict between the Irish heroes, *Bricriu's Feast* also contains many other components.

The most important of these for the present study is the involvement of the heroes' wives in the conflict over the champion's portion. The *bríatharcath na mban* (the women's war of words), which forms part of the dispute at Bricriu's hall, is a rare but vivid depiction of female identification with and involvement in the heroic honour code that plays such a crucial role in the Ulster Cycle tales. Not only does it afford a glimpse of the qualities valued in aristocratic women by the society which produced the texts, it also constitutes a 'fleshing out' of the legal provision that a woman's status was directly dependent on that of her husband, and implies that her honour, as well as her status, was a reflection of that of her spouse.

Yet the 'women's war of words' in *Bricriu's Feast* provides more than just an illustration of medieval Irish attitudes towards honour and status. It also depicts the relationships between women in this society as parallel to those of their men in that they are essentially *competitive* in nature.

There is no solidarity or sisterhood here, at least between females of the same status.[1] On the contrary, every woman is determined to win for herself Bricriu's tempting prize of *banrígnacht úas bantrocht Ulad uli* (queenship over all the womenfolk of Ulster). Each of the three noble women – Emer, Fedelm, and Lendabair – operates as an entity unto herself in the shadow of her husband. Moreover, it is clear that Bricriu bases his strategy on this principle of competition, and on the absolute assurance that the women will not discuss his flattering words with each other.

As we might expect from her portrayal in *The Wooing of Emer*, Emer emerges the victor in the 'women's war of words.' She also shares the reflected glory of her husband Cú Chulainn when he ultimately wins for himself the champion's portion. A modern audience may find Emer's wholesale adoption of the heroic ethos disappointing, especially in light of her determined rejection of her father's marital choices for her in *The Wooing of Emer*. However, *Bricriu's Feast* offers us a glimpse of what she has become as a fully integrated member of this (of course, fictional) Ulster society. Although Emer fits into the framework of expected values and behaviour here, she also demonstrates her superior skill in eloquence and word-play. Her masterful speeches recall the wooing dialogue in *The Wooing of Emer* and break new ground in their audacious content and style.

The tale thus appears to portray Emer positively, as a woman of strength and eloquence. Within the larger context of the narrative as a whole, however, the representation of women is more problematic. Sencha's misogynistic reaction to the women's verbal combat, the deceitfulness of Medb in judging the three heroes later in the tale, and the specific mention of Cú Roí's (eventually treacherous) wife Bláthnat near the end of the story, all combine to form a subtly negative subtext in the tale.[2]

A full-scale examination of *Bricriu's Feast* is clearly beyond the scope of this study, but such an analysis would have to take into account the tale's many ambiguities. Chief among these is the tension between the overtly comic agenda of many scenes and the tragic-heroic discourse which lies submerged just beneath the text's surface.[3] The fact that this tale incorporates so many elements from other Ulster Cycle narratives suggests that this subtext would have been recognized by contemporary audiences.

The ambiguous nature of the tale includes its representation of women. Indeed, *Bricriu's Feast* would seem to illustrate the ongoing tension between positive and negative portrayals of women which characterizes much of medieval Irish literature. Women are free to speak, but their words are often censored or ignored, even when they are clearly right. Often the objection raised is simply that 'women's words are deceitful,' whether or not they prove to be so in the context; this simplistic judgment reflects the sentiments of the widespread misogynistic discourse of medieval Europe.[4] Although ostensibly powerful, women's words are frequently undercut or robbed of their impact by the reactions of men or by the narrative structure itself.

Thus although Emer's portrayal in *Bricriu's Feast* is essentially positive, and is consistent with the depictions of her in other tales, this larger, more problematic context must not be overlooked. Ultimately, Emer's impact on the narrative trajectory is minimal. Her speech acts do not *change* the world in *Bricriu's Feast* as they do in *The Wooing of Emer* or the other two tales discussed here, but merely confirm her importance as one of the chief aristocratic women of Ulster. Her role in this tale is more subtle and ambiguous. More than just her husband's 'cheerleader,' yet robbed of any real influence in the plot of the tale, Emer emerges as an eloquent but ultimately powerless voice for woman's right to speak.

Summary of *Bricriu's Feast*

Bricriu builds an extravagant new hall so that he can host a great feast for all of the Ulstermen. When the Ulstermen receive their invitations, they are unwilling to attend because of their strong suspicion that Bricriu intends only to make trouble between them. They finally agree to come only when Bricriu threatens dire consequences if they do not. Predictably, Bricriu sets the stage for conflict by speaking to each of the heroes before the feast and promising each one the 'champion's portion,' which signifies preeminence above all the other heroes. When the Ulstermen arrive at the feast, and each of the heroes claims his prize, a brawl ensues. Sencha, the wise man, negotiates a temporary peace by deciding that the champion's portion will be divided equally this time and the issue of preeminence will be adjudicated later by Medb and Ailill.

Disappointed at the temporary peace, Bricriu turns to the wives of the heroes. He approaches each of them in turn as they leave the house, promising that the first of them to return will win the right to preeminence over all the other women. When the crowd of women come thundering back to the hall, each one running to outdistance the others, the heroes inside take up arms again. Once again Sencha intervenes, decreeing that the women should debate the matter in a war of words, rather than of weapons. Emer, Fedelm Noíchride, and Lendabair, the wives of the three greatest heroes, boast of their own beauty and the valour of their husbands. On hearing their wives praise them, the three heroes become enraged again. Lóegaire and Conall Cernach break holes in the walls of the house to let their wives through; but Cú Chulainn lifts up the entire side of the house, so that not only Emer but also her retinue and the retinues of the other two wives can enter. Bricriu is enraged that his house is now askew, and at last only Cú Chulainn is able to set it right. At that, the feast resumes.

However, the women presently resume their boasting about their heroic husbands. Sencha rebukes them, using strongly antifeminist language and apparently blaming them for causing dissension between the warriors. Emer objects, claiming her right to speak on account of her husband's reputation. Conall calls on Cú Chulainn to speak on his own behalf, but Cú Chulainn complains that he is too weary because he has spent the day catching his horse, the Grey of Macha.

The remainder of the tale concerns the many new outbreaks of fighting among the heroes over the champion's portion, and the repeated attempts to have the issue arbitrated by objective authorities, including Medb and Ailill. Conall and Lóegaire refuse to accept the verdicts, claiming that the trials were not fair. Finally, the issue is settled when Cú Roí mac Dáire, in the form of a huge churl (*bachlach*), challenges the heroes to a contest in which anyone may behead him on one night, if he may return to behead the hero on the next. Conall Cernach and Lóegaire both back out of the second part of the bargain. Only Cú Chulainn keeps both parts of the bargain and offers his head to the resuscitated giant. He is publicly awarded the champion's portion, and Emer is simultaneously granted the right to precede the women of Ulster into the hall from that time forward.

Bricriu's Feast is a long and episodic tale, and much of it is irrelevant to an examination of the representation of women's speech. This study will focus on the first part of the story, in which the women of Ulster figure prominently. The relevant portion depicts Emer's participation (and apparent victory) in the boasting contest with the two wives of the other rival heroes Lóegaire Buadach and Conall Cernach. This boasting contest clearly forms an integral part of the story as a whole, since the phrase 'in Bríatharchath ban Ulad' ('the war of words of the women of Ulster') is included in the title at the beginning of the tale.[5] Significantly, Emer here demonstrates the eloquence which we saw in the wooing dialogue in *The Wooing of Emer*. Although her words in the 'women's war of words' are more highly structured, she uses them to maintain and consolidate her position as a woman of great verbal skill.

Before analysing these passages, it is important to establish the legal and literary context of the narrative.

Context: Law and Honour

The apparently complete identification of the women with their husbands in this tale can be explained in large part by women's position in medieval Irish law. Although Irish women enjoyed relatively high status compared to their continental counterparts in the Middle Ages, they were still defined in relation to the males in their society. According to the laws, a married woman's honour-price was half that of her husband, unless he were a foreigner or an outcast, in which case he derived his honour-price from that of his wife.[6] An unmarried woman was assigned an honour-price in relation to that of her father or brother. As a result, as Nancy Power points out in her discussion of the classes of women dealt with in the Irish law tract, *Senchas Már,*

From the *cétmuinter* to the *bé nindlis*, all the women mentioned ... stood in a clearly defined relation to some one man, in a relation which, in default of a more exact English term, must be described as a marital relation. Their status and privileges varied, but all of them had certain rights and duties in relation to the man.[7]

However, the distinction between status (and the honour-price that accompanied it) and *honour* must be kept in mind. T.M. Charles-Edwards has discussed the implications of this distinction for the understanding of some medieval Irish and Welsh narratives. He notes:

Honour is opposed to shame: they are the publicly declared valuation put upon a person by those who know him ... Status, on the other hand, implies a hierarchy of social ranks within which individuals have their place. It implies systematic social differentiation using some general scheme of valuation according to occupation, wealth or whatever it may be. Honour and status are distinct ...; where they co-exist they are determined by different criteria: for example, sexual conduct, often a criterion of honour, especially for women, is normally irrelevant to status.[8]

At the same time, as Charles-Edwards goes on to show through an examination of several literary texts, honour or shame brought on by certain situations could change one's status, at least temporarily. Public shame in particular could destroy the *value* of status; only when this shame was in some way redressed could the injured person be restored to his or her former status in the eyes of the community. Two of Charles-Edwards's most telling examples of this involve women: Rhiannon from the medieval Welsh *Mabinogi*, and the nameless wife of Rónán in the Irish tale *The Kin-slaying of Rónán*. At one point in the First Branch of the *Mabinogi*, Rhiannon is believed to have killed and eaten her newborn child; the allegation is false and unproven, but until she is *publicly* exonerated Rhiannon must undergo punishment. During this time, her social inferiors address her as *gwreicda* (woman) and *eneit* (literally 'soul,' a term of address used by superiors to inferiors when they were on friendly terms) rather than *arglwydes* (lady), even when they know she is innocent. Only when Rhiannon has been publicly exonerated does she regain her title of *arglwydes*.[9] In the Irish tale a much more complicated situation obtains, in which the son Mael Fothartaig must tactfully resist the sexual advances of his young stepmother in order to avoid insulting her. This avoidance is particularly crucial because to insult her is also to insult her husband, the king – Mael Fothartaig's father Rónán.[10] Mael Fothartaig ultimately fails to negotiate this delicate situation and dies as a result.

Although both of these situations exist within literary texts, Charles-Edwards argues that they must represent something approximate to the actual social situations of their respective societies. If he is correct in this, these tales afford us a glimpse of the paramount importance of honour in early Irish and Welsh society. Such an emphasis on honour as one's social persona sheds important light on the behaviour and words of Emer in *Bricriu's Feast*.

Context: Boasting Contests

As we might expect, most of the boasting contests in medieval Irish texts are contests between men. One well known example is the boasting contest in *The Story of Mac Datho's Pig* (*Scéla Mucce Meic Dathó*). As in *Bricriu's Feast*, the conflict in this tale arises over how a choice pig is to be divided among the heroes at a feast.[11] In this tale, the heroes boast of their exploits before resorting to physical fighting over the pig. Cet mac Mátach of Connacht prevails for a time by insulting the other heroes one by one, offering physical proof of their unworthiness. The following excerpt will serve as an example:

'In comram beus!' ol Cet. 'Rot•bia són' ol Cúscraid Mend Macha mac Conchobair. 'Cuich so?' ol Cet. 'Cúscraid' ol cách; 'is adbar ríg ar deilb.' 'Ní buide frit'
ol in gilla. 'Maith' ol Cet. 'Cucainni ceta•tudchad-so do chétgaisciud, a gillai.
Imma•tarraid dún issin chocrích. Fo•rácbais trian do muintire, ocus is <s>am-
laid do•cúadaiss ocus gaí tríat brágit conna•étai focul fort chenn i córai; ar
ro•loitt in gaí féthi do brágat. Conid Cúscraid Mend atot•chomnaic ónd úair-
sin.' Do-rat tár fon n-indas-sin forsin cóiced n-uile.

'On with the contest!' said Cet. 'You shall have it,' said Cuscraid the Stammerer
of Macha son of Conchobar. 'Who is this?' said Cet. 'Cuscraid,' said each one;
'the material of a king is in his shape.' 'I have no regard for you,' said the young
man. 'Well,' said Cet. 'You came to us first for your first raid, O young man. We
met at the boundary. You left behind a third of your people, and it is thus you
came with a spear through your throat, so that you don't get a word out of your
head properly; for the spear wounded the sinews of your throat. So that it is
Cúscraid the Stammerer of Macha that you are called ever since.' He brought
disgrace in that manner on the whole province.[12]

Cet seems assured of victory until the arrival of Conall Cernach, who
proves his own superior warrior skill by offering the evidence of the
severed head of Cet's brother Anluan as proof of his right to carve the
pig.
    In this boasting contest, both Cet and Conall substantiate their claims
to precedence in the warrior hierarchy either by pointing out the physical
signs (wounds, scars, debilities) which testify to the damage they have
inflicted, or by explaining the embarrassing reasons behind a challeng-
er's nickname. Conall's decisive proof – Anluan's bleeding, severed head
– is the most dramatic of all. Thus, the deeds of these heroes are verifiable, and their proof depends on evidence, not simply the testimony of
the boasters. Cet and Conall combine their verbal darts with the physical
evidence of past injuries and suggest, in the process, that similar damage
will result in the future if their opponents do not capitulate.
    Another interesting example of a boasting contest is found in the early
Hiberno-Latin text *Hisperica Famina*. Here the combatants are apparently
scholars of rhetoric, not warriors, and their weapons are cleverly manipulated words:

Quos edocetis fastos?
Cuique adheretis rhetori?
Hinc lectorum sollertem inuito obello certatorem,

qui sophicam pla<s>mauerit auide palestram.
Nam trinos antea dimicaui athletas,
inertes mactaui duelles,
ac robustos multaui coaeuos,
fortioresque prostraui in acie ciclopes;
hinc nullum subterfugio aequeuum.
Dum truculenta me uellicant spicula,
protinus uersatilem euagino spatham
quae almas trucidat statuas;

What texts do you recite
and what rhetor do you adhere to?
Thus do I challenge the adroit wrangler to a
    verbal duel,
to engage in rhetorical gymnastics with eagerness.
For previously I contended against three athletes:
I slaughtered helpless warriors,
punished powerful peers,
and brought down stouter giants in the fray;
hence I shun none of my age-mates.
When their cruel darts begin to prick me,
straightaway I unsheath my dextrous sword,
which hacks up sacred pillars ...[13]

In this battle it is clearly the *verbal* skill of the participants that is at stake; the 'uersatilem ... spatham' ('dextrous sword') referred to here is not to be understood literally but is a metaphor for dazzling eloquence. Unlike the contest in *The Story of Mac Dathó's Pig*, this struggle seems to be waged on the rhetorical level alone, without any physical damage being inflicted on the combatants. Yet pride in one's battle skills and the honour at stake are clearly at issue here too.

This passage in the *Hisperica Famina* is an interesting intertext for other verbal battles in medieval Irish literature. Its focus upon eloquence and its use of battle imagery in describing purely verbal conflict inevitably links it with contests like the 'women's war of words' in *Bricriu's Feast*, even though both the speaker and his foes in the *Hisperica Famina* are understood to be male scholars. It is not clear how widely known the *Hisperica Famina* was in medieval Ireland – indeed, the difficulty of the Latin may have ensured its restriction to a small, scholarly audience.[14] Nevertheless, it is an instructive example of a verbal battle between *men*, implying that purely verbal conflict is not simply the preserve of women.[15]

Context: Women Competitors

Not surprisingly, most of the battles in medieval Irish literature are those fought with real weapons, not with words, and involve groups of competing men, not women. Another important group of intertexts for the 'women's war of words' are, therefore, tales involving competitions between women.

These are exceedingly rare. Conflicts between women do occur, but in different contexts. *The Wooing of Ailbe* contains the hint of a competition between the daughters of Cormac as to who can answer the questions of the suitor, Finn. However, Ailbe is the only woman who can answer his questions; beside her, all the other sisters are silent:

'A ingena' ol Find, 'an•fil uaib si nech rot•fessead anniso .i. Cia lind as lethi cac rian?' – 'Leithi drucht' or Ailbi Gruadbreac ingen Cormaic. as i ro•frecair, ar ni•boi astig nech bad glica a leth o mnaib 7 dino as furri ro•saided an medair.

'Maidens,' said Finn, 'is there any among you who knows this? What lake is wider than any sea?'
'Dew is wider,' said Ailbe of the Freckled Cheek, daughter of Cormac. It is she who answered, for none of the women in the house was cleverer than she. It was with her, then, that the rest of the conversation took place.[16]

The implied contest turns out to be a non-competition after all.

In *The Wooing of Étaín* Fúamnach, the first wife of Mider, does her best to destroy her rival Étaín, her husband's beautiful new wife. Fúamnach is skilled in magic and succeeds in turning Étaín into a pool of water, which in turn transforms itself into a beautiful scarlet fly. Étaín survives in this form despite Fúamnach's best efforts to destroy her until Fúamnach is killed.[17] The rivalry of the two wives is dramatic, but it is essentially non-verbal and therefore provides only a very general example of female competition. A similar instance is the competition of the women for a view of Cú Chulainn in the *Táin*.[18]

A more interesting example of female competition occurs at the beginning of *The Wasting Sickness of Cú Chulainn* (*Serglige Con Culainn*). In this portion of the tale the name of Cú Chulainn's wife is Eithne Ingubai; later on in the tale she is called Emer, as she is in the other Ulster Cycle tales.

The scene in question occurs while the people of Ulster are assembled for a great gathering at Samain, the festival of the new year. Cú Chulainn insists that the proceedings be delayed until Fergus and Conall arrive. While everyone is waiting, a flock of birds settles on the lake nearby.

Batar imtholtanaig na mná imna héonu imdarubart fair. Gabais cách díb immarbáig a mmuin a céli im gabáil na n-én. Asbert Ethne Aitencháithrech, ben Chonchobair; 'Asagussim én cechtar mo dá gúaland dind énlaith ucut.' 'Assagussem uli,' ol na mná, 'aní sin.' 'Má gabthair do neoch, is damsa cetagébthar,' ol Ethne Inguba ben Chon Culaind.'

The women grew very excited over the many birds on the lake. Each began to argue with her companion over who should have them. Eithne Aitencháithrech, Conchubar's wife, said, 'I desire a bird for each of my two shoulders from that bird-flock,' but the other women replied, 'We all desire that too.' 'If birds are caught for anyone, it is for me first that they will be caught,' said Eithne Ingubai, Cú Chulainn's wife.[19]

An angry and reluctant Cú Chulainn is eventually persuaded to capture the birds for the women, and each one gets a pair of birds except for his own wife. Her response to this is surprisingly generous:

Tánic de íarom coa mnaí fessin. 'Is olc do menma,' ol Cú Chulaind fría. 'Ní holc,' ol Ethne, 'úair is úaim fodáilter dóib. Is dethbir dait,' ol sí. 'Ní fil diib mnaí náchit charad no ná beth cuit dait. Úair mád messi, ní fil cuit do nách ailiu inniumsa acht duitsiu th'óenur.'

Then he came to his own wife. 'You are in an evil mood,' said Cú Chulainn to her. 'I am not,' she replied, 'for it is by me that the birds are distributed to them. You did right,' she said, 'for there is not one of those women who does not love you or give you a share of her love. But as for me, I do not share my love with anyone but you alone.'[20]

As in *Bricriu's Feast*, the women argue here for precedence based on their status, which is based in turn upon the status of their husbands. The real dispute seems to be between the wife of the king and the wife of the most illustrious hero. Which criterion will prevail – one's social rank, or the heroic reputation of one's husband? In the end, the hero's wife finds a way of graciously reformulating her loss into a statement of generosity through complete identification with her husband's act of gift-giving. It is a manoeuvre worthy of both the clever potential bride of *The Wooing of Emer* and the self-assured Emer who boasts of her beauty in *Bricriu's Feast*. Yet the outcome of this dispute is predicated not on the verbal dexterity of its combatants, but on Cú Chulainn's distribution of the birds – a factor which seems to be outside his wife's sphere of influence.

The most horrific example of a competition between women occurs in *The Deaths of Lugaid and Derbforgaill* (*Aided Lugdach ocus Derbforgaille*). This tale, which is closely connected with stories about Cú Chulainn,[21] depicts a group of women (presumably the women of Ulster) engaging in a bizarre urination contest.

Laa and didiu i nderiud gemrid. Snec[h]ta mór and. Doniat na fir corthe mór don tsnechtu. Lotar na mna forna corthe. Ba he a tuscurnud. 'Tabram ar mún isin coirthe dús cia as sia ragas ind. IN ben o ría triit isí as ferr congaib úan.' Ni roacht didiu uadib. Congairther Derbforgaill uadib. Nir bo áill lea or nir bo baeth. Téit arai forsin corthe. Roselaig uade co talam.

'Dia fessatar trá ind fir so ní congrádaigfider i fail na óinmná. Gatair a súile assa cind 7 a sróna 7 a da nó 7 a trilis. Ni ba soaccobraite ón.'
Dognither a pianad amlaid sin 7 berair iartain da tig.

On a certain day at the end of winter there was deep snow. The men make great pillars of the snow. The women went up on the pillars. This was their device. 'Let us make our water upon the pillars to see which will enter the farthest. The woman from whom it will enter, she is the best of us to keep.' However it did not reach through from them. Derbforgaill is called by them. She did not like it, because she was not foolish. Nevertheless she goes on the pillar and it poured from her to the ground.

'If the men knew of this, no woman would be loved in comparison with this one. Let her eyes be taken from her head, and her nose, and her two ears and her locks. She will not be desirable then.'
She is tortured in this way and afterwards brought to her house.[22]

Horribly disfigured, Derbforgaill locks herself inside and refuses to admit either her husband Lugaid or Cú Chulainn. She laments her fate and dies, and when the men finally gain entrance Lugaid dies at the sight of her.

This story seems designed to highlight the evils of female jealousy. Clearly, Derbforgaill is perceived to have proven herself more sexually desirable to men than the other women, and can therefore be justifiably targeted for abuse. It is interesting to note that although Emer *claims* to be the most sexually attractive female in the house in her boastful speech at Bricriu's feast, her claim is *verbal* only. Derbforgaill's reluctant participation in the women's trial provides visual *proof* of her superiority, and this is unforgivable.[23]

These intertexts serve to establish the literary context of the 'women's war of words.' Several general observations can be made at this point. First, competitions between women are usually not verbal, and are often dangerous – even fatal. Second, jealousy between women is assumed to be as natural as physical combat between warriors. And third, it is worth noting that although some of these intertexts portray boasting contests among men, and others show competition between women, none depicts a *verbal* contest among women. *Bricriu's Feast* appears to be unique in its inclusion of a 'war of words' between women.[24]

Bricriu's Flattery

The scene is set for conflict from the outset of the tale. When Bricriu realizes that his plan to incite the warriors has failed, he turns to their wives instead. He promises precedence in entering the feasting hall to the woman who reenters it first.

An examination of Bricriu's flattering words to the three women offers insights into the values, assumptions, and priorities of the fictional world of this narrative – and, indeed, of the other Ulster Cycle tales as well. Bricriu greets each of the three women – Fedelm Noíchride the wife of Lóegaire Buadach, Lendabair the wife of Conall Cernach, and Emer the wife of Cú Chulainn – in turn. Fedelm Noíchride is the first:

Maith sin innocht a ben Loegairi Búadaig ní lesainm dait dano Fedelm Noíchride ar febas do chrotha 7 do ceille 7 do ceneoil. Conchobar rí cóicid Herend do athair. Loegaire Buadach do chéle. acht nammá níbo ró lim dait conna tissad nech di mnaib Ulad ríut hi Tech Midchúarda 7 combad hit íarsála no beth bantrocht Ulad uile.

'Glad I am to see you tonight, wife of Lóegaire Buadach, for Fedelm 'of the nine hearts' is no misnomer for you on account of your excellence of form and wisdom and lineage. Conchobar, king of a province of Ireland, is your father and Lóegaire Buadach is your husband. Indeed I should not consider it too great an honour for you that none of the women of Ulster should precede you into the Hall of Mead-circuit, but that they should instead all follow in your train.'[25]

Bricriu praises Fedelm's physical and personal qualities first, and then quickly moves to the cornerstones of her high status: the identity of her father and her husband. As the daughter of a king, she has enjoyed a high rank from birth, and is probably the highest-born of the three women. Moreover, she has married one of the three most famous young heroes in the province, and the honour he has won by his valorous deeds clearly reflects on her.

Lendabair is the second woman to emerge from the hall with her retinue. Bricriu addresses her in similar terms:

Maith sin a Lendabair or se ní lesainm dait ind Lenabair at banlendan 7 at menmarc fer ndomain uli. ar do aíne 7 t'urdarcus. A n-ed ruc do chéli do ócaib domoin ar gaisciud 7 cruth roucaiseo di mnáib Ulad.

I am glad to see you, Lendabair, for the name Lendabair is no misnomer for you:[26] you are the darling and the loved one of the men of the whole world for your fame[27] and distinction. As much as your husband surpasses the warriors of the world in valour and appearance, so do you surpass the women of Ulster.[28]

Lendabair is apparently not of such high birth as Fedelm but her husband's distinction makes up for this lack. In fact, it is worth noting that Bricriu explicitly states that her husband's valour excels that of every other warrior in the world! This tends to confirm the idea that although rank or status was important, one's position in medieval Irish society was also influenced by one's reputation in the public sphere.

Bricriu reserves his most extravagant flattery for Emer:

Slán seiss a Emer ingen Forgaill Manach ol Bricriu a ben ind fir as dech i nÉren. Ní lesainm dait ind Emer Foltchaín is húariud do rígaib 7 rígdomnaib Herend immut. A n-ed rucc grían do rennaib nime rucaisiu de mnaib domain ule. ar chruth 7 deilb 7 cenel. ar oíti 7 áni 7 irdarcus. ar allud 7 érgna 7 aurlabra.

'Hail to you,'[29] said Bricriu, 'Emer daughter of Forgall Manach, and wife of the best man in Ireland. Emer of the Beautiful Hair is no misnomer for you, you for whom the kings and potential kings of Ireland are in contention. As the sun surpasses the stars of heaven, so do you outshine the women of the whole world in form and shape and lineage, in youth and brilliance and dignity, in fame and wisdom and eloquence.'[30]

There is no doubt that just as Cú Chulainn is meant to surpass the other heroes in every way, so is his wife intended to eclipse the other women. In contrast with his other speeches, Bricriu here begins with brief praise of the husband and goes on to elaborate at some length on Emer's own qualities. Not only does he call Cú Chulainn 'ind fir as dech' ('the best man') in Ireland – in valour and in every way – but he calls Emer the best woman in the whole world, and compares her brilliance to that of the sun. This is high praise indeed. Like the other women, she is flattered for her beauty and lineage; but – as in *The Wooing of Emer* – she is also credited with wisdom and eloquence.

Bricriu's rhetorical patterning thus reinforces the progressive force of his flattery. Fedelm's greatest asset is her lineage; Lendabair's husband surpasses the warriors of the world; but Emer herself outshines *mnaib domain ule* (the women of the whole world). In fact, Bricriu's greeting to Emer differs from his greeting to the other two women. To Emer he says, 'Slán seiss a Emer,' a phrase which echoes the opening line in an early hymn to Saint Brigit.[31] The connection with Ireland's most famous female saint is thus made with subtlety, but might well have been recognized by a contemporary audience.

Although Bricriu seems to describe each woman in glowing terms, his assumption that they are easily deceived through flattery and motivated by jealousy – an assumption which the subsequent narrative proves correct – undermines their positive representation. Moreover, the dignified images of the women presented by Bricriu here are comically undercut a few paragraphs later, when the women race each other for the hall on their return. Yet they regain their composure in the war of words which follows. The representation of the women here seems to shift back and forth, no doubt for comedic effect. Yet underneath the humorous agenda is inscribed a subtly negative portrayal of women as jealous and easily manipulated.

The Bríatharcath

In this 'women's war of words,' each woman sets forth her boastful claim to preeminence in a highly alliterative and often obscure verse form called *rosc* (plural *roscada*). These obscure alliterative passages tend to occur in dialogue or speeches spoken by the characters, particularly at moments of heightened emotion, and are often marked by the marginal notation '.r.'[32] The nature and significance of *roscada* is still a subject of some debate. Earlier scholarship which claimed that these passages were older and more archaic than the surrounding prose, and therefore were composed much earlier in an oral context,[33] has been increasingly challenged. In commenting on an example of *rosc* in *The Death of Conchobar* (*Aided Conchobair*), James Carney writes:

Nativist scholars would do well to reflect upon the fact that this Christian chronologist sat down and deliberately composed the difficult, obscure, and archaic-seeming rhetoric which Conchobar was supposed to have uttered when he heard of the Crucifixion. From this it would emerge that we can never assume that merely because rhetorics contain linguistic archaisms they are older in point of composition or 'writing down' than the text in which they are incorporated ... the incorporation of archaic monologue or dialogue would give a story an appearance of realism and authenticity.[34]

Proinsias Mac Cana expresses reservations about some of Carney's arguments but agrees with the essential point that some passages marked with the marginal '.r.' may be artificially obscure.[35] More recently, Liam Breatnach has concluded that the difference between passages of *rosc* and the prose around them is not one of age but of style, and that the composition of *roscada* continued (at least in the law texts) at least as late as the eighth century.[36] With this in mind, Aitchison suggests that the *roscada* are, in some cases, deliberate archaisms composed by the poet/ redactor as 'showpieces' or manifestations of his poetic craft and thus of his higher status in society.[37]

Certainly the most well known *roscada* in Irish narratives are those which mark moments of heightened emotion and conflict, and particularly conflict between the sexes. The verbal sparring in the *Táin* between Fergus, Ailill, and Medb, after Fergus and Medb have been discovered sleeping together (discussed in chapter 1) is the most famous example. The *bríatharcath* in *Bricriu's Feast* is another example of the use of *roscada* in a prose tale to mark dramatic moments of conflict and tension, although in this case the conflict is primarily between three women, and not between men and women.

In this section of the tale, each woman begins by praising her own beauty, but then quickly turns to an account of her husband's attributes and warrior deeds. Emer's speech excels those of her rivals in sheer space alone.[38] The content of Emer's speech likewise goes far beyond those of the other women, for she includes taunts and insults as well as boasts.

Fedelm is the first to speak:

Cotombertsa brú sóer
sruith dim chlaind comceneoil
cinsiu di churp ríg sceó rígnai
richt for caíni costud
conid cruth buidech berar úaim
noíthium cruth caín
consert la feba Féne
fogart geinsiu genas.

A noble womb bore me,
An equally noble lord begot me.
I was born from the body of a king and queen
and shaped in the image of beauty,
so that I am esteemed to be pleasing of form;
beauty of form makes me famous.
It is well known among the distinctions of the Irish
that I was born with honour and chastity.[39]

Just as Bricriu has done in his flattering comments earlier, Fedelm focuses on her high birth as the daughter of a king and queen, and on her physical beauty. The use of the word *genas* (chastity, restraint) here is somewhat puzzling, but certainly does not mean that Fedelm is the product of a virgin birth. It may signal the idea that Fedelm's mother is the ecclesiastically sanctioned *cétmuinter*, the chief wife of her father – that is, his first wife rather than any of the subsequent wives permitted under traditional Irish law but abhorred by the Church.[40] This would identify her as the true legal offspring of her royal parents.

After describing her high status and good looks, she turns to glorifying her husband:

áurslaid crícha comnart comnámat
cen Ultu imbi.
Imúsdích immustecrathar imgoin airriu
airdercu laechaib Loegaire
lín a búada bías úas cech láech.

He defends the borderlands of neighbouring enemies
without the support of the Ulstermen.
He covers and protects them and wages war for them.
Lóegaire is more illustrious than all other heroes
By the number of his victories which will be beyond
[those of] every other warrior.[41]

As we might expect, the qualities she describes in her husband are
related to his heroic, martial activities. Fedelm does not describe his
physical attractions, although detailed descriptions of men by women
are not uncommon in the Ulster Cycle tales.[42] Nor does she mention her
husband's lineage.[43] We might infer that in the context of this boasting
contest, such details are irrelevant to a man's status. What counts here is
his heroic reputation: what he *does* rather than what he *is*.

Lendabair, in her turn, wastes little time dwelling on her own qualities:

Ar is mése cruth chéill chongraimmim
coiblethar céim cruth caín caurchasta
i Tech Midchúarta ríg
ría mnáib Ulad.
Ar is mo chéle cáem
Conall coscorach credmair
coibledar céim n-ard n-adguide
i n-uchtu ergal n-eirrind ría cach.
Caín tintaí chucum co cernaib co cennaib
co ruccai calca crúaidae comraicthi Ulad
arsaid cach n-áth conid día thuil targlaí
arslaidh a n-áthu arfich a ngressu
comaig láech arabí lecht líac
laimethar meic áin Amorgin accalldaim
ar is Conall ar lín a cherd
cinnges ría cach laech.

For it is I who by virtue of my beauty, good sense and bearing
shall turn my step, beautiful and graceful,
into the House of Mead-Circuit of the kings,
before the women of Ulster.
For it is my dear husband,
Conall triumphant and mighty,
who directs his noble and stately step

to the forefront of deadly battles before all others.
Splendidly he returns to me with spoils and heads
bringing with him shields from the hard-fought battles of the Ulstermen.
He holds every ford so that it is by his consent that
he permits passage.
He defends their fords and fights their battles.
He is a battle-hero standing before his own grave-stone
who dares to challenge Amorgin's illustrious son;
for it is Conall who for the multitude of his feats
marches ahead of every other warrior.[44]

Lendabair omits all mention of her own lineage and quickly turns to praising her husband. Like Fedelm, she dwells on his warlike deeds as the basis for her (and his) claim to preeminence. She does mention Conall's lineage; presumably being the son of the great poet Amorgin contributes to his status.[45]

Emer's speech is so clearly the most cleverly crafted and audacious of the three that we are left with no doubts as to which of the women has won this battle. It is worth quoting in full, even though it is a lengthy speech.

Cotomgabasa chéim cruth cheill congraimmim
coibliud búada báigthir cach delbchaín chucum
conid mo rosc sóer setta doíne dom gnúis gné
ní fríth cruth ná córai ná congraim
ní frith gáes ná gart ná genus.
Ní frith luth seirce sóerligi
na celle conom thicse
ar is immumsa ochsatar Ulaid uile
is mé a cnú chridi
glé diammbése báeth fíad etarlu.
nimmar mbith ben úadib lía céle
on trath sa co alaile
is Cu Chulaind mo chéle
ní cú ches
crithir fola fora crund
cobur fola fora claediub.
Caín forondar a chorp hi crú
créchta ina chaíncnis
álta ina thóeb liss

caín feid a rosc rocheim inna chend síar
caín fúalaing fuither glaini sair
sírderg a sella
ógdérg a fonnaid
fordeirg a fortgae
arfich ó aíb ech 7 analaib fer
foceird ích n-erred ind aíb
atetha cles dond cless dall cless n-eóin
immelig loa usci
atetha cless nonbair
conboing catha cróchombág
falgai betho borrbuidne
brissid úath n-adarccna
is fer seirgeis i lligu
is crón chutma cúaride
iss i richt mná siúil
sedda Ulaid uli
co rrici mo chélese Coin Culaind
cró dond glé sin samlaitir
at salaig úantaind
at húanaind chrisalaig
at gairb chaithlig
at cróna cutrumma
at crothle garmilíne
at búanaind bodelbae
is i rrechtaib bó 7 dam 7 ech
settai mná Ulad uli conom thicisea.

I have established myself as a standard for carriage, beauty, sense, bearing
and vigour;[46] every fair form is exalted until compared with me
and men are attracted by my noble eye, face and appearance.
There has not been found beauty or grace or bearing,
there has not been found wisdom or honour or chastity,
there has not been found movement of love in a noble sexual union[47]
nor intelligence[48] to equal mine.
For it is for me that all the Ulstermen sigh
I am their darling [lit. the nut of the heart].
Clearly, if I were wanton in the presence of opportunity,
hardly would a woman of them be with her husband
between this hour and the same time tomorrow.

Cú Chulainn is my husband,
not a hound of weakness.
A drop of blood upon his spear-shaft,
a froth of blood upon his sword.
Splendidly is his body reddened with blood,
wounds upon his beautiful skin,
gashes on his side.
Splendidly does he bring his eye back deep into his head;
Splendidly in frenzy does he send his jawbone forward.[49]
Crimson red his eyes,
full-red his chariot bearings,
deep red his chariot rug.
He fights above the ears of horses and the breaths of warriors,
he performs the hero's salmon-leap over spear-points,
he accomplishes the brown feat, the blind feat and the bird-feat,
he treads the water,
he accomplishes the nine-man feat,
he smashes battalions in bloody combats,
he lays low the mighty troops of the world,
he overthrows the horror of Adarcna.[50]
He is the man who lay in wasting-sickness;
he is heroic (even) in his dark-stained collapse.[51]
Like women in childbirth
sit all the men of Ulster
except for my husband, Cú Chulainn.
They are like dark gore compared to that bright one[52];
they are dirty and scummy [?]
scummy and unkempt
rough and rubbishy
swarthy and coarse,
noisy and vociferous [or base-born?][53]
long-lived and bovine.
It is in the guise of cows and oxen and horses
that all the women of Ulster sit there,
     except for me.[54]

Emer's speech is a *tour de force* of eloquence. Although the other two women's speeches are also in the form of *rosc*, Emer's words are even more highly wrought than theirs. She uses repetition for emphasis and heightened drama, as in her repetition of 'ní frith ... ní frith' ('there has not been found') near the beginning of the speech, and the six short lines just before the end describing the Ulstermen which all begin with 'at' ('they are'). She uses word-play, as in 'is Cu Chulaind mo chéle / ní cú ches' ('Cú Chulainn is my husband / [he is] not a hound of weakness') in which she plays on her husband's name, 'The Hound of Culann' and thereby invokes the story of how he got his name by killing the giant hound of Culann the smith. She repeats compound words for a cumulative effect, as in 'sírderg ... /ógdérg ... / fordeirg' ('crimson red ... / full-red ... / deep red').

While the other women rely mainly on abstract terms, Emer includes an astonishing number of very concrete images in her speech. She reserves many of these for her description of her husband Cú Chulainn. Unlike the other women, she describes not only her husband's deeds but also his physical appearance:

> crithir fola fora crund
> cobur fola fora claediub.
> Caín forondar a chorp hi crú
> créchta ina chaíncnis
> álta ina thóeb liss
>
> A drop of blood upon his spear-shaft,
> a froth of blood upon his sword.
> Splendidly is his body reddened with blood,
> wounds upon his beautiful skin,
> gashes on his side.[55]

The repetition of 'f's and 'c's here is woven skilfully through the first three lines. The central image in the passage is that of blood – both the blood of defeated opponents and of the hero himself. Emer's imagery moves deftly here between the blood upon Cú Chulainn's weapons and the blood upon his own skin. Her intense focus on blood carries with it an aesthetic sense of the body as object decorated with the patterning of blood and wounds, as well as the idea of the beautiful hero suffering from the effects of battle. In this series of blood images, Emer conveys both the famed physical beauty of her husband and his prowess in combat.[56]

After describing Cú Chulainn's distortions when gripped by battle rage (his sunken eye and protruding jawbone), Emer returns to the imagery of blood, but this time less literally, by using the word *derg* (red) in several compounds:

> sírderg a sella
> ógdérg a fonnaid
> fordeirg a fortgae

> Crimson red his eyes,
> full-red his chariot bearings,
> deep red his chariot rug[57]

Here Emer moves in the opposite direction, from an image of her husband's physicality (the redness of his eyes, presumably from battle-rage) to images of his war chariot and its accoutrements. In these lines the reference to combat is more oblique, with the colour of his chariot equipment carrying the suggestion of blood. She thus maintains the vivid connection between Cú Chulainn's physical appearance and his warrior identity.

Emer treads a fine line between vaunting herself above the other women and actually insulting them. In comparing the other wives with cows and oxen and horses, she comes extremely close to impugning their honour. Charles-Edwards points out that 'it was hardly possible to insult a woman without also insulting her husband; the value of her face was dependent upon the value of his.'[58] Yet Emer also devotes ten lines of her speech to insulting the men, calling them *salaig* and *crothle* (dirty and vociferous?) and taunting them with the lines 'iss i richt mná siúil / sedda Ulaid uli' ('like women in child-birth / sit all the men of Ulster'), an allusion which deliberately recalls the Ulstermen's strange debility the 'ces noínden.'[59] The mention of this condition could not help but remind the audience of the *Táin*, in which Cú Chulainn defends Ulster against the forces of Medb and Ailill of Connaught single-handed because the other Ulstermen are incapacitated by this debility. Thus, in the space of two lines Emer manages to conjure up the whole context of Cú Chulainn's most famous combat, at the expense of the other heroes.

Perhaps Emer's most audacious move in this speech is her claim not only to superior beauty, intelligence, and nobility, but to *sexual* attractiveness as well. She signals this early on in the speech when she declares, 'Ní frith luth seirce sóerligi' ('there has not been found [my equal in] movement of love in a noble sexual union').[60] This seems to be an explicit statement of her skills in bed as well as an assertion of her high status. She then reinforces the image of herself as a sexual threat to the other women with the statement, 'ar is immumsa ochsatar Ulaid uile / is mé a cnú chridi' ('For it is for me that all the Ulstermen sigh / I am their darling [lit. the nut of the heart]'),[61] and delivers the final blow with the declaration 'glé diammbése báeth fíad etarlu / nimmar mbith ben úadib lía céle / on trath sa co alaile' ('Clearly, if I were wanton in the presence of opportunity / hardly would a woman of them be with her husband / between this hour and the same time tomorrow').[62] The phrase 'fíad etarlu' ('in the presence of opportunity') implies that not only do the other Ulstermen want her, she has had many opportunities for encounters with them. Although she seeks to emphasize her chastity and restraint, and therefore her nobility in not succumbing to temptation, Emer also clearly intends this as a challenge to the other women's sexual pride.

Despite her depiction of herself as sexually desirable, Emer's boastful words are, in the final analysis, just words. She provides no physical proofs to back up her arguments – a point which might have had special resonance for an audience familiar with *The Deaths of Lugaid and Derbforgaill*. This, coupled with the fact that *Bricriu's Feast* is clearly intended to be a humorous, entertaining tale rather than a tragedy, may account for Emer's apparent exemption from reprisals for her insulting words to both the men and women of Ulster.

Emer's boasts about her beauty and desirability provide yet another instance of her presentation of herself in her own terms. In this context, as in *The Wooing of Emer*, her illocutionary act of boasting is also a perlocutionary act calculated to have an effect on the listeners.[63] In this situation, however, the intended effect is quite different; the enhancement of her public persona is designed to reflect on her husband and to confirm his status as the greatest hero.

Emer's speech in the 'women's war of words' provides yet another powerful demonstration of her skills in eloquence. It reinforces the impression left by her deft manipulation of speech during the wooing dialogue with the hero in *The Wooing of Emer*, and shows her extending her verbal skills to include insults and challenges to the honour of the other nobles of Ulster.

Sencha's Misogyny

Emer's demonstration of her eloquence does not end with the *bríatharcath*. In a coda to the episode, after the heroes have admitted the women to the house, the debate between the women breaks out anew. Sencha, the 'wise man' who initially called for a war of words between the wives in place of a battle between their husbands, has apparently grown tired of this strategy. In calling a halt to the women's words he trots out some of the well-worn misogynistic sentiments about garrulous women found in many classical and medieval writings:

Cotobsechain a laíchessa
ána áurdairce airegda Ulad.
anat for mbriatra bági
na banaiter fergnúsi
i ccruadaib comraicthib
tria úalle a nglond.
ar is tria chin mban
bit fernai fer dlochtai
fir i n-irgalaib
immad már galgat
comlud ferglunni
ar is dia mbrígaib báesaib
bés dóib dofurcbat nad íccat
imsuídet nad rairget
cotobsechain a laicesa
ana urdairci.

I avoid you, glorious, famous,
noble laywomen[64] of Ulster;
cease your boastful words.
Do not turn pale the faces of the men
in harsh combats
through the arrogance of their deeds;
for it is through the guilt of women
that men's shields are lacerated;
[that] men [are] in battles
in which there is great strife of champions,
setting in motion manly exploits;
for it is through their powers and follies
that they habitually instigate what they do not mend
and attack what they are unable to obtain
I avoid you, glorious, famous,
noble laywomen of Ulster.[65]

Of course, Sencha's insinuation that the words of women are responsible for the conflict in Bricriu's hall is patently ridiculous; the audience knows that it was *Bricriu's* words that started the conflict in the first place, and that in fact the *bríatharcath* was Sencha's idea. To then blame the women for the conflict is absurd.

Emer responds to Sencha's charges immediately. She does not, however, address the assumptions behind his misogyny, nor attempt to refute them. Instead, she falls back on the honour code and claims her right to speak on the basis of her husband's reputation:

Deithbir damsa a Sencha uair isam bensa curad caín cotngabthus cruth ceill o ro damnad a forcetul cen díchill. eter chles for análaib 7 ubullchles 7 siaburcles 7 cles cúair 7 cles cait 7 dergfilliud erred nair 7 gai bolcai 7 bai brasi 7 bruth ngene 7 sían curad 7 rothchles 7 faeburchles 7 dreim fri fogaist 7 dírgiud cretti for cach n-aí.

Ní faigbistar fer and conmestar
a aes 7 a ás 7 a anius.
a guth a gáes a chenel.
a anius a urlabra.
a ág a gal a gaisced.
a bruth a búaid a búadirse.
a foraim a fómsige.
a déni a tharpige
a fíanchoscur co cles nónbair
fo Choin Culaind comchosmail.

It is fitting for me, O Sencha, since I am the wife of a fair hero who contains beauty [and] sense, since his education was easily completed, between the over-breath-feat, apple-feat, sprite-feat, screw-feat, cat-feat, valiant champion's whirling-feat, the *gáe bolga*, quick stroke, raging heat of the mouth [?][66], heroes' fury, wheel-feat, sword-edge-feat, climbing against spikes and straightening his body on each of them.

No man will be found who will equal
his age, his growth, his splendour,
his voice, his intelligence, his race,
his splendour, his eloquence,
his valour, his fury, his weapons,
his heat, his victory, his frenzy,
his bearing, his accuracy in estimating,
his swiftness, his violence,

his killing of game with the feat of nine men.
[No one] is similar to Cú Chulainn.[67]

Emer's statements here tend to repeat the descriptions of her husband's heroic skills that she has given earlier. The significance of this passage lies, instead, in the forceful way in which she counters Sencha's rebuke to the women. It is not only Emer's eloquence that is on display here – it is also the sheer force of her personality, rooted in a profound conviction of her right to speak simply on the basis of her status as Cú Chulainn's wife. She is not cowed by Sencha's antifeminist diatribe but instead brushes it aside and proceeds to the reiteration of her husband's glories. This forceful insistence on her right to speak will continue to mark Emer's interventions in the other two Ulster Cycle tales discussed in this book.

Whether because of the comic agenda of *Bricriu's Feast*, or the compilatory nature of the tale, the force of Emer's words is undercut by the behaviour of her heroic husband. When the Ulstermen call on Cú Chulainn to speak for himself, he complains that he is too tired for duelling. He has, he explains, spent the day capturing the Grey of Macha, one of his two chariot horses. In a sense, his statement, 'Ferr cach cles cotlud diliu lim longud oldás cach ni' ('I would prefer the feats of sleeping and eating to everything else'),[68] undermines everything that his eloquent wife has been trying to establish through her words. The humorous possibilities of this little scene are cut short by Bricriu's impatience to resume the feast, and the hero's refusal to participate further ultimately has no effect on the remainder of the story. It does, however, point out a certain disjunction between women's words and men's deeds.[69] This is an issue which resurfaces again in *The Wasting Sickness of Cú Chulainn*, in more serious circumstances.

Emer's verbal dexterity in the passages cited underscores and enhances the impression of skill and intellect which is first evidenced in the the wooing dialogue of *The Wooing of Emer*. Her ability to construct highly rhetorical statements in the alliterative *rosc* form confirms her identity in the text as a woman of culture rather than an untamed, natural force. Moreover, she rebuffs Sencha's attempt to portray women's words as disruptive and disastrous for men.

The tension between Emer's generally positive representation and the latent misogyny in the narrative nevertheless remains problematic. Although she proves herself worthy of the prize of precedence through her beautifully crafted speech, Emer's eloquent words ultimately carry little weight within the narrative structure. Her praise of Cú Chulainn is not sufficient to convince anyone of his worth; he must travel to the remote regions of Ireland to be judged by a powerful male, Cú Roí, before his claim to the champion's portion is validated. And although Cú Roí specifically awards Emer precedence over the women of Ulster when he proclaims Cú Chulainn the winner of the contest, he does so almost as an afterthought. In the end, Emer's victory – like her honour – is inextricably bound up in that of her husband, and has little if anything to do with her own verbal skills.

Nevertheless, Emer's speeches in this text do leave the impression of a woman in complete control of her thoughts and words, well able to manipulate language to her advantage and audacious enough to risk pushing at the boundaries of acceptable speech in order to enhance her own honour and that of her husband. Moreover, in her rebuttal of Sencha's misogynistic words she implicitly denies their validity. She has the 'last word' against Sencha, and in doing so acts as a bulwark against the sentiments conveyed in his speech. Her behaviour creates – for the audience, at least – the impression of a forceful woman who knows her rights within society and who is not afraid to insist on them. Her speeches provide a space in which a latent female subjectivity, however circumscribed by custom and patriarchal discourse, can be glimpsed and recognized.

3

The Death of Aífe's Only Son: 'Do not slay your only son'

In the two tales discussed so far we have seen Emer playing the roles expected of an aristocratic woman in her society. Although she exerts great influence through her speech, and occasionally comes close to transgressing the boundaries of acceptable discourse, she has been seen operating within the parameters of her heroic, male-centred society. In *The Wooing of Emer* she awaits the return of the hero, guarding her chastity and keeping her promises to him, and in *Bricriu's Feast* she joins the other heroes' wives in expressing her self-worth in the heroic vocabulary of her social milieu.

Yet in two other tales, *The Death of Aífe's Only Son* and *The Wasting Sickness of Cú Chulainn*, Emer emerges as a force of opposition, challenging the customs and attitudes of her society and opposing her husband's choices. In *The Death of Aífe's Only Son* (*Aided Óenfir Aífe*) her challenge is directed specifically towards the heroic honour code that plays such an important role in the fictional world of the Ulster Cycle tales – a code in which she herself has participated. In this story, Emer distances herself from the violent, male-centred discourse of the Ulster warriors and turns her verbal skills against her husband and the heroic ethos he represents.

The Death of Aífe's Only Son is one of the briefest of the Ulster Cycle tales and has attracted little comment. Yet it is the tale which depicts most vividly the tragic flaw both in Cú Chulainn's own character and in the warrior ethic which imbues the Ulster Cycle tales. Cú Chulainn's invincibility both protects Ulster and ultimately deprives it of the survival of his martial brilliance into the next generation. In killing his only son, Cú Chulainn cuts himself off from the continuation of his own bloodline.

By vigorously opposing her husband's decision to fight the boy, Emer becomes the locus of meaning in the tale and the voice for its powerful critique of the warrior ethic. In the process, she inscribes the absence of women in this tale and in its intertexts. She acts as a symbolic mother to Connla, articulating the absence of the real mother Aífe and embodying the maternal values that promote stability and the survival of society. Although her intervention ultimately fails, Emer's speech opens up a space in which change is possible. Her words compel the audience to 'rewrite' the tale in light of their meaning.

While *The Death of Aífe's Only Son* may be a somewhat later addition to the body of stories about Cú Chulainn's career, its depiction of Emer is consistent with that of the other Ulster Cycle tales. On the one hand, this story continues to portray her as the intelligent and outspoken woman we have come to know from *The Wooing of Emer* and *Bricriu's Feast*. On the other hand, this tale develops these characteristics further, and ultimately pits Emer against her husband and against the heroic values which he embodies.

Summary of *The Death of Aífe's Only Son*

The opening paragraph explains the background of the encounter with Aífe and the conception of Cú Chulainn's son, referring to events narrated in *The Wooing of Emer*. The story then resumes seven years later, when Connla comes to Ireland seeking his father (strangely, without the gold ring that Cú Chulainn left for him at his birth). He travels in a marvellous bronze boat, dealing stunning blows to the birds overhead (just as his father did at the same age in the *Táin*). Upon seeing the boy approach, the Ulstermen fear an invasion by adult warriors of his race and send a man of wisdom, Condere son of Echu, to meet him. Condere offers him the hospitality of all the Ulstermen but the boy refuses his welcome and sends him back to the others with the demand that the Ulstermen decide whether they wish to fight him singly or as a host. Condere returns and reports the conversation.

Offended by the shame such a refusal has brought on the Ulstermen, Conall Cernach offers to fight the boy. Connla knocks Conall down and defeats him. When he limps back to them, the rest of the Ulstermen refuse to fight against the boy.

Cú Chulainn approaches with Emer and sees the newcomer. In a fierce and desperate speech, Emer warns him not to fight the boy because he is Cú Chulainn's only son, the son of Aífe. Cú Chulainn responds that even if this is so, he cannot let the Ulstermen be shamed in this way. Cú

Chulainn confronts the boy and does battle with him. Connla succeeds in throwing the great hero in wrestling, and when they fight in the water he ducks his father twice. Enraged, Cú Chulainn then uses his deadly weapon, the *gáe bolga*. He mortally wounds Connla, who laments that the *gáe bolga* was the one weapon that Scáthach did not teach him to use. Cú Chulainn carries the wounded boy back to the Ulstermen and acknowledges that he is his own son. Connla laments, embraces each of the great heroes, and dies. The Ulstermen mourn him, and separate the calves from the cows for three days to commemorate him.

Clearly, the key event in this tale is Cú Chulainn's encounter with his only son and its tragic outcome. What, then, is the significance (if any) of Emer's exceedingly brief involvement in the story and her opposition to Cú Chulainn's course of action? To begin to answer this question we must first place the tale in its context.

Literary Context

The Death of Aífe's Only Son operates within a web of intertexts, many of which refer to Connla as 'Óenfir Aífe' ('the only son of Aífe') and thus suggest strong literary connections. The central event recounted in *The Death of Aífe's Only Son* – Cú Chulainn's slaying of his son – appears in three different literary genres: as a literary tale, as part of the *dinnshenchas* material (the lore of places), and as a legal *exemplum*. Each of these genres carries different assumptions about the tale's meaning and has a different agenda for interpreting it. We shall examine each of these in turn.

As a literary tale, *The Death of Aífe's Only Son* is part of two distinct networks of stories: those containing the motif of father-son conflict, and those recounting an imagined history of Cú Chulainn's heroic career. The first group includes *The Second Battle of Mag Tuired (Cath Mag Tuired)*, an early Fenian tale of the quarrel between Finn and his son, and *The Death of the Children of Tuireann (Oidhe Cloinne Tuireann)*.[1] These tales are not concerned with Cú Chulainn, but they do depict situations strikingly similar to the confrontation between him and Connla. The second group could include Cú Chulainn's entire 'heroic biography,' but this discussion will limit itself to the tales immediately relevant to an analysis of *The Death of Aífe's Only Son*: the *Táin* as a whole, Cú Chulainn's 'Boyhood Deeds,' and *The Wooing of Emer*.

First, the tales containing the motif of father-son conflict establish an important context for our tale in that, unlike *The Death of Aífe's Only Son*, they depict *alternative* solutions to kin-slaying. In *The Second Battle of Mag*

Tuired, Bres is the son born of a union between Ériu and her Otherworld lover Elatha, who leaves a ring for the son she will bear him. Father and son eventually meet, but combat between them is avoided when Elatha sees the ring and recognizes Bres.[2] The situation portrayed here, with its union of two people from different races and the potential conflict between father and son, is remarkably similar to that in *The Death of Aífe's Only Son*. Yet in this case the ring does serve its intended purpose as a badge of identification, while in *The Death of Aífe's Only Son* the ring is never mentioned once Connla comes to Ireland.[3] 'The Quarrel between Finn and Oisín,' a ninth-century text, tells of a dispute which drives Finn's son Oisín out of the Fenian band for a year. On his return he fails to recognize his father and the stage is set for conflict; however, father and son spar with words rather than swords, and when Finn identifies himself further combat is avoided.[4] In *The Death of the Children of Tuireann*, Lug (who is, significantly, Cú Chulainn's father) manages to avenge the murder of his own father Cían at the hands of his kinsmen by arranging for others outside the kin-group to kill the murderers instead.[5] It is significant that in all of these examples, *fingal* (kin-slaying) is avoided.

In her analysis of the parallels between Lug and Cú Chulainn, Elizabeth Gray points out how differently Lug approaches the dilemma of law versus honour in avenging his father's death:

Lug's stratagem benefits the tribe and meets his personal desire to destroy his father's murderers ... he causes the death of the sons of Tuirenn through fair and lawful combat. It is a brilliant solution, supportive of law as a substitute for violence, but acknowledging the alternative ideal of physical retribution.[6]

Cú Chulainn's options are more limited, and perhaps Gray has a point when she claims that 'To fail to meet his son in battle would be even more profound a betrayal of Cú Chulainn's own honour, rooted in his identity as Ulster's defender, than the act of *fingal* itself.'[7] However, when compared with these other tales (which would likely have been familiar to an eleventh- or twelfth-century Irish audience) Cú Chulainn's refusal to consider other options appears foolhardy. Furthermore, the legal text discussed below suggests a greater concern with the crime of *fingal* – at least among certain sections of the tale's audience – than Gray would seem to allow.

The second group of literary tales, those concerning Cú Chulainn, relate specifically to Cú Chulainn's combat with his son. The briefest intertextual reference occurs in the Fer Diad episode in the Book of Leinster version of the *Táin*, where Cú Chulainn says he has not met a warrior of such prowess since he encountered 'Óenfer Aífe.'[8] More important for our discussion is the section of the *Táin* where Cú Chulainn's boyhood deeds are recounted by the exiled Ulstermen.[9] Cú Chulainn, technically an outsider, forces his way into the Ulster camp and through his persistence and brilliant fighting skill wins a place at his maternal uncle's side. His initiatory deeds culminate in his return from the wilderness after slaying the three sons of Nechtán Scéne; he approaches the fortress with a flock of swans he has stunned and captured and a stag he has similarly subdued. Half-crazed with warrior fury, he challenges even the Ulstermen to combat:

Conid samlaid siu luid do Emain Macha: dam allaid i ndíaid a charpait 7 íall gésse oc folúmain úassa 7 trí cind inna c[h]arput. Recait iar sin co Emain ... Ocus asbert Cú Chulaind: 'Tongu do dia toingte Ulaid mani étar fer do gleó frim-sa, ardáilfe fuil lim cach áein fil isin dún.' 'Mná ernochta ara chend!' ar Conchobar.

In this wise he went to Emain Macha with a wild deer behind his chariot, a flock of swans fluttering over it and three severed heads in his chariot. They reached Emain then ... And Cú Chulainn said, 'I swear by the god by whom Ulstermen swear that, unless some man is found to fight with me, I shall shed the blood of everyone in the fort.' 'Send forth naked women to meet him!' ordered Conchobor.[10]

The opening of *The Death of Aífe's Only Son* is strongly reminiscent of this scene. Connla is also an outsider who attempts to force his way into the Ulster warrior band. He approaches Ulster from the sea instead of by land, but his display of heroic prowess is very similar to Cú Chulainn's. The text of *The Death of Aífe's Only Son* reads as follows:

Carn cloch aici isin luing. Dobered cloich ina crandtabaill 7 dosléged tathbé[i]m forsna héonu, congebead na airberthe díb, it é béoa, condaléigid úad isinn aér doridisi. Imfuirmed a carpad clis itir a dá láim conátairthed súil. Noglésed a guth dóib, condafoilged indara fecht. Dondiusced in fecht aile.

A heap of stones was in the skiff with him. He would put a stone in his staff-sling and launch a stunning shot at the birds, so that he brought them down unconscious [?],[11] and alive. Then he would let them up into the air again. He would perform his palate-feat between both hands so that it [his upper jaw?] reached his eye [?]. He would tune his voice for them, and bring them down for the second time. Then he revived them a second time.[12]

It is clear that the young hero Connla is modelled after his father – boastful, precocious, and master of many warrior feats. The two heroes' control over birds is a particularly striking feature in both texts.

Yet the evocation of Cú Chulainn's youth in Connla's arrival scene also highlights the differences between the careers of father and son. Despite his warrior frenzy, Cú Chulainn is ultimately accepted into the Ulster warrior band, chiefly through the favour of Conchobar, his maternal uncle. Connla is not so fortunate; the one man who *could* integrate him into the Ulster band is his father, who does not recognize him – and indeed seems almost determined *not* to recognize him. As a result, Connla's potentially brilliant career ends just as it begins.

The Death of Aífe's Only Son has especially strong links with *The Wooing of Emer*. In fact, it is dependent upon *The Wooing of Emer* for both its existence and its meaning, for it provides a sequel to events recounted in that tale. As discussed in chapter 1, the wooing tale describes the adventures of the young hero Cú Chulainn in a far-away land where he defeats Aífe, the foe of his foster-mother Scáthach. In return for her life, Aífe grants three promises to him, one of which is that she will bear him a son. At this point the narrative in *The Wooing of Emer* tells us:

Luid dano Cú Chulainn la Aífe 7 fois lee in n-aidchi sin. Asbertsi íarom indí Aífe ba torrach 7 is mac do bérad. 'Cuirfedsa íarom dia secht mblíadan co hÉrinn é,' ol sí, '7 fácaibse ainm dó.' Fácbaid Cú Chulainn dornaisc óir dó 7 asbert fria co tísed dia chuindchidseom co hÉrinn in tan bad lán in dornaisc dia mér. 7 asbert combad é ainm dobretha dó Connlae, 7 asbert fria nacha sloinded do óenfer 7 nacha mbérad óenfer dia sligid 7 náro opad comlonn óenfir.

Then Cú Chulainn went with Aífe and slept with her that night. Aífe said then that she was pregnant and that she would bear a son. 'I will send him after seven years to Erin,' she said, 'and you leave a name for him.' Cú Chulainn leaves a fist-ring of gold for him and says to her that he should come to seek him in Erin when the fist-ring fit. And he said that this was the name that should be given to him, Connla, and told her that he should not name himself to any man and that no man should turn him from his path and that he should not refuse battle to any man.[13]

This scene is summarized and the dialogue changed slightly at the beginning of *The Death of Aífe's Only Son*. Here it is the hero who tells Aífe that she will bear a son, rather than *her* telling *him* as in the *The Wooing of Emer* version – a change which diminishes her power somewhat. However, the prohibitions on the son are the same in both texts: he should not identify himself, should turn aside for no one, and should not refuse battle to any one.

These prohibitions set the stage for the tragic outcome of *The Death of Aífe's Only Son*. In fact, the nature of the restrictions actually *guarantees* conflict when the boy reaches Ireland – and clearly that is what Connla's father had in mind. They not only ensure conflict with the other warriors of Ulster but also raise the possibility of combat with Cú Chulainn himself.

The other crucial link with *The Wooing of Emer* is the issue of whether or not Cú Chulainn has an heir. At the beginning of that tale one of the reasons cited for the Ulstermen's insistence that Cú Chulainn find a wife is that

ba sáeth 7 ba homan leo mocherchrae do bith do Choin Chulainn, corb accobur leo arin fáth sin tabart mná dó, fo déig co fárgbad comarbae. Ar rofetatar is úad fessin no bíad a aithgein.

They were sorrowful and fearful that Cú Chulainn would die an early death, and they desired for that reason to get a wife for him, so that he would leave an heir. For they knew that it was from him himself that his rebirth would come.[14]

This passage is inevitably recalled in *The Death of Aífe's Only Son*. There is no evidence in any of the other Ulster Cycle tales that Emer bears Cú Chulainn a son, or indeed any children at all.[15] In her desperate warning to Cú Chulainn in this tale, she specifically urges him not to kill his only son. We can thus assume that the hope of the Ulstermen that the marriage to Emer would produce a successor for their greatest hero has proven elusive. The tragedy of Cú Chulainn's slaying of his only heir is thus deepened by the background provided by this other tale, which would surely have been known to the audience of *The Death of Aífe's Only Son*.

Turning from the literary texts, we find that the story is also summarized in the metrical and prose versions of the *dinnshenchas*, both of which relate the essential features of Cú Chulainn's battle with his son to explain the name of the grave *lecht oen-fir Aife* (The Grave of Aífe's Only Son).[16] Another fuller summary is found in a legal text, which will be discussed below. These summaries are all much shorter than our tale and imply the existence of a longer version or versions. Perhaps most significantly, these summaries all omit Emer's intervention and speech. None of them mentions Emer at all, and since she alone seems able to discern Connla's true identity, all of the summaries assume that Cú Chulainn is ignorant and therefore not guilty of the crime of *fingal*.

First we will consider the *dinnshenchas* material. In his extensive introduction to *The Metrical Dindshenchas*, Edward Gwynn discusses the two recensions of this legendary lore, which recounts stories of how various geographical places got their names. It is clear that the *dinnshenchas* about 'The Grave of Aífe's Only Son' is found only in manuscripts of the later, second recension, and not in the Book of Leinster version. Consequently, Gwynn lists the literary tale, *The Death of Aífe's Only Son*, as a *source* of the poems and prose concerning Connla's grave.[17] This need not diminish the value of the *dinnshenchas* material in this discussion. If *The Death of Aífe's Only Son* is indeed the source, we can see the way the story has been shortened and reshaped; if, on the other hand, both our tale and the *dinnshenchas* material derive from some earlier (either oral or written) source, we have a glimpse of the context of variants in which our tale developed.

The rather moralistic version in *The Metrical Dindshenchas* seeks to lay the blame for the boy's death on both Cú Chulainn and Aífe as just punishment for their sexual sin.[18] The text calls Connla the 'mac lánamna lán-baíthe' ('the son of a very wanton couple') and says:

Rafaíd a máthair anair
ocus rombí a athair:
olc dóib ar óen díb línaib
bás a meic a mígnímaib.

His mother sent him from the east and his father slew him: wrong of them both together was their son's death through their misdeeds.[19]

This passage suggests that Cú Chulainn and Aífe are culpable for both the sexual encounter which led to Connla's conception and for their actions later. The implication is that not only was Cú Chulainn wrong to kill the boy, but Aífe was wrong to send him to his father in the first place, even though he had instructed her to do so. This is the only one of the summaries which comments on the role of Aífe, and it is perhaps not surprising that it portrays her in a negative light. The moralistic tone is typical of the clerical editorializing which marks much of the eleventh-

and twelfth-century revisions of and additions to the *dinnshenchas* material.[20] However, it is important to note that despite this text's attention to
Aífe's role, it makes no reference to Emer's presence on the scene.

The summary of the tale is even briefer in the prose version of the
dinnshenchas, relating the events of the father-son combat in the sketchi-
est manner and concentrating on the boy's dying words and Cú Chulainn's
response. It is worth quoting in full:

Oenfer Aife mac do Choinculainn dorocht tar muir co Traigh mBaile no co hAth
mBec i Conaillib Murthemne, como farnaic do fria athair, co ron-íarfacht a athair
cia bui and, 7 ni dernai a sloindedh dó. Nói mbliadna ba slán dó. Imuforbair doib
co ndrochair in mac. Conid and isbert in mac: 'Andsu labroind [aní] bíis no [a]ni
thoas.' Conid and asbert Cú culainn:

'Oenfer Aife ciarba du
do diclith 'na athardu,
bidam bithchuimnech rem re
dom gleo fri hOenfer Aife.'

Oenfer Aife the son of Cú Chulainn came across the sea to Traig Baile or to Little
Ford in Conaill Muirthemne, where he met with his father; and his father was
asking who he was, and he would not name himself. He was a full nine years
old. They attacked each other so that the son fell. Then the son said: 'It is difficult
for me to say what is or what turns.'[21] Then Cú Chulainn said:

'Oenfer Aife, even if it was [his] native place/due
that he went unrecognized in his native land[22]
I will be ever mindful during my time
of my fight against Oenfer Aife.'[23]

Unlike the *Metrical Dindshenchas*, this prose version contains no moralistic comments on the situation. The verbal exchange between Cú Chulainn
and his son is strange and obscure. In any case, this version is clearly
interested only in providing an explanation for the place-name 'Lecht
Oinfir Aífe' ('The Grave of Aífe's Only Son').

The legal version of the tale presents yet another viewpoint. This text is
found in a manuscript which contains a number of law tracts and tales.[24]
It begins with a summary of the tale which is much more detailed than
those of the *dinnshenchas* versions and which includes more dialogue
between Cú Chulainn and the boy. There are interesting differences in
detail between the literary tale *The Death of Aífe's Only Son* and this

summary. In this version, Aífe is Scáthach's daughter instead of her enemy or her sister, the boy's sex is not known right after conception, and his father leaves for him the name 'Aenfer Aífe'[25] instead of 'Connla.' Aífe herself seems to be responsible for teaching him feats of arms, except for that of the deadly *gáe bolga*, which, the text explains, Cú Chulainn has taken with him back to Ireland.

However, the most interesting portion of the text is the legal discussion which follows the summary of the tale. Here the text asserts that Cú Chulainn was sued by the men of Ulster for half the body-fine for his son. The summary of the tale is thus set in the context of a discussion of *fingal* or 'kin-slaying,' and becomes a vehicle for explaining a point of law. The legal implications of this, and their significance in the context of the tale, are discussed in greater detail below.

Despite the obvious connections between *The Death of Aífe's Only Son* and these other texts, the concerns of the former are quite different. The crucial divergence lies in the role of Emer herself. Emer's impassioned verbal intervention in *The Death of Aífe's Only Son* shifts the tale's focus onto the tragic consequences of a conflict between law and honour. Emer emerges as the representative of law, and the social stability it represents and purports to protect, in opposition to the inexorable demands of the heroic honour code. To appreciate the significance of this clash it is necessary to examine more closely the contexts of early Irish law and the honour code.

Context: Law

Emer knows that the boy on the beach is the son of her husband and the warrior woman Aífe. Thus, if Cú Chulainn kills him he will be committing *fingal*, 'kin-slaying.' As Fergus Kelly has pointed out, the early Irish laws and wisdom texts stress the disastrous nature of *fingal*, a crime which 'strikes at the heart of the kin-based structure of early Irish society.'[26] *Fingal* did not fit into a legal system in which crimes were atoned for through payment to the victim's kin-group. No compensation could be paid to the victim's kin, because the perpetrator was also of that kin. Revenge by members of the victim's kin-group would only constitute further kin-slaying.

The penalties listed for *fingal* are generally heavy. The laws specify that a fort which has been the site of a kin-slaying can be destroyed without penalty,[27] and a king who commits the crime loses his honour-price.[28]

One commentary prescribes that the kin-slayer be set adrift in a boat with one paddle and a little food as punishment; if he is washed ashore he is condemned to servitude.[29]

Although *fingal* is mentioned with some frequency in the Irish Annals, the examples cited are always instances of brother killing brother or kinsman killing kinsman – never of a father killing his own son. In the Annals of Ulster, instances of *fingal* seem to increase with the intensifying Viking raids and the inter-tribal wars which apparently accompanied them. A similar but less dramatic increase can be observed in the Annals of Inisfallen.[30] Yet a scan of the entries reveals no mention of a father slaying his own son, and we can assume that this was a rare and particularly heinous act.

That the crime of *fingal* is a major concern of *The Death of Aífe's Only Son* is confirmed by its treatment in the legal text mentioned above. The literary version of the story ends with the heroes mourning the death of Cú Chulainn's only heir. Yet the shorter version of the tale found in the legal manuscript attempts to deal with the legal ramifications of the slaying of Connla by his father. After a brief summary of the story, this text launches into a discussion of how the men of Ulster sued Cú Chulainn for half the *corpdíre* ('body-fine') of his son. The text explains:

Uair a nimraichni romarbustar é, 7 inddilsec a rricht dilsigh é, ciarbo comracc[.] Cid fodera lethcorpdire uad ind, 7 a marbad a nimraichne 7 conid comracc dorígnestar. IS in fath fodera: ger comracc é. Uair ni haititi in tuaithe na cineoil dorindé[.] Cid fodera lethcorpdire d'íc do choin culainn ina mac. uair ropo deóraig a nulltaib é mád roba hi sídaib do-sein. Fead trichaid cet muirthemne dobói d'feronn dilis aicce ind ulltaib, 7 urrad essem 7 deorad a mac 7 a breith do concobhur in lethcorppdire[.] Cid fodera a breith do concobur, in leth-corpdire? .ní. iss ed fodera. Fingalach cu chulainn, 7 nocha beirind fingalach dibad na corpdíri; iss é coibdelach is nessa dó concobar, ocus in lethcorpdire do breith dó[.]

For he [Cú Chulainn] had slain him in error, and he was an innocent person in the guise of a guilty person, although it was combat. What causes half the body-fine [to be exacted] from him in this case, both his killing him in error, and that it was combat that he made? This is the reason which caused it: it was an intense fight. For [the son] made no acknowledgement of tribe or family. What causes Cú Chulainn to pay half body-fine for his son? Because [Connla] was an alien in Ulster, even if he was from the síd-mounds.[31] The extent of thirty hundreds of Muirthemne was the land belonging to [Cú Chulainn] in Ulster, and thus he was a person of legal standing,[32] and his son an alien, and thus he brought to Conchobar the half body-fine. What caused the half to be given to Conchobar? Not difficult. This is the cause. Cú Chulainn was a kin-slayer, and the kin-slayer does not take inheritance or body-fine. Conchobar was the nearest kin to him, and the half body-fine was given to him.[33]

This legal commentary provides insight into the concerns raised by the tale, concerns which were surely shared by any audience who heard the story. It is worth noting that the solution worked out here depends entirely on Cú Chulainn's ignorance of the identity of the boy whom he kills – the text states, 'Uair a nimraichni romarbustar é, 7 inddilsec a rricht dilsigh é' ('For he had slain him in error, and he was an innocent person in the guise of a guilty person'). The summary which precedes this discussion omits any mention of Emer's intervention and warning to her husband. In this version Cú Chulainn is unaware even of the *possibility* that the boy is his son, and this ignorance enables him to pay only half the body-fine to Conchobar and to remain a functioning member of his society. In early Irish law, ignorance of wrongdoing often reduced the penalty for an offence by half, and this principle appears to influence the legal solution worked out here.[34] Knowing the boy's identity would complicate matters considerably.

The situation between Cú Chulainn and his son Connla is exacerbated by the fact that by not identifying himself Connla is not recognized immediately as Cú Chulainn's kin. The ring given to Aífe, which is clearly meant to function as a token of identification, is not mentioned (in any version) once Connla arrives in Ireland. This omission would perhaps be all the more noticeable to an audience well acquainted with the scene between Bres and his father, in which the ring *does* function as a badge of identification. One could easily argue that Connla's boastfulness and bombast, not to mention his superior fighting skill, all mark him as the son of his father. His actions repeat those of Cú Chulainn in the 'Boyhood Deeds' episode of the *Táin* and recall the older hero's development. All evidence points to his identity as Cú Chulainn's son. But he will not confirm this by revealing his name to anyone, not even to his father. And since he comes to Ireland from across the sea, apparently from a distant unknown land, he is an outsider and thus possesses none of the rights of a member of the *túath* (tribe).

According to the law texts, the rights of such an outsider were very restricted. The laws refer to various types of strangers; the *ambue* seems to have been someone from another kingdom within Ireland, while the *cú glas* was apparently from overseas.[35] Neither had any status in the community. They could be killed or injured without compensation, and no one could act as valid surety or give pledges for them.[36] If such a person married, he was assigned half the honour-price of his wife but still had very restricted legal rights.[37] He was, in short, marginalized and compelled to live without the full legal rights and protections of Irish society.

Connla is thus in a very vulnerable position. His death would not incur the standard punishments for the slaying of a member of the *túath*. One might expect his death to require no payment at all; yet this idea was obviously a disturbing one that demanded amendment in light of the boy's parentage. The legal commentary makes the point that Cú Chulainn pays only half the body-fine normally due because Connla was an 'alien' in Ulster.[38]

This legal commentary highlights the concern with law in *The Death of Aífe's Only Son*. The legal implications of the situation would have been clear to a medieval audience, and the existence of the commentary points to a vital, interactive relationship between at least some members of the tale's audience and the text itself.

Yet Emer's conspicuous absence in the legal *exemplum* remains to be explained. We could speculate that the summary is based on a version which also omitted Emer's intervention. Yet there is another possible explanation. In the medieval society depicted in the law tracts, women had virtually no legal voice. They could not normally act as witnesses,[39] except in a few exceptional circumstances – most notably in sexual matters.[40] In fact, with regard to their right to speak in a legal context, women in Ireland seem to have been subjected to the same anti-feminist censure as their British and Continental sisters. One glossator explains the inadmissibility of female evidence by describing it as 'biased and dishonest.'[41] In the early Middle Ages, women could make contracts only with the permission of their superiors (that is, their fathers or husbands), although this situation clearly improved over time.[42] But in general, women's voices were absent from the legal arena. Emer's intervention in our tale could thus be regarded as without weight and therefore without relevance in a legal argument. Her words would be as insubstantial in a legal text as they are to Cú Chulainn in the tale.

Context: The Honour Code

Complicating the situation even further is the heroic code of honour, which seems to have existed – at least, in the literary world of the texts – alongside the laws. The legal tracts themselves deal only with the honour-prices of various persons according to rank, and prescribe the payment of honour-price to wounded parties in a variety of circumstances.[43] However, the obsessive concern with honour and shame evident in the tales does not emerge from the legal record.

In contrast, the medieval tales depict a warrior society in which being shamed is literally a 'fate worse than death.'[44] As we have seen, the plot of *Bricriu's Feast* hinges on this obsessive concern with honour. The need to preserve one's public reputation and avoid shame informs a great number of medieval Irish tales, especially those concerning Cú Chulainn, Conchobar, and the other Ulster heroes.

Several scholars have recently explored the workings of the honour code in a number of medieval Irish tales. Philip O'Leary says:

The society depicted in early Irish literature seems to have allowed little if any scope for the exercise of individual conscience, the agent of an internalized personal code of ethics. Instead, standards of right and wrong were traditional, external, and public, determined and imposed by the society, with shame and disgrace the major sanctions and honour and glory the ultimate rewards.[45]

The situation presented in *The Death of Aífe's Only Son* illustrates this vividly. Connla's arrival is witnessed by a large number of the Ulstermen; therefore, all responses and reactions are visible and open to public approval or disapproval. After offering hospitality to Connla, the wise man Condere warns him of bringing shame to the Ulstermen by refusing their welcome:

bad búada brón la Blaí brigiu bem sechai. Cia so laech daig nimardraic ilar ruice

it would be a triumph of sorrow for Blaí Briugu if you journeyed beyond him. Although he is a fiery hero ... shame [would come?] to a multitude.[46]

Connla's treatment of Condere is clearly perceived as shameful, for when Condere gives his account of the conversation Conall Cernach says, 'Ní ba fír ... enech Ulad do breith céin am beó-sa' ('It would not be right ... for the Ulad to be shamed while I am alive')[47] and goes down to meet the boy himself. Then when Conall is thrown and defeated, Cú Chulainn insists on fighting Connla despite Emer's words, for he says, 'Cid hé nobeith and, a ben ... nangonaind-se ar inchaib Ulad' ('Even though it be he who is there, O woman, ... I will kill him for the honour of the Ulstermen.'[48]

This is a shocking declaration, for it implies that Cú Chulainn prizes honour more highly than the survival of his own bloodline. A similar situation occurs in the *Táin*, when Cú Chulainn must decide whether or not to fight his foster-brother Fer Diad.[49] In both of these instances, the high value placed on honour both raises the stakes of the conflict and heightens the emotions in the tale.

Perhaps the closest analogue to the situation in *The Death of Aife's Only Son* is found in *The Kin-slaying of Rónán*. In this tale, discussed briefly in chapter 1, a complex web of events leads to a situation in which Rónán must have his son Mael Fothartaig killed for allegedly attempting to seduce his young wife. In fact, the wife has been soliciting Mael Fothartaig since she married Rónán, and she takes revenge on the son for repudiating her by accusing him of trying to seduce her. Rónán is reluctant to believe her accusations but the possibility of damage to his honour causes him to accept a public ordeal by 'verse-capping' to determine the truth.[50] In his detailed examination of the issues of honour and shame in this tale, Charles-Edwards concludes:

In Rónán's case a public ordeal has been employed, and a public decision reached. Rónán has, therefore, been formally shown to have been insulted by his son Mael Fothartaig. Compensation, however, is out of the question: the feud is intra-familial. Rónán must either forfeit his honour or have his son killed.[51]

Although in *The Death of Aife's Only Son* the honour being defended seems to be that of the Ulstermen as a group, Connla's public defeat of his father in single combat would also dishonour Cú Chulainn personally.

Whether or not the preoccupation with honour portrayed in these texts reflects actual social conditions at any point in the Irish past must remain a matter for speculation. Recent scholarship has tended to emphasize the process of *rewriting* the past by the *literati* of medieval Ireland.[52] In discussing the *Táin*, N.B. Aitchison remarks, 'the epic literature does not present a reflective impression of contemporary society in north-eastern Ireland. Rather, it comprises contemporary perceptions of the past projected back into prehistory.'[53] Thus, a society obsessed with honour in which men murder even their own sons may be a literary construct shaped by redactors with a moral case to make against the so-called glories of the secular Irish past, or indeed the abuses of power in the present.[54] This might have been especially true as the church consolidated its power in Ireland and began a process of reform.[55] A tale in which the heroic ethos leads to chaos and tragedy might also have been deemed timely and appropriate in the eleventh and twelfth centuries, when intertribal wars and political upheaval had become the norm. It is interesting to note, then, that the voice of moral order in this tale is that of a woman.

Keeping in mind this social and legal context, as well as the intertextual links between literary tales, let us look more closely at the role of Emer's intervention in *The Death of Aífe's Only Son*.

Words of Warning

Emer and Cú Chulainn arrive on the scene immediately after Conall Cernach has been defeated by the boy Connla. The account of their arrival, and Emer's response, are worth citing in full:

Bái Cúchulaind immorro oc a cluichiu oc dul adochum in gillai, 7 lám Emeire ingine Forgaill dar a brágaid. 'Ná téig sís!', ar sí. 'Mac duit fil tís. Ná fer finga[i]ll 'mot énmac. Co sechnom a maic saigthig soailte. Ní soáig ná soairle coimérgi frit mac mórgnímach mór n-esad artai o riad cnis focloc ót biliu bai cotaith fri Scáithci scél. Mád Conlai cesad clár clé comad fortemen taidbecht. Tinta frim! Cluinti mo chlois! Fó mo cosc. Bad Cúculaind cloodar! Adgén-sa cid ainm asind ón masa Conlai énmac Áifi in mac fil tís,' or in bean. Is andsin asbert Cúculaind: 'Coisc, a bean! ní coisc mná admainiur mórgnímaib asa coscaib glé. Ní gníthear do bancobro bam gním búadach nó buideach na ruisc na ruireach de fola form chnis crú cuirp Conlai. Cain sug set gai in cleitíne cain. Cid hé nobeith and, a ben,' ar sé, 'nangonaind-se ar inchaib Ulad.'

Moreover Cú Chulainn was at his game, approaching the boy, with the arm of Emer daughter of Forgall across his throat. 'Do not go down there!' she said. 'It is your son who is below. Do not commit kin-slaying against your only son. May we avoid [each other] O impetuous well-bred boy [?]. It is neither a fair fight nor good counsel to rise against your son of great deeds. Turn away from the skin-torture of the sapling of your tree, severe against the words of Scáthach. If the left board [of the chariot] of Connla were turned, your bombast[56] would be a very obscure protection. Return to me! Hear me! My prohibition is good! Let Cú Chulainn listen! I know what name he bears, if that boy below is Connla the only son of Aífe,' said the woman. Then Cú Chulainn said, 'Forbear, woman! I do not request a woman's prohibition regarding great deeds [and] prohibitions of brilliant splendour. Triumphant deeds are not performed through the feminine assistance of women; nor is there gratitude in the eye of a king because of it, the blood of the body of Connla on my skin. Beautifully will spears consume the fair little javelin.[57] Although it were he who is down there, O woman,' he said, 'I would kill him for the honour of the Ulstermen.'[58]

The initial image in this passage is highly ambiguous. Emer's arm is around her husband's throat or neck and Cú Chulainn is 'oc a chluichiu' ('at his game') – a detail which echoes both the previous mention of 'games' by Condere and Conall Cernach (earlier on in this text) and Cú Chulainn's own behaviour as a young boy in the 'Boyhood Deeds' section of the Táin.[59] Cú Chulainn's identification with his former (childish, immature) self through his 'games' both accentuates the impression of doubling between him and Connla and recalls the potentially destructive forces that Cú Chulainn embodied as a child. Emer's part in this image depends to some extent on how one translates the word brágaid. If we render the phrase 'dar a brágaid' as 'across his neck,' we have a picture of a relaxed, loving gesture. However, this impression dissolves if we translate the word as 'throat, gullet,' for such a translation conveys a physical intervention, an attempt to restrain the hero, which matches the desperation of her words.[60]

Emer's speech and Cú Chulainn's reply are among several roscada scattered throughout the tale. As we saw in Bricriu's Feast, these highly alliterative passages tend to mark moments of heightened emotion and conflict, and particularly conflict between the sexes. Perhaps the most striking analogue to our passage in The Death of Aífe's Only Son is the trio of roscada spoken by Lí Ban in welcoming her husband Labraid in The Wasting Sickness of Cú Chulainn (which begins, 'Welcome, Labraid').[61] Twice she welcomes him and praises his warlike abilities, but he does not respond. After the third welcome he finally speaks, but rejects her characterization of him as a brilliant hero. Like Cú Chulainn in The Death of Aífe's Only Son, Labraid pointedly disregards the words of his wife.

The rosc passages in The Death of Aífe's Only Son include Condere's welcome to Connla and the boy's reply, as well as Emer's warning and Cú Chulainn's response. A closer look at these four passages reveals some interesting features which have important implications for the meaning of the tale and Emer's role in it. The first pair consists of Condere's welcome and warning and Connla's rejection of both. The second pair contains Emer's warning to Cú Chulainn and his rejection of her advice.[62] This sets up a parallel situation in which Condere and Emer both seem to represent wisdom and prudence, and Connla and his father Cú Chulainn embody the warrior ethic. The identification of Emer with the wise man Condere, through these links between her warning and his, serves to strengthen her role as the voice of moral authority in the tale. By aligning her with a male from within the tribe, the text makes her less marginal and gives weight to her words.[63]

That these four *roscada* are meant to function as parallel units is further emphasized by the clear verbal connections between them. Condere's admonition, 'Tinta frim, a mo maic' ('Turn to me, O my boy') is echoed in Emer's more desperate 'Tinta frim!' ('Turn to me!'). Both use similar phrasing to stress the boy's warrior skills; Condere says to him, 'Tinta frim, a mo maic, ad mórgníma ... cucad' ('Turn to me, O my boy, you are capable of great deeds ...'), while Emer tells Cú Chulainn 'Ní soáig ná soairle coimérgi frit mac mórgnímach' ('It is neither a fair fight nor good counsel to rise against your son of great deeds'). Both Condere and Emer use the phrase *clar clé* (the left board [of the chariot]) to signify the potential danger in the encounter. There are similar verbal echoes between Connla's response to Condere's warning and Cú Chulainn's response to Emer's; for instance, in the word *morgnimaib* repeated in both answers and in Connla's use of *cletínib* (javelins) and Cú Chulainn's use of *cleitíne* (javelin). These verbal correspondances reinforce the connections between the two pairs of speeches.

Clearly the *roscada* in *The Death of Aífe's Only Son* express conflict between different men (Condere and Connla) as well as that between men and women (Cú Chulainn and Emer). They are thus used in both the expression of heightened emotion and the accentuation of male-female conflict. It is also worth noting that a redactor who sought to reshape the tale with a pointed moral agenda might have been tempted to embed his message in deliberately archaic *roscada* to give the impression of age and authority to his additions.[64]

The *rosc* passages in *The Death of Aífe's Only Son* serve to bind together the warnings of Condere and Emer to Connla and his father, thereby reinforcing the opposition between reason and warrior fury in the text. But does Emer's use of this type of language merely trap her in the same web of patriarchal discourse which governs her headstrong husband, a discourse of violence to which there is no alternative? Perhaps on the surface it appears so. On the other hand, through the particular construction of her speech, Emer diverts attention *away* from issues of honour and shame, and concerns herself instead with lineage and family connections. In doing this, she succeeds in introducing a more humane, perhaps even female mode of speaking – if only for a moment.

The Role of Emer's Words

Emer is the pivotal figure in whose words the meaning of the encounter with the foreign boy takes shape. Although the action continues along its tragic course to the inevitable conclusion, Emer's warning speech creates a pause in the action during which events are suspended and the choices and their implications are made clear. Only she possesses the key piece of information which could influence the outcome of the conflict – that is, that Connla is Cú Chulainn's son.

Emer's warning contains, in Searle's terms, both representatives and directives. Through representatives, statements which 'commit the speaker ... to something's being the case,'[65] Emer supplies the missing pieces of information which Cú Chulainn sorely needs: that this boy is his son, that he is a mighty force to be reckoned with, and that killing him will constitute *fingal*. She combines these statements with directives, a series of passionate imperatives in which she commands her husband to refrain from violent action.[66] The force of her commands hinges on the truth of her statements about the boy, and the two types of illocutionary acts are woven together in an eloquent warning against the consequences of violent action.

Emer is the only person in the tale who is able to interpret the meaning of Connla's arrival and the riddle of his identity. Like so many other women in Irish literature – like Fedelm in the *Táin*, for instance – she is the decoder of signs, the interpreter of meaning. Yet the silencing of her voice which takes place (deliberately or not) in the summaries discussed above is dramatized forcefully here by Cú Chulainn's sharp retort. Cú Chulainn rejects her words with the statement, 'Ní coisc mná admainiur mórgnímaib asa coscaib glé. Ní gníthear do bancobro ...' ('I do not request a woman's prohibition regarding great deeds [and] prohibitions of brilliant splendour. Triumphant deeds are not performed through the feminine assistance of women ...').[67] He thus discounts past evidence of the value of women's reading of signs – not least of which is Scáthach's prophecy of his role in the *Táin* – and stubbornly persists in his own blind adherence to the honour code.[68] This behaviour contrasts sharply with his acceptance of women's words in *The Wooing of Emer* when he explicitly follows Uathach's instructions about how to approach her mother, and later follows Scáthach's advice as to how to trick Aífe. In rejecting Emer's advice in this tale, he implies an unbridgeable chasm between words (especially those of women) and deeds (which he sees as a male preserve).

This is somewhat ironic in light of Scáthach's role in both his and Connla's training at arms. An audience familiar with *The Wooing of Emer* would surely be aware of the contradictions implied here; indeed, the point is driven home when Cú Chulainn uses the *gáe bolga* and the narration adds 'are ní romúin Scáthach do duine ríam in gaisced sin acht do Coinculaind aenur' ('for to no man had Scáthach ever taught the use of that weapon save to Cú Chulainn alone').[69] The fatally wounded Connla cries out, 'Is ed ón tra ... ná romúin Scáthach dam-sa!' ('That is what Scáthach never taught me!')[70] Thus, despite his words, Cú Chulainn's ability to defeat Connla is due entirely to 'the feminine assistance of women.'[71]

Emer's most potentially persuasive argument is a legal one: Cú Chulainn will be committing *fingal* if he kills the boy, since Connla is Cú Chulainn's son. There is surely a subtle irony in the the legally 'voiceless' woman introducing the legal term *fingal* here. Emer also appeals to the principles of *soáig* (fair fight) and *soairle* (good counsel). She calls the boy the 'focloc ót biliu' ('sapling of your tree'), an image designed to symbolize both their close biological tie and the survival of Cú Chulainn's blood line into the future. Finally (perhaps in an attempt to muster support from a greater authority), she alludes to a warning from Scáthach against this fight, a warning which does not, unfortunately, appear in any of the versions of *The Words of Scáthach* (*Verba Scáthaige*) which survive today.[72] Her invocation of Scáthach's prophecy – and its failure to move her husband – only heightens the impression of the weightlessness of women's words in this situation.

In taking a stand on the side of the law, Emer aligns herself with the desire for stability in her society and against the demands of the honour code. In the context of the tradition as it appears in medieval Irish tales, this is a difficult position to take. It means defying a whole range of assumptions and customs which regulate society. Such a rupture with custom is very rare in the literature; the private bargain between Cú Chulainn and Fergus to withdraw from each other in the *Táin* is one of the few exceptions.[73] A woman would likely be doubly reluctant to oppose her husband, since her status depended upon him and the stability of her marital life rested on his continuing good will.[74] Emer's courageous stand against the honour code articulates the catastrophic

implications of following the demands of honour to their logical conclusions. Her defiance of the code as an unchangeable imperative opens up
a space in which change and repair are possible. Although the hero
rejects her advice, his actions and their tragic consequences are completely coloured by Emer's words and their implications.

Although she cannot change the events of the past (her husband's
liaison with Aífe and the injunctions he has laid on the boy), Emer can
attempt to change the present and draw the boy and his father together.[75]
In opposing Cú Chulainn's misplaced priorities, Emer aligns herself with
all mothers and children. Although she has no children of her own, in
this scene she assumes the protective role of mother and speaks for the
absent mother, Aífe. While I disagree with O Hehir's view that Emer and
Aífe are both different aspects of the same goddess, there is certainly a
sense of symmetry between the two women as literary figures in this
scene.[76] Aífe has provided Cú Chulainn with the heroic successor that
Emer could not produce. Emer, in turn, acts as a symbolic mother, arguing for the protection of the young against the ravages of combat and
acting as a voice for the absent mother who remains a shadowy figure in
the background.

In aligning herself with all mothers, Emer places herself in the company of other protecting mothers in Celtic literature such as Branwen in
the Middle Welsh tale *Branwen Daughter of Llyr*. Honour is also at issue in
this tragic tale, which once again pits a woman against the male honour-
code of her society. When her son Gwern is thrown into the fire by her
half-brother Efnisien, Branwen attempts to save him but is held back by
her brother. It is as if the death of this child is an imperative that tran-
scends all familial ties.[77]

In both of these cases, the text assumes that the audience's sympathies
will be with the protecting woman. The death of the son is seen as foolish
and wasteful, and the woman functions as the voice of reason, protecting
the present and future interests of society. Tragically, Emer's attempt to
change the course of events fails; ultimately the male honour code triumphs and Cú Chulainn and the Ulstermen must suffer the loss of a
brilliant new warrior.

Woman as Culture

In representing the law and its sanctions against *fingal*, Emer is once
again acting as a culture figure. Although both law and honour appear to
belong to the realm of culture, the honour code can be seen as a more

emotional and less rational side of culture. In this tale the overwhelming desire to preserve honour is portrayed as a dangerous and potentially destructive force in society. While the law enjoins people to live up to their obligations and to use reason and temperance in their interactions with others, the obsession with honour often militates against this ideal, with disastrous consequences. Emer represents the realm of reason in contrast to that of emotion and action.

The conflict between reason and action is reinforced by the structure of the tale. *The Death of Aífe's Only Son* begins with a brief account of Cú Chulainn's relationship with Aífe in Alba, then moves to Ireland where the milieu is one of male action.[78] Emer disturbs the pattern of that action with her speech and inserts a discourse of reason which offers an alternative to combat. Her words are ignored, and the trajectory of male violence resumes its course, proceeding to its inevitable conclusion. The implication here is that heroic deeds, performed without the guidance of reason within the framework of culture, are destructive and dangerous.

Female Absence

Despite Emer's strong presence in the tale, *The Death of Aífe's Only Son* is haunted by the *absence* of women. Aífe is perhaps the most notably absent because her name is present both in the title of the tale and in the way the boy is referred to ('the only son of Aífe'). She is mentioned in the beginning as a part of Cú Chulainn's past, but then disappears from the narrative stage. Scáthach is mentioned several times as the foster-mother of young heroes and the best teacher of martial arts, and (by Emer) as the one who has warned Cú Chulainn against combat with his son. Emer's presence is powerfully conveyed in her impassioned speech, but with Cú Chulainn's rejection of her advice she fades from view and we never see her reaction to Connla's death. These women all hover in the background while the heroes pursue their heroic male goals. Through her words and actions, Emer draws the shadows of Aífe and Scáthach to herself and speaks for them. Yet by the end of the tale, all three women have faded from view.

The story alludes to and reinforces this absence of women in the unusual way that the Ulstermen commemorate the boy: the text says 'co cend trí tráth nicon reilgthe láig día mbúaib la hUltu ina díaid' ('to the end of three days no calf was allowed to their cows by the Ulstermen after [to commemorate] him').[79] Through the ruptured relationship of cows and calves, all the ruptured mother-son connections – between Aífe and Connla, between Emer and the son she will never have as well as the surrogate son Connla, and between Scáthach and her foster-sons Cú Chulainn and Connla – are woven together with subtlety and emotion. This is a powerful image, evoking the bawling of cows and calves when the two are separated at weaning. This anguished bellowing becomes a kind of keening when transferred to the dead boy Connla. At this point in the tale, the only females left to raise the death lament are the cows.[80]

Although Emer's intervention in *The Death of Aífe's Only Son* ultimately fails to prevent tragedy, her words radically alter the meaning of the tale. As a speaking subject, she powerfully inserts herself into the heroic discourse and communicates her own fears for a young boy's future. As the representative of all absent and grieving mothers, she presents a compassionate alternative to male violence. As the voice of law and stability, she warns of the disastrous effects of pursuing heroic goals at the expense of family and society. As the spokesperson for culture and reason, she argues against the emotional and destructive obsession with honour. And as a reader of signs and the bearer of the knowledge of Connla's true identity, she changes forever the meaning of Cú Chulainn's foolish *fingal* by naming his deed openly.

While Emer's role in this tale is brief, she is nevertheless the pivotal figure in its construction of meaning. If *The Death of Aífe's Only Son* as we now have it was indeed crafted by a writer with a moral agenda, Emer is the figure who carries the weight of that agenda. Although she fails to dissuade her heroic husband from his folly, her words embody the tale's stinging indictment of the old heroic honour code.

4

The Wasting Sickness of Cú Chulainn: The Language of Desire

The story of Cú Chulainn's debilitating love-sickness and Emer's corresponding jealousy is one of the most unusual tales in medieval Irish literature. Not only does the narrative manage to subvert many of the norms of both heroic and romantic stories, it also opens a window onto the emotional lives of its female characters. Through the device of a potion of forgetfulness, *The Wasting Sickness of Cú Chulainn* (*Serglige Con Culainn*[1]) contrives to tell an anomalous tale within an established tradition without jeopardizing the essential outlines of that tradition. At the same time, the text presents both Emer and her Otherworld rival, Fand, as speaking subjects who articulate their desires clearly and forcefully. Few other medieval texts contain such a vivid portrayal of a female perspective on the nature of love. And few others depict a woman's verbal intervention as altering the narrative trajectory so decisively. Emer's words actually change her world.

The Wasting Sickness of Cú Chulainn is perhaps the most interesting tale in which Emer plays a major role. It is a complicated text which toys with the conventions of 'heroic age'[2] literature and presents Cú Chulainn as an ambiguous hero. The ultimate *effect* of this play is to make possible a discourse about the potentially disastrous tensions in male-female relationships and the consequences of love and jealousy. Crucial to this discourse is the central role of women in the narrative, and particularly of Emer. Through a network of inversions and ambiguities, the tale probes the limits of society's ability to deal with active women, inactive heroes, polygyny (the possession of more than one wife at a time),[3] and spousal abandonment.

Summary of *The Wasting Sickness of Cú Chulainn*

One year when the Ulstermen and their wives gather on the Plain of Murthemne to celebrate the feast of Samain, a flock of beautiful birds settles on a lake nearby. Each woman wants a pair of the birds, and they argue over which of them are most worthy to possess them. They persuade a reluctant Cú Chulainn to catch the birds, but when he distributes them there are none left for his own wife (called Ethne at this point in the tale). Ethne denies being angry at being left out, and Cú Chulainn promises that the next birds which arrive will be hers.

A pair of birds does appear, but they are joined together by a chain and Ethne and the charioteer Lóeg urge Cú Chulainn not to shoot at them. He ignores their advice, misses twice, and finally strikes one bird on the wing. In an angry mood, Cú Chulainn falls asleep sitting against a pillar stone and has a terrifying dream of two women who laugh at him and beat him with a horse-whip. When he awakes, he is unable to speak. He lies sick in bed for a year.

The next Samain (the last day of the Celtic year), Óengus, the son of Áed Abrat from the Otherworld, appears to Cú Chulainn and his companions. He invites the hero to the Otherworld, where his sister Fand is longing for his company. Cú Chulainn rouses himself and, at the Ulstermen's urging, returns to the pillar stone where the encounter with the women occurred. One of the two women meets him there. She says she is Lí Ban, the sister of Óengus and the wife of Labraid, a warrior who needs his help in battle. She tells him that Fand's husband Manannán mac Lir has left her, and that she has set her love upon Cú Chulainn instead. If he will come and fight alongside Labraid, Fand will be his reward.

Cú Chulainn sends his charioteer Lóeg with Lí Ban to learn about her country. There Lóeg sees the wonders of the Otherworld and meets both Fand and Labraid. Lóeg returns and describes the marvels of the Otherworld. Cú Chulainn is temporarily revived by his account and sends Lóeg to Emer to ask her to visit him.

Emer rebukes Lóeg for failing to bring back a cure for her husband from the Otherworld. She travels to Cú Chulainn's bedside, and urges him to rise from his love-sickness and resume his warrior deeds. Her words revive him, and after further deliberations (and another foray into the Otherworld by Lóeg) Cú Chulainn finally travels there himself. There he fights a battle and apparently defeats Labraid's enemies, although his own assessment of his triumph is more equivocal. Fand praises his deeds and he becomes her lover. They spend a month together in the Otherworld and then make a tryst to meet again in Ulster.

Emer learns of the tryst and arrives along with fifty female servants, all of them armed with sharp knives with which to kill Fand. Fand sees the women approaching and warns Cú Chulainn. He vows to protect her and rebukes Emer for taking up arms. Emer in turn reproaches him for dishonouring her before all of Ulster. Cú Chulainn wonders why she objects to his tryst with Fand, enumerating the other woman's virtues and noting her wealth and high status. Emer responds by suggesting that he is merely bored with her, and reminds him that she and he were happy together once and could be so again if he still desired her. He confirms that he does still desire her. On hearing this, Fand says, 'Leave me then.'

Emer and Fand then debate which of them ought to be abandoned by Cú Chulainn. Fand decides that it is she who must withdraw and laments her parting from the hero. Her husband, Manannán, approaches from the Otherworld and speaks to her without being perceived by the others. He persuades her to return with him and she leaves reluctantly.

When Cú Chulainn realizes that Fand has departed he goes mad and wanders the mountains until Emer persuades the Ulstermen to find him. The druids give both Cú Chulainn and Emer a potion of forgetfulness, and Manannán shakes his cloak between Cú Chulainn and Fand so that they should never meet again.

Before beginning to explore the complexities in this tale we must first consider the context in which it took shape and in which it would have been received by a medieval audience.

Context: Romantic Tales

The particular gender operations in this tale distinguish it from the medieval Irish literary tradition. *The Wasting Sickness of Cú Chulainn* defies classification in any of the genres dealing with male-female relationships mentioned in the tale lists.[4] It certainly is not a *tochmarc* (wooing), for there is no bride who must be won by marvellous deeds. And it is certainly not a *táin* (cattle-raid), the other type of (admittedly, less romantic) wooing tale common in the medieval Irish tradition.[5] In fact, *The Wasting Sickness of Cú Chulainn* seems to be in some ways an inversion of the 'elopement' plot, the kind of tragic story engineered by a strong woman like Deirdre or Gráinne, in which two rival males battle

for the love of one female.[6] Instead, we have here two determined women
fighting over the love of one man.

Perhaps the most important of the early tales for comparison with *The
Wasting Sickness of Cú Chulainn* is *The Wooing of Étaín*.[7] This tale also
contains the striking motif of a jealous first wife's attack on a female
rival. Whereas Fúamnach, the first wife of Mider, is ultimately destroyed
for her magical revenge on Étaín, Emer is rewarded with the withdrawal of Fand when she arrives with her retinue of armed women to
challenge her. Fúamnach is portrayed as a wicked sorceress in *The Wooing of Étaín*, but Emer clearly has the sympathies of the redactor and
occupies the 'moral high ground' in *The Wasting Sickness of Cú Culainn*.
This is partly due to Emer's passionate articulation of the reasons for
her opposition to Fand – reasons which include her public dishonour as
well as Cú Chulainn's apparent rejection of her personally.[8] But the
differences could also be due to differing literary agendas on the part of
the redactors who shaped the tales. This point will be discussed in
greater detail below.

The Wasting Sickness of Cú Chulainn also toys with the 'fairy mistress'
motif so common in early Irish literature. In these stories an Otherworld
woman comes to woo a mortal hero, usually declaring that she has long
loved him although she has never seen him. Examples of this story type
include an alternate version of *The Wooing of Étaín, The Voyage of Art Son
of Conn*, and *The Voyage of Connla*. The brief version of *The Wooing of Étaín*
is found at the beginning of another tale, *The Destruction of Da Derga's
Hostel* (*Togail Bruidne Da Derga*).[9] The first section of the story tells of an
encounter at a well between king Echu Feidlech and a woman of incom-
parable beauty. She is Étaín, a fairy woman from the Otherworld, who
says she has come seeking Echu himself; she has loved him since childhood, she says, on account of his noble reputation. He agrees to wed her
and pay her bride-price. In *The Voyage of Art Son of Conn* (discussed
briefly in chapter 1)[10] Bécuma comes to Ireland from what appears to be
the Otherworld. She seeks Art son of Conn, with whom she has fallen in
love, but instead meets Conn himself, whose wife has just died. Bécuma
decides to wed Conn instead of the younger Art, and persuades him to
banish Art from Tara for a year. Her presence as the wife of the king
brings disaster, and the rest of the story concerns various efforts to
restore peace and equilibrium to the kingdom. *The Voyage of Connla* also
contains the fairy mistress motif.[11] In this story, Connla is visited by a
beautiful Otherworld woman who tries to persuade him to go with her to
the land of immortality. When he hesitates, she leaves him a magical

apple which only increases his longing for her. In the end, he cannot resist and departs with the woman, never to be seen again.

In all of these tales a king is wooed by an Otherworld woman, and some scholars have read these female figures as sovereignty goddesses whose function is to legitimize the kingship of the man they come to woo.[12] Whether or not this mythological reading is valid, the tales do tend to be concerned in various ways with the consequences of an alliance between a mortal man and an Otherworld woman.

But in *The Wasting Sickness of Cú Chulainn* the 'fairy mistress' expectations raised by Fand's overtures unravel as the tale progresses. Cú Chulainn forms a union with her in the Otherworld, but does not remain there. Nor can their relationship continue in the mortal world. The anomaly here may be due to Cú Chulainn's identity as a hero *tout simple*, rather than a candidate for kingship. But on the structural level, the impediment to the development of the theme is the intervention of the determined wife, Emer. Because of Emer's powerful presence in the tale, the normal narrative trajectory of the fairy mistress story is frustrated, and what unfolds instead is a very human drama of love and jealousy and loss.

Because these other romantic tales would likely have been well known to a contemporary audience, it is reasonable to expect that the similarities and differences would have been taken into account in any assessment of *The Wasting Sickness of Cú Chulainn* by readers or hearers. These tales would form part of a network of intertexts for the story of Cú Chulainn's love-sickness.

Context: Marriage Laws

Another important set of intertexts for this tale are the medieval Irish marriage laws. In fact, it is difficult to read the final scene of confrontation between Emer and Fand without recognizing its legal subtext. Implicit in Cú Chulainn's defence of his decision to sleep with Fand is the idea that he has the legal right to have relationships with more than one woman at a time. The early Irish marriage laws list several forms of marital union of varying degrees of formality, and make it clear that a man could be married to 'wives' of different categories simultaneously.[13] Naturally, such marriage practices did not meet with the approval of the Christian church. However, the evidence suggests that even within ecclesiastical circles this issue was a matter of some debate in early Ireland. The law tract *Bretha Crólige* refers to a dispute in Irish law as to whether monogamy or polygyny is the better choice, citing the polygyny of the Old Testament patriarchs.[14] For the early Irish, who saw in their own society strong parallels with the ancient Hebrew culture represented in the Old Testament, monogamous Christian marriage was not necessarily the ideal.

Ireland's non-conformity to canonical marriage laws in this matter, as well as in its remarkably liberal divorce laws, were cause for complaint and rebuke for centuries, but particularly from reforming churchmen in the eleventh and twelfth centuries. A letter from Lanfranc, Archbishop of Canterbury, to the Irish king Toirdelbach Ua Briain in 1074 vividly illustrates the reformers' concerns about divorce and remarriage:

However among many things that please us some things have been reported to us that displease us: namely that in your kingdom every man abandons his lawfully wedded wife at his own will, without the occasion of a canonical cause; and with a boldness that must be punished takes to himself some other wife who may be of his own kin or of the kindred of the wife whom he has abandoned, or whom another has abandoned in like wickedness, according to a law of marriage that is rather a law of fornication.'[15]

Although we cannot be certain about exactly when *The Wasting Sickness of Cú Chulainn* took its present shape, the text does seem to have undergone some revision during this period, particularly at the hands of the scribe known as the Reviser, who reshaped the LU text in the twelfth century.[16] It is possible that the tale in its present form was reshaped to reflect the views on marriage being propagated by the English and Continental church.

Certainly, the legal intertexts provide important insights into the tensions in this tale. The laws allow a *cétmuinter* (chief wife) to beat her new rival with impunity for the first three nights after the husband brings her into the home; the second wife can retaliate, but only by scratching or pulling hair or with verbal abuse.[17] The existence of these provisions shows an attempt by lawmakers to deal with a potentially explosive situation in the home. But of course, real life is always problematic, as Emer's behaviour in *The Wasting Sickness of Cú Chulainn* suggests. Obviously, Emer does not care that murdering Fand is illegal and will likely result in her having to pay a fine.[18] The anger and jealousy which such a situation would provoke would likely often override legal obligations.

Both *The Wooing of Étaín* and *The Wasting Sickness of Cú Chulainn* show

how close to chaos such a situation can bring both the family unit and society as a whole, and how inadequate the legal framework really is for containing that chaos. Cú Chulainn's madness after Fand's departure highlights the disastrous nature of his Otherworld encounter. It is only through drinking a druidic potion that both Cú Chulainn and Emer find forgetfulness and the strength to continue their lives within their society. Significantly, any audience would know that such a remedy is not available to real human beings.

Context: Audience

Any discussion of inversions and anomalies implies a norm which can be violated. It is clear that for medieval Irish readers or listeners to have recognized the extent of play within this tale, they had also to be familiar with other tales, both those concerning Cú Chulainn and those concerning women. As noted earlier, we are probably safe in assuming that at least the upper classes, who frequented the courts of chiefs and kings where tales were told, were familiar with a body of tradition about Cú Chulainn (including the *Táin* in some form). Secular audiences were also likely familiar with *The Wooing of Étaín* and a range of other wooing tales. Thus, the audience of *The Wasting Sickness of Cú Chulainn* can be assumed to have known a significant number of intertexts which they could recall and compare when faced with a telling or reading of this tale.

This audience would also have been a Christian one. Yet its Christian character would have coexisted with a number of archaic survivals in society, such as the native marriage customs. While we will never be able to reconstruct completely the social milieu in which our tale was redacted as we now have it, there is ample evidence that it evolved in a society marked by competing voices and traditions. For instance, the colophon at the end of *The Wasting Sickness of Cú Chulainn*, in which the scribe attributes Cú Chulainn's adventures to the delusions of demons, serves to highlight the uneasy marriage of pre-Christian tradition and Christian sensibility.[19]

This split between alternative points of view is further illustrated in the double colophon of the twelfth-century Book of Leinster version of the *Táin*, where the scribe first pronounces a blessing (in Irish) on those who memorize the *Táin* as he has written it, and then goes on to express grave doubts (in Latin) about the truthfulness and value of the epic.[20] This is perhaps symptomatic of an audience (among both the *literati* and the secular hearers of the tales) capable of achieving some distance from their tradition. As Donnchadh Ó Corráin has noted, the medieval period saw a rise in literary satire in Irish texts:

Indeed, in the case of the *Táin Bó Cúalgne* we reach that stage of literary self-awareness which gives us literary satire: *Scéla mucce meic Dáthó*, dated to AD 800, seems to be a sophisticated parody of the heroic genre as represented by *Táin Bó Cúalgne* – whilst the principal characters remain the same, a new tale is built about the dog of the king of Leinster in the place of the divine Brown Bull of Cúalgne and heroic combats become boorish boasting and mindless slaughter – so redolent of Irish learning and so stylishly executed within the conventions of the genre that most modern scholars and not a few of their medieval predecessors have entirely missed the point of the jape.[21]

If Ó Corráin's assessment is correct, it would suggest a self-aware audience capable of perceiving and enjoying ambiguity.

While it is impossible to draw definite conclusions about audience responses, the violation of traditional norms in *The Wasting Sickness of Cú Chulainn* and the resulting emergence of a strong female discourse within the narrative may have been difficult for a medieval audience to ignore. A careful examination of the text reveals a whole range of intertextual signals which open up the discourse to ambiguity and uncertainty.

Inversion and Ambiguity

There are so many anomalous incidents in this narrative that attributing them to a 'momentary lapse' on the part of any one redactor seems hardly credible. What emerges from the text is a subtle yet sustained critique of the hero and the treatment of women in the society he represents.

Considering the substantial amount of revision which marks the text's earliest manuscript version (LU), it is tempting at first glance to speculate that the scribe known as the Reviser reshaped our tale to introduce this critique of the hero. There is certainly no doubt that this scribe erased a number of leaves and copied new material onto them.[22] Whether he was merely combining existing elements as a redactor or adding his own inventions (as Cecile O'Rahilly has suggested he may have done in *Táin*)[23], the Reviser had definite ideas about what the finished product should be.[24] It is important to note that whether or not Cú Chulainn's instructions to his foster-son (the *bríatharthecosc*) were part of the original text, they are there now; they were either inserted or retained by the

Reviser.[25] It is also worth observing that it is the interpolated passages, attributed to the Reviser, which contain many of the elements which undermine Cú Chulainn's heroic reputation.

On the other hand, the fact that the powerful final scene between Cú Chulainn, Emer, and Fand was present in the *uninterpolated* eleventh-century text suggests that the major concerns of the tale were already articulated in some measure before the Reviser came along. There is also evidence that the *briatharthecosc* formed part of the earlier, ninth-century recension,[26] while the colophon at the end is also part of the uninterpolated eleventh-century version, and apparently untouched by the Reviser.[27] All of this suggests that the Reviser was only one of several agents who undertook the literary reshaping of this tale.

Whether or not any of the medieval redactors who worked on *The Wasting Sickness of Cú Chulainn* would have termed its present form 'ironic,' the narrative as it stands does create critical distance between itself and its audience by defamiliarizing the familiar.[28] Several recent studies have pointed to the presence of a 'critical self awareness' in the works of eleventh- and twelfth-century British authors.[29] Siân Echard's study of Welsh, Latin, and Middle English Arthurian texts demonstrates how a creative author could manipulate a traditional genre for his own ends.[30] The goal of the game is to allow a portion of the audience to share a 'sympathetic superiority' with the narrator. In the case of *The Wasting Sickness of Cú Chulainn*, the audience finds itself looking down on Cú Chulainn as his reputation is progressively undercut, a process which ultimately creates a stance akin to Frye's 'ironic mode.'[31] Although the most overtly ironic works in Irish, such as *The Vision of Mac Conglinne* (*Aislinge Meic Conglinne*) and *The Banquet of the Fort of the Geese* (*Fled Dúin na nGéd*), date from later than our tale, there is enough evidence of a sense of 'critical self awareness' in earlier texts to suggest that some understanding of irony was in operation at least by the eleventh century, if not earlier.[32]

The Wasting Sickness of Cú Chulainn can certainly be read or heard 'straight,' and indeed it always has been.[33] Anomalies can be ascribed to the blending of two different versions over the centuries. Since we do not know which of its handlers introduced the ambivalences into the tale, we have difficulty ascribing ironic intention to one individual. On the other hand, intention is not necessary for irony to occur, and indeed recent scholarship has stressed the crucial role of the interpreter(s) in the production of irony.[34] Yet it is possible (and, I would argue, likely) that one or more of the tale's redactors shaped the text so as to introduce inversions and ambiguities that would be apparent to discerning members of the audience.

Parody, such as that operating in the medieval Welsh tale *Culhwch and Olwen*,[35] would not have served to undercut Cú Chulainn as decisively as does the kind of irony discernible here. Parody relies on exaggeration,[36] but Cú Chulainn as superhero is traditionally described in exaggerated terms. Exaggeration is his *norm*. He can hold off hosts of thousands and slay dozens of men with one blow; even his appearance is pure hyperbole. *The Wasting Sickness of Cú Chulainn* relies instead on the incongruity between traditional expectations about the hero and his actual behaviour in the tale. The key here is that the expectations be present in the first place and that they be echoed in the text. The audience then perceives the incongruities and is distanced from him, made to feel superior to him in judgment and intelligence. The fact that the women are *never* represented in the 'ironic mode' allows the audience to perceive the implied meanings in the text and its criticisms of its own 'heroic' society.

In light of the other Ulster Cycle tales, it is difficult to ignore the ambiguous treatment of the hero in this text. While the narrative refers to Cú Chulainn's reputation as the superhuman hero of the tribe (embodied in the traditions of the *Táin* and other Ulster Cycle tales) it constantly undermines that reputation.[37] His incredible strength is reduced to weakness, his vision and judgment are almost consistently faulty, and his dealings with women are fraught with disaster. The audience, and even the other characters in the tale, see much more clearly than he does and his reactions are frequently at odds with the reality presented.

An examination of the tale reveals many situations in which inversions and anomalies occur. At the beginning of the narrative, the stated purpose of the assembly of the Ulaid in Mag Murthemne is to give the warriors a forum for boasting about their warrior triumphs. This situation immediately invites comparison with *Bricriu's Feast*, in which the heroic agenda is, more or less, adhered to in the course of the tale. In *The Wasting Sickness of Cú Chulainn*, however, the purpose of the assembly is quickly derailed; Conall Cernach and Fergus mac Roich are late, and Cú Chulainn refuses to start the assembly without them. As a result Sencha calls for songs and games of *fidchell*. Into this festive, non-warlike scene comes the first flock of birds, and the whole assembly is distracted by the desires of the women to possess them. The contrast here between the expected course of the tale and what ensues is the first signal in the text of something unusual. The ambiguous space thus created by the delay of warrior boasting is invaded first by female concerns and then by Otherworld women. The Ulsterwomen's desire for the birds effectively separates Cú Chulainn from the company of the other warriors and perhaps makes him more vulnerable. Yet even this isolation recalls a similar situation in which Cú Chulainn found himself in 'female space' and yet remained in control – that of the land of Scáthach and Aífe in *The Wooing of Emer*.[38] In that tale, the hero's behaviour is more typical, as when he forcibly extracts three wishes from the warrior-woman Scáthach:

Luid iarom Cú Chulainn co hairm i mbaí Scáthach. Dobert a dí choiss for dá bord in chléib chliss 7 nochtais a chlaideb ém 7 doberar a rind fo chomair a cridi 7 asbert: 'Bás úasut,' ol sé. 'Do thrí hindroisc duit úaimse,' ol sí.

Then Cú Chulainn went to the place where Scáthach was. He placed his two feet on the two edges of the basket of feats, and bared his sword, and put its point against her heart and said, 'Death over you!' 'Your three wishes from me,' she said.'[39]

An audience familiar with *The Wooing of Emer* would recall this type of behaviour when presented with the contrasting portrait of Cú Chulainn in *The Wasting Sickness of Cú Culainn*.

Cú Chulainn's reactions in this situation are also at odds with audience expectations. He erupts into a rage at Leborcham's plea for the birds on behalf of the women of Ulster. He even draws his sword to strike her.[40] Although Cú Chulainn appears in the tradition as a volatile, somewhat mercurial personality, this particular behaviour is unusual. He says in the *Táin* that he never kills women; in fact, in that tale he spares even Medb.[41] In this scene his anger seems completely out of proportion to the request, and his labelling of the women as the 'merdrecha Ulad' ('whores of Ulster') seems extreme and out of place. Leborcham is the voice of reason when she objects, 'Ní coir duit ém ... fúasnad fríu ...' ('It is not right for you indeed to rage at them')[42] and reminds him of how the devotion of those women who love him leads them to blind themselves in one eye in the likeness of his distorted fury. Although this passage is hyperbolic, employing the type of exaggeration frequently found in these early tales, Leborcham's point is clear: Cú Chulainn's attitude is improper.

The second incident is very reminiscent of the first section of the Middle Welsh tale *Pwyll*.[43] When two supernatural birds linked by a chain arrive at the lake, Cú Chulainn, like Pwyll, fails to perceive that these birds are different from the previous ones. What is to the audience an unmistakable sign of the Otherworld – the chain linking the two birds – is lost on him.[44] Unlike Pwyll, Cú Chulainn even has the benefit of perceptive companions (Ethne and Lóeg) who warn him and state the obvious. Cú Chulainn responds 'In dóig bat dom éligudsa ón?' ('Is it likely that I will be refuted?')[45] He shoots and misses twice. Only then does he realize his folly. Yet he insists on a third cast, and this time strikes the wing of one of the birds. The dire events that follow – the dream of the two women beating him and the sickness that incapacitates him – are thus set in motion. But the audience sees that he has brought the disaster upon himself through his own folly.[46]

The passage labelled 'Cú Chulainn's words of instruction' ('bríatharthecosc Con Culaind')[47] would have reminded the medieval reader or listener of other examples of this type of didactic, gnomic utterance, such as *The Instructions of Cormac (Tecosca Cormaic)*,[48] *The Bequest of Morann (Audacht Morainn)*,[49] and others. There would likely have been the recognition that such a speech is normally associated with wise old men and kings speaking words of wisdom to their heirs. But Cú Chulainn is a young man at the height of his powers and is bedridden not because of old age but from love-sickness. He is the wrong speaker for this speech. The scene thus violates normal expectations and draws attention to this echo of a familiar type of speech by its unfamiliar context. An attentive reader or listener would also notice the gap between Cú Chulainn's wise words of advice and his own behaviour thus far in the tale. The speech begins:

Nírbat taerrechtach debtha déne dóergaire.
Nírbat díscir doichlech díummasach.
Níbbát ecal ocal opond esamain.

Do not be seeking fierce, uncouth combat
Do not be fierce, churlish, arrogant.
Do not be fearful, violent, sudden, bold.[50]

Yet Cú Chulainn has recently displayed violent, churlish, and rash behaviour both in his reaction to Leborcham and in his insistence on shooting at the supernatural birds despite advice to the contrary. The incongruity between the hero's words and his behaviour in the tale would likely have been evident to the audience.

Although his voyage to the Otherworld is supposed to provide the cure for his sickness, Cú Chulainn still suffers from impaired vision and prowess while there.[51] While the prose description of the battle against Eochaid Íuil and his host seems to indicate that Cú Chulainn's victory was decisive, his own assessment of his performance afterwards is laden with ambiguity and uncertainty.[52] He says:

Tarlucus urchur dom sleig
i ndúnad Éogain Inbir:
nocon fetur sochla sét
in búaid dorignius nó in bét.

Cid ferr cid messu dom nirt,
co sse ní tharlus dom chirt
urchur anfis fir hi céo:
bés ná n-árlaid duni béo.

...

Rochúala cneit Echach Íuil
is ó chraidi[53] labrait bíuil:
mad fir co fír bes níp cath
int urchur ma tarlacad.

I have hurled a throw of my spear
into the camp of Eogan Inbir:
I do not know, famous path,
if I made a success or a calamity.

Whether better or worse for my strength,
up to now I never missed my aim;
a throw of ignorance of a man in the mist:
perhaps it did not pierce a living being.

...

I heard the groan of Echaid Iuil
from the heart lips speak[54]
if it be a true attestation perhaps there may be no battle;
if the cast was thrown.[55]

These stanzas imply that Cú Chulainn is unsure of the extent of his victory. Here again, his vision is impaired; he has been forced to shoot from within the mist, and is confused about what really happened. For an audience that was certainly familiar with Cú Chulainn's self-assured assessments in other tales, this anomaly would be unsettling. We need only look to the *Táin* for an utterance more typical of the hero:

Fó mo cherd láechdachta
benaim beimend ágmara
for slóg síabra sorchaidi.
Certaim ág fri isluagaib.
im díth erred anglondach
scéo Medbi 7 Ailella.

Splendid is my heroic deed. I strike fearsome blows against a brilliant spectral army. I wage battle against many hosts to destroy valiant warriors together with Ailill and Medb.[56]

Later on in *The Wasting Sickness of Cú Chulainn*, Cú Chulainn's response to Emer and her knife-wielding servants reinforces the ironies of his portrayal. He says to Emer:

'Not sechaimsea, a ben, amal sechnas cách a chárait. Ní rubimsea do gáe crúaid crithlámach nach do scían tím thanaidi nách t'ferg thréith thimaircthech, ar is mórdolig mo nert do scor ó nirt mná.'

'I avoid you, o woman, as everyone avoids his friend. I do not strike your hard spear in your trembling hand, nor your feeble slender knife, nor your weak restrained anger, for it is very grievous to unyoke my strength on account of the strength of a woman.'[57]

These confident words are ironic in light of the power women have over him in this tale, both up to this point and in the imminent climax. Cú Chulainn seems not even yet to realize that words can be as deadly as weapons. Emer may not be strong enough to hurt Cú Chulainn or Fand physically, but her words have power against both of them. For her part, Fand has proven only too well her ability to control Cú Chulainn. This last attempt at recreating himself in the heroic mould fails within the context of the rest of the tale.

The ambiguous portrayal of Cú Chulainn in this text seems to highlight the problems inherent in polygyny, and may reflect the continuing debate about marriage customs. Perhaps we can also see here the emergence of a 'critical self-awareness' born, in part, from the transfer of traditional stories to a contemporary, literary form – not just from oral to written form but from written to 'literary' form. Scholars increasingly stress the links between literacy and the growth of a critical stance among medieval authors.[58] As we saw earlier, evidence from British texts suggests that across the Irish Sea the trend was established well before the twelfth century.[59] Modern Celtic scholarship now recognizes the importance of medieval Ireland's links with European culture, and it seems likely that the Irish *literati* were aware of literary developments beyond their shores at least by the eleventh century, and were increasingly able to view their traditional material within a broader, more critical context.[60] What emerges in *The Wasting Sickness of Cú Chulainn* is a portrait of a hero who violates his own traditional norms at every turn.

Cú Chulainn's incapacity certainly has a literary purpose in the tale. His sickness makes possible an exploration of issues crucial to the text – the power of sexual desire, the implications of polygyny, and the potentially destructive nature of love and jealousy. Only with Cú Chulainn temporarily sidelined can the women take centre stage. And only when the women begin to speak can the text explore the conflicts inherent in male-female relationships.

The Language of Desire

The Wasting Sickness of Cú Chulainn can be read as a narrative of desire. It primarily concerns the desires of women, but also explores the impasse created when a man desires not one woman but two simultaneously.

On a structural level, it is obvious that the plot of *The Wasting Sickness of Cú Chulainn* is generated entirely by women. At the beginning of the tale the women of Ulster desire to possess the beautiful birds that land on the lake. Cú Chulainn's reluctant compliance with their wishes and his provision of the birds to all but his own wife sets the stage for his subsequent unwise cast at two clearly supernatural birds. These birds are indeed two Otherworld women who incapacitate Cú Chulainn by beating him speechless in a dream-vision, depriving him of his strength and ensuring his dependence upon them for a cure.[61] The eventual journey to the Otherworld, first by Lóeg and then by Cú Chulainn and Lóeg together, is really a matter of necessity and not of choice. In the latter part of the tale it is Cú Chulainn's own wife Emer who wrests control of the plot by challenging her Otherworld rival for influence over her besotted husband. And when Cú Chulainn goes mad over the loss of Fand, it is

Emer who persuades Conchobar to send druids to the wilderness to rescue him.

This narrative framework suggests one of the major inversions within the text – namely, the reassignment of Cú Chulainn from an active to a largely passive role. The normally aggressive hero has become the classic object of desire, a role largely reserved in medieval literature for females. The ambiguities in the narrative detailed above reinforce this undercutting of the hero's traditional role. He spends a large portion of the tale sick in bed, stripped of the strength and sexual power which define him as the great Ulster hero. When he does take action, it is usually unwise action (such as the foolish casts at the supernatural birds). His impaired vision and understanding cause him to seem often confused and uncertain.

On the other hand, the women in *The Wasting Sickness of Cú Chulainn* are clear about their actions and their motivations for them. Fand and Emer both want Cú Chulainn's love, and are prepared to do anything to win or keep it. The surprising degree of control that these women exhibit here serves to highlight the incapacity of the great hero whom they desire.

As this text plays with the expectations of the audience, both regarding the patterns of male-female relationships and the reputation of the hero, it opens up a new zone of women's discourse which functions on an emotional level rather than a simply structural one. This type of discourse first appears in the middle of the tale, in Emer's lament for her sick husband, where she reproaches Lóeg for failing to bring back a cure for Cú Chulainn from the Otherworld.[62] Here Emer expresses her feelings clearly:

Uchán do galur nom geib
ó Choin cherda Conchobair:
is sáeth rem chridi is rem chnes,
día tísad dím a leges.

...

Is de ná tic a hEmain
dáig na delba ro ndedail:
is merb is is marb mo guth,
dáig atásom fó drochcruth.

Mí 7 ráthe 7 blíadain
cen chotlud fó chomríagail
cen duini bad bind labra –
ni chúala, a meic Ríangabra.

Alas! Your sickness seizes me
O Hound of the smith of Conchobar.
It is grief to my heart and to my breast;
if [only] his healing had come from me.

...

He comes not from Emain
because of the shape[63] that has parted us.
My voice is weak and dead
because he is in an evil state.

A month and a season and a year
without sleeping in wedlock
without a man who was pleasing of speech –
I have not heard [such], o son of Ríangabur.[64]

These words leave no doubt about Emer's emotional state as an abandoned wife. Indeed, as the narrative states earlier, her home itself has been rejected as a place of convalescence by her husband. Cú Chulainn's request that he be taken to An Téte Brecc, rather than to Dún Delca where he and Emer live, may serve to highlight both his physical and emotional separation from his wife. It also reinforces the idea that Cú Chulainn's sickness is not simply a physical ailment, but sexual desire for another woman (Fand).[65]

But Emer's words here are far more than a passive lament for her sad and lonely state. Emer reveals herself as a speaking subject, powerfully articulating her experience and feelings from a woman's point of view. In doing this she is performing an illocutionary act – a 'representative' – which describes her lonely isolation.[66] Yet she is also performing a perlocutionary act designed to goad Lóeg into action by shaming him and the other Ulstermen. Emer begins her speech by reproaching Lóeg for returning from the Otherworld without a cure for her husband, and then spends many lines accusing the other Ulstermen for not doing more to help him. This stanza is typical:

Diambad hé Conall chena
fris mbetís créchta is chneda,
no sirfed in Cú in mbith mbras
co fagbad líaig dá leges.

If it were Conall moreover
on whom were wounds and gashes
the Hound [Cú Chulainn] would search the wide world
until he found a doctor to cure him.[67]

By linking her own personal complaint with this reproach, Emer seeks to goad Lóeg (and by extension, the other Ulstermen) into taking action on Cú Chulainn's behalf. The perlocutionary effect which she desires is that a cure for her husband's sickness be found – an outcome which would, she presumes, restore him to her side. Thus, in her passionate speech here Emer not only describes her own state of mind, but in the act of telling attempts to effect change in her world.

This female discourse finds its fullest expression in the extraordinary final scene with its verbal struggle between Emer, Cú Chulainn, and Fand. Here all the tensions of the story tangle in a knot of surprisingly intense feeling. By depicting Emer and Fand as emotional beings, the narrative addresses the issues of love and jealousy at a very personal level.

The scene takes place after Cú Chulainn has returned from a month with Fand in the Otherworld, and has agreed to meet her again. Emer is told of the tryst, and arrives at the trysting place accompanied by fifty female servants armed with sharp knives. Fand sees her approaching, and warns Lóeg and the hero:

'Fég, a Loíg, dar th'éis. Oc coistecht frit filet mná córi cíallmathi co scenaib glasgéraib ina ndeslámaib co n-ór fria n-uchtbrunnib. Cruth caín atchíchither amal tecait láith gaile dar cathchairptiu. Glé ro soi gné Emer ingen Forgaill.'

'Look behind you, Lóeg. Listening to you are upright,[68] skilful women with sharp grey knives in their right hands and gold on their breasts. A fair form will be seen, [as] when warriors come across battle-chariots.[69] It is clear that Emer daughter of Forgall has changed her form.[70]

Emer appears as a warrior, leading her troop of armed women like a male hero advancing into battle. Here, in her moment of greatest crisis, she has abandoned her reliance on the power of speech alone, and comes prepared to reinforce her words with deeds. The hints of masculine imagery present in *The Wooing of Emer* (as in Emer's image of herself driving a chariot) are finally given substance in this passage. Although Emer has not yet spoken at this point, her presence and appearance speak eloquently of the threat she presents, both to Fand and to the hero.[71]

In the same way that she fearlessly confronted Sencha in *Bricriu's Feast*, so Emer confronts Cú Chulainn in the presence of his new lover:

'Ceist trá,' ar Emer, 'cid fódrúair latsu, a Chú Culaind, mo címiadsa fíad andrib ilib in chúicid 7 fíad andrib ilib na Hérend 7 fíad áes enig archena?'

'A question then,' said Emer, 'what has caused you, Cú Chulainn, to dishonour me before the many women of the province, and before the many women of Ireland, and before people of honour in general?'[72]

She complains that he has dishonoured her publicly, an objection which would seem to carry some weight in the context of Ulster Cycle society.[73] But Cú Chulainn ignores the issue of Emer's honour. He asks instead why she objects to his meeting Fand, enumerating the Otherworld woman's qualities as if this were all that mattered. Emer then resorts to more personal, emotional language. She laments that 'is gel cach núa ... is serb cach gnáth' ('everything new is bright ... everything familiar is bitter'), and adds, 'Cáid cech n-écmais, is faill cech n-aichnid, co festar cach n-éolas' ('What is absent is honoured, what is known is neglected, until everything is known').[74] Here she chooses a series of gnomic sayings which purport to express well-known truths, but harnesses them to her own personal complaint.

Emer then utters what proves to be the crucial speech act in the tale, a perlocutionary act which provokes the desired response in her husband, but an unexpected response from Fand:

'A gillai,' ar sí, 'ro bámarni fecht co cátaid acut, 7 no bemmis dorísi diambad áil duitsiu.' ... 'Dar ar mbréthir trá,' ar sé, 'isatt áilsiu damsa 7 bidat áil hi céin bat béo.' 'Mo lécudsa didiu' ol Fand.

'Ah, youth,' she said, 'we were together with honour once, and we would be again if you still desired me.' 'By my word,' he said, 'I do desire you, and I will desire you as long as you live.' ... 'Leave me then,' said Fand.[75]

Emer's consummate skill with words is evident once again here. Her reference to past marital happiness is designed to turn Cú Chulainn's thoughts away from his new lover and back to Emer herself. Her cleverly worded punch line, 'diambad áil duitsiu' ('if you still desired me'), begs a response. And she gets one – the hero's admission of his continuing desire for her. But his statement, in turn, provokes a response in Fand, whose words, 'Mo lécudsa didiu' ('Leave me then'), seem to be an admission of defeat.

Emer and Fand then turn to each other and debate which one of them should be abandoned by the hero they both love. Not only is this a surprising move in itself, it is also an inversion of the initial scene by the lake where the women of Ulster debate who should have the birds. There, each woman argues for her own right to possess a pair of birds in accordance with the status of her husband; here, each argues in favour of *her own* abandonment. Fand states her case most strongly, arguing that leaving her is more fitting since 'is me ro baeglaiged o chein' ('I am the one who was threatened just now').[76] While this is clearly a reference to the Ulsterwomen and their knives, her remark has another significance. In the two lengthy poems which follow, Fand implies that the real reason for her withdrawal is Cú Chulainn's admission of his continuing desire for Emer:

> Mairg dobeir seirc do duni,
> menes tarda dia airi:
> is ferr do neoch a chor ass,
> mane charthar mar charas.

> Woe to her who gives love to a person,
> if he takes no heed:
> it is better for that person to be cast aside
> if she is not loved as she loves.[77]

Fand clearly interprets Cú Chulainn's declaration of his continuing desire for Emer as a lack of love for her, and it is this that she views as the greatest threat to her. Like Emer, Fand apparently believes that a man can only truly love one woman at a time, and thus she feels she has no choice but to relinquish him.

Fand's discussion of the nature of love and its perils here opens a window on female subjectivity which is very rare in medieval literature. This final section of the tale is completely dominated by her voice; even

Emer falls silent while Fand speaks. Fand utters two long poems, the first of which is directed towards Emer. In these verses she mourns her own imminent departure from the hero. She gently rebukes Emer for her threat of violence, but nevertheless acknowledges her as a worthy opponent. Part of Fand's speech reads as follows:

Messe ragas for astur
cé dech lim ar mórgestul:
cé tora[78] nech, lín a blad,
ropad ferr lim tairisem.[79]

Robad ferr lim bith hi fus,
dobér fót láim cen dobus,
ná dula, cid ingnad lat,
co gríanan Áeda Abrat.

A Emer, is lat in fer
7 ro mela, a deigben:
aní ná roich lám cidacht,
is écen dam a dúthracht.

It is I who will go on a journey,
though I prefer our great adventure:
though someone may come, full of triumphs,
I would prefer to remain.

I would prefer being here,
I admit it without grudge,[80]
than going (though it be wonderful to you)
to the sun-house of Áed Abrat [her Otherworld home].

O Emer, the man is yours
and may you enjoy him, good woman:
what [my] hand does not yet attain,
it is necessary for me to desire.[81]

Although Fand clearly still desires Cú Chulainn, she reluctantly relinquishes him to Emer of her own free will.

The second, lengthier poem is spoken as Fand's invisible husband, Manannán mac Lir, returns from the Otherworld for her. There is a greater depth of feeling in this poem, and it has the quality of a lament. Here Fand probes the nature of love more deeply. Her own feelings for her husband have changed (perhaps as a result of his abandonment of her, noted earlier in the tale). Whatever the cause of the rift between them, Fand expresses her feelings clearly:

Mád indíu bá dígrais núall,
ní charand mo menma múad:
is éraise in rét int serc:
téit a héol cen immitecht.

As for today, [my] lament is keen,
my proud spirit does not love him:
Love is a vain thing
knowledge of it vanishes quickly.[82]

Fand contrasts this admission with a picture of former marital happiness with Manannán; she was a fitting bride for him, she claims, for they were equally matched, even at playing *fidchell*. Their happy times together were unmarred by thoughts of future discord:

Lá ro bása 7 mac Lir
hi ngríanan Dúni Inbir,
ropo dóig lind cen adad
noco bíad ar n-imscarad.

When the son of Ler and I were [together]
in the sun-house of Dún Indber
we thought always
that we should never be separated from each other.[83]

Now, she has fallen in love with Cú Chulainn and she feels he has betrayed her. Ultimately, she blames herself for her folly:

Mad messe bá dethbir dam,
dáig at báetha cíalla ban:
intí fo charus co holl
domrat sund i n-écomlond.

As for me, it was natural,
for the senses of women are foolish:

he whom I loved greatly
has brought me here into unequal combat.[84]

This is one of the rare instances where a woman in this tale lapses into anti-feminist clichés; here Fand blames herself as a weak female for succumbing to love.

Fand's final words in the tale come after her lament has ended. She sets out to meet Manannán, whom only she can see. The short exchange between the two of them captures all the ambivalences of her earlier words:

'Maith, a ingen,' ar sé, 'in oc urnaidi Chon Culaind bía fodechtsa, nó in limsa doraga?' 'Dar ar mbréthir ém,' ol sí, 'fil úaib nech bad ferr lim a chéli do lenmain. Acht,' ar sí, 'is letsu ragatsa, 7 ní irnaidiub Coin Culaind, ar rom thréc. Ocus araill and, dano, a degduini, ní fil rígain chátamail ocotsu, atá immurgu la Coin Culaind.'

'Well, woman,' he said, 'Will you be awaiting Cú Chulainn now, or will you return with me?' 'By my word,' said she, 'there is one of you who would be a better spouse for me to follow. But,' she said, 'I will go with you, and I will not await Cú Chulainn, for he has abandoned me. And there is moreover another thing, good man: there is no dignified queen with you, but there is [one] with Cú Chulainn already.'[85]

Fand here discusses the situation honestly and rationally. She makes no secret of her preference of Cú Chulainn over Manannán, but has clearly concluded that a relationship with the former is impossible. It is worth noting that it is Fand's decision to leave the hero, and *not* any decision on his part, which brings about a turning point in the narrative here.

In this final scene Emer and Fand are speaking subjects discussing the world from their own viewpoints. Despite their functions as opposing forces, Emer and Fand really have much in common. Both are clearly aristocratic women of high status. And both are trying to cope with abandonment by husbands. Emer's husband has abandoned her in spirit if not in body. In Fand's case, we are told that her husband Mannanán mac Lir has left her.[86] Indeed, early on in the tale Lí Ban implies that Fand has sought Cú Chulainn as a *result* of her abandonment, suggesting that the real culprit in this affair is Manannán.[87] Fand seeks a man to replace her husband, while Emer's response is to fight to win Cú Chulainn back. Both strategies likely reflect medieval Irish women's social dependence upon males for their status in society.

The desires of women are articulated powerfully in this scene, and as such it forms a fitting culmination of the discourse of desire which dominates the tale as a whole. That at least one redactor also saw this as a tale about desire can be inferred from the presence of a quatrain at the top of the page which begins with the poem Fand speaks to her approaching husband Manannán. This poem, written in the hand of the original scribe but glossed by the Reviser, is very obscure and can only be tentatively translated, but it does seem to deal with the desires of supernatural women and its destructive effect upon men.[88] The fact that the poem is written on one of the pages where Fand describes her desire for both her departed husband and for Cú Chulainn suggests that the story was perceived by its scribes and redactors as being concerned with the dangers of female desire.

As speaking subjects, both Emer and Fand reveal themselves as self-aware individuals. Through their speeches, they construct their own identities as women with pasts who remember the good times in their relationships while acknowledging the uncertainties of love. In contrast, Cú Chulainn never verbalizes his own desires and seems unaware of anything but the moment. During the climactic exchange, and during Fand's laments, he seems unable to understand what is happening. And his charioteer Lóeg is of no help; when Fand leaves to join Manannán, and Cú Chulainn asks 'Crét sút?' ('What's that?'), Lóeg replies 'Fand ic dul la Manannán mac Lir ar nocorb álic duitsiu hí' ('Fand is going with Manannán mac Lir, for she was not desired by you').[89] This is not true, of course; she *was* desired by him, but faced serious competition. Here Cú Chulainn is portrayed as a confused, inarticulate man. He is unaware that in revealing his desire for his wife, he has committed himself to her and must forfeit the other woman. Within the context of this situation, he cannot have both.

Women's Words

What then are the roles of women's words in this tale? Emer certainly acts as Cú Chulainn's foil, here as in other tales, and her speeches in the narrative reinforce this; he is rash and easily angered, while she is cautious and generous in spirit. Her reason counters his imprudence and lack of understanding. In the final scenes, she also acts as his conscience, reminding him of their happy past and pointing out the ramifications of his affair with Fand.

Significantly, Emer is the only one who is able to break Fand's hold over her husband. She achieves this by getting Cú Chulainn to say one significant thing: that he still desires her, and always will. The answer lies not in the standard heroic solution of martial activity but in emotion admitted and articulated. This is perhaps not surprising, since Cú Chulainn's sickness is clearly more of a psychological state than anything else. Thus, the cure must also be psychological. But it must also be *articulated*, put into words.

It is also no surprise that Emer's most effective weapons are her words, for we remember that in *The Wooing of Emer* one of Cú Chulainn's main reasons for choosing her as his wife is her *bindius* (sweet speech) and her ability to debate with him. There is perhaps a subtle irony within the Ulster Cycle tradition that it is this attribute, so valued by the courting hero in the initial stages of his relationship with Emer, which ultimately proves his undoing in his affair with Fand. Here, within a discourse strikingly different from the arcane riddling of the wooing scene, Cú Chulainn is no match for his wife. Her clear apprehension of the situation and its implications for her, her courage in confronting her rival, and her ability to ruthlessly speak the truth, give Emer the clear advantage. Significantly, verbal prowess is the only one of Emer's qualities *not* possessed by Fand.[90]

Yet ultimately it is not the speech acts of Emer or Fand, but the druidic potion of forgetfulness, which restores Cú Chulainn to himself. Emer's words provoke a response in her husband, which in turn provokes a response in Fand; but even Fand's withdrawal from the scene cannot heal Cú Chulainn's love-sickness. In fact, it has the opposite effect, plunging him into a frenzy of madness which drives him from civilization and into the wilderness. Emer's intervention on his behalf, which eventually prompts the druids to find him, is certainly crucial; yet it is the potion itself which restores order. Even the powerful speech of these two women is inadequate to deal with the chaos unleashed by excessive desire.

Despite this, Emer is clearly the winner in this narrative. Whether her victory is to be read as a triumph of the mortal, Christian world over the immortal, pagan one, or simply as an affirmation of stable monogamous marriage over polygyny, it seems clear that Emer is the one with whom the audience is to identify. She is a moral agent, arguing forcefully against the chaotic forces of fragmentation unleashed in male-female relationships by uncontrolled desires. She is perhaps the paradigm of the loyal, aristocratic wife who knows her rights and has the strength of mind to insist on them.

Yet much of the story's power also lies in Fand's sympathetic portrayal. She is never overtly condemned within the tale itself, unlike Sín in the later tale *The Death of Muirchertag mac Erc* (*Aided Muirchertaig meic Erca*).[91] Indeed, through her honest and heartfelt laments Fand implicitly refuses to be dismissed as a wicked adulteress. She is, on the one hand, the beautiful denizen of the Otherworld so common in early Irish tales, seductive and powerful. Yet in this text, her powers are limited in ways only too familiar to human beings living in the 'real' world.

Emer and Fand contain within them many layers of meaning. On the structural level, they create and sustain plot and action through their desires. On the symbolic level, Fand signifies the Otherworld, with all its magical power, while Emer represents the mortal world and Cú Chulainn's connections to it. While the question of the 'Otherworld as literary device' is a complicated one, I will simply suggest that here it provides a safe explanation for Fand's awesome powers of seduction and enslavement.[92] That is, it is easier psychologically for both author and audience to blame Otherworld enchantment (which supposedly no longer exists due to the triumph of Christianity) than to acknowledge the ongoing threat to peaceful relationships posed by human physical attraction.

Clearly, *The Wasting Sickness of Cú Chulainn* is not a traditional tale. Its inversion of audience expectations signals the possibility of something new. Is it then a misogynist text intent on demonstrating that even the mighty Cú Chulainn can be brought down by dangerous female desires? Are Emer and Fand mere mouthpieces for the patriarchal discourse of ecclesiastical reform? Although a superficial examination might suggest this, the text itself seems to resist such a reading. Despite one or two antifeminist phrases, such as Cú Chulainn's reference to the Ulster women as the 'whores of Ulster' and Fand's lament over her weak 'female' senses, the text generally represents women positively. Fand's sympathetic portrayal, in particular, militates against such a reading. A text with a relentless antifeminist agenda would be more likely to represent Fand as an evil mistress like Sín, the destructive second wife of *The Death of Muirchertag mac Erc* (*Aided Muirchertaig meic Erca*). In *The Wasting Sickness of Cú Chulainn*, we are encouraged to set Fand's negative effects on the hero alongside her personal statements which give us 'her side of the story.' The remarkable space afforded to Fand as speaking subject in the text ultimately dilutes the negative aspects of her portrayal as dangerous Otherworld siren.

In fact, the tensions between law and 'real life,' between monogamy and polygyny, are embedded in the very text itself. By treating Fand and Emer with equal dignity the tale grapples with the issues it raises, and can only resort to a potion of forgetfulness to restore equilibrium. The unease likely to be generated in any potential audience is confirmed in the scribal comment at the end:

Conid taibsiu aidmillti do Choin Chulaind la háes sídi sin. Ar ba mór in chumachta demnach ria cretim, 7 ba hé a méit co cathaigtis co corptha na demna frisna doínib 7 co taisféntais aíbniusa 7 díamairi dóib, amal no betis co marthanach. Is amlaid no creteá dóib. Conid frisna taidbsib sin atberat na hanéolaig síde 7 áes síde.

That is the destructive vision [shown] to Cú Chulainn by the people of the síd [fairy mounds]. For the devilish power was great before the faith, and it was so great that demons used to fight bodily against men, and used to show pleasures and hidden things to them as if they really existed. It is thus they were given credence. Thus the ignorant call these apparitions[93] *síde* and *áes síde* [the people of the síd].[94]

In other words, we are asked to believe that Fand was a demonic apparition and that Emer and her retinue were, like Cú Chulainn, deceived by these devilish images. By recasting the Otherworld in a Christian framework, the scribe attempts to convert *The Wasting Sickness of Cú Chulainn* from a story about love and jealousy into a cautionary tale about the Otherworld as a manifestation of evil.[95] However, this 'rewriting' of the text's meaning only barely contains its tensions and ambiguities. The powerful speeches of Emer and Fand, Fand's positive representation, and the complexity of the interactions of the main characters all militate against such a simplistic reading.

The Wasting Sickness of Cú Chulainn may be a warning against excessive desire in both men and women. It may have evolved as it did in the context of accelerating tensions between native marriage customs and the demands of canon law in the eleventh and twelfth centuries. Read in light of this conflict, the tale portrays Emer as a voice of protest against polygyny, as the spokeswoman for all abandoned and rejected wives. But in toying with heroic norms and expectations the tale also suggests a broader questioning of traditional social customs and attitudes – at least of those portrayed within the Ulster Cycle tales. The inversions and ambiguities in the narrative serve to distance the audience from its own legendary past, and thus open the way for a critique of the society depicted in those traditions. Perhaps this vivid picture of passion and barely contained violence was intended as a warning against the dangers unleashed by all misdirected desires. In the world of this text, even the superhuman Cú Chulainn is vulnerable to folly and the ravages of love and jealousy.

Whatever the tale's evolution, its power lies in its honest exploration of the grief and turmoil caused by unfulfilled desire, and its vivid articulation of women's concerns. Fand seems to speak for all women when she laments:

Mairg dobeir seirc do duni,
menes tarda dia airi.

Woe to her who gives love to a person,
if he takes no heed.[96]

Conclusion

Throughout this study, we have seen how Emer's speech plays crucial roles in the Ulster Cycle narratives. In each of the tales discussed here, the representation of Emer's speech in the text shapes either the narrative trajectory itself or the construction of the text's meaning for the audience, or both.

In *The Wooing of Emer* and *Bricriu's Feast*, Emer emerges as a paragon of medieval Irish womanhood, distinguished from her female peers by her beauty, her intelligence, and her unique ability to manipulate language effectively. Her verbal skills enable her to shape her world through the judicious use of speech acts, and her words encompass a much wider range of genres than those traditionally used by women in other medieval literatures. Although she appears to conform to the expectations of the heroic, patriarchal society depicted in these two tales, Emer also demonstrates her strength of mind and her determination to insist on her rights as an aristocratic wife. She holds her own against male attempts to rebuke her or to ignore her right to speak. While the representation of Emer in these tales recalls a number of other women from the Irish tradition, Emer far surpasses these other female figures in confident speech.

If Emer is presented as an ideal in these first two tales, she is a far more complex figure in *The Death of Aífe's Only Son* and *The Wasting Sickness of Cú Chulainn*. In these narratives she interrogates the norms of her patriarchal society with its heroic code of honour and its laws concerning marriage. She intervenes passionately in the events of these tales, marking with her words the danger zones where honour and custom collide with more compassionate human values – the pressure points where the heroic society depicted in the texts threatens to rupture under its own internal strains. In *The Death of Aife's Only Son* she acts as a symbolic mother, attempting to protect her husband's foreign-born son from his father's overriding need to defend his own honour and the honour of Ulster. Although her attempt to avert disaster fails, Emer's words 're-write' the meaning of the tale for the audience, and in the process affirm the values of family and society over the obsessive concern with honour. In *The Wasting Sickness of Cú Chulainn* Emer fights a more personal battle, as she confronts her Otherworld rival Fand and struggles against the power of excessive sexual desire. Implicit in her challenge of Cú Chulainn's behaviour towards her is a critique of her culture's marriage laws and the disruptive forces which they only barely contain. The ambiguities within this narrative distance the audience from the story and thus allow for an interrogation of the traditional society portrayed within the text. In both of these tales, Emer acts as a moral agent, presenting and defending options which are more just, reasonable, and compassionate than the norms of her male-dominated culture.

In all of the narratives discussed in this study, Emer emerges as a female figure of some complexity, reacting to life situations which would likely have been recognizable to the real, historical human beings who heard or read the texts. Throughout this study, we have seen Emer consistently identified with the 'mortal' world with its human civiliza-tion. We have also seen the many points where the concerns of the narratives intersect with what we know of the legal and historical context of medieval Ireland. Each narrative is indeed, to use Kristeva's phrase, an 'intersection of textual surfaces' – including the 'textual surface' of medieval Irish society.[1] Although it is at this point impossible to pinpoint the original composition dates of these texts, we can be sure that the hearers or readers of these narratives saw in them reflections of their cultural past, if not of their cultural present. Whether or not the abduc-tion of women, boasting at feasts, combat for the sake of honour, or the taking of second wives were common occurrences in the present moment of any given audience, these things were surely recognized as a part of a general cultural inheritance and therefore as part of the ever-present tradition.

Current trends in the analysis of literary texts from medieval Ireland suggest a new awareness of the importance of historical context. It may be possible at some point to link the events in these tales with actual events in the 'real' past, or to see in Emer a literary reflex of some identifiable woman in history. Certainly, these are fruitful areas for investigation in the search to shed greater light on the representation of

women in medieval Irish literature. However, the lack of precise historical models for Emer need not prevent us from seeing in her words
reflections, however dim, of the concerns and tensions of medieval Ireland, and particularly of the eleventh and twelfth centuries.

Equally important in any thorough assessment of medieval Irish
female characters is an awareness of the models provided by biblical
women and female saints (particularly Saint Brigit). Emer's (albeit tenu-
ous) connection with Brigit raises the possibility of a network of connections between sacred and secular female figures in the medieval Irish
tradition. Patricia Kelly's suggestion of an Old Testament archetype (or
anti-type) for Medb is the first step in this direction.[2] Ann Dooley's recent
remarks about the existence of 'a system of typology governing saintly
women in Irish ecclesiastical thinking' which could be transferred with
ease to secular women is also highly suggestive of a complex web of
correspondences between literary genres.[3] This is certainly an area which
merits more detailed investigation.

Although Emer is presented as an ideal in the tales discussed here, she
is never essentialized as a mythic archetype or confined to the restrictive
roles of a goddess. Nor is she ever identified with the chaotic forces of
nature, as is common in the representation of divine females. This may
be partly due to her status as the spouse of a hero and not of a king – a
role which carries with it considerable mythic weight. However, considering the many superhuman traits of her husband, this is not necessarily
a satisfactory explanation.

Clearly, the representation of Emer goes beyond both the paradigm of
the sovereignty goddess and other archetypes of female divinity in the
Irish tradition. Accordingly, this study has sought to demonstrate alternative methods of analyzing female characters in medieval Irish texts.
This is not to suggest that what I term 'mythological' analysis should be
abandoned or ignored. It is, rather, to insist that female figures in medieval Irish texts must be assessed on their own terms: as women, as
literary constructs, as potential symbols, and then, in some cases, as
possible reflections of half-forgotten pre-Christian divinities. Viewing
these women only through the lens of mythological models results in
short-sighted and narrow conclusions, both about the female characters
themselves and about the beliefs and attitudes of the society which
inscribed them in its texts. This is to do a grave injustice to an evolving,
literate, Christian culture which was well aware of historical, ecclesiastical, and literary developments both within Ireland itself and beyond its
shores.

Within the larger context of medieval literature, Emer stands out as a remarkable example of a strong female figure. Most surprising is her ability to escape the type of censure by male characters (and their authors) which her female counterparts in other medieval literatures endure so often. She does this, moreover, in spite of being enmeshed in a tradition which strongly condemns another aristocratic Irish woman – Medb – for her independent behaviour and forthright speech. Instead, Emer occupies an intriguing middle ground between the sirens of the Otherworld and the disruptive mortal women like Medb, Deirdre, and Rónán's wife. She resists categorization and manages to escape the two common female paradigms noted by Ní Bhrolcáin: 'one beneficial, positive and passive, the second malevolent, negative and independent.'[4]

It might be argued that, in the final analysis, the parameters of Emer's life, and therefore the space in which she can speak, are still ruthlessly controlled by the male-dominated society which constitutes her fictional world and by the patriarchal discourse which gives that fictional world its life. Despite her ability to speak out, she is hopelessly trapped within the traditional female roles of wife, helpmate, and (surrogate) mother. Like other female characters in medieval literature, she has few options outside of these.

On the other hand, as this study has sought to show, a careful reading of these texts reveals deep fissures in the discourse of male heroism and a marked anxiety over the traditional gendered codes of honour. And it is often within or near the speeches of Emer that these gaps reveal themselves. By reading these texts attentively, we can catch glimpses of the unease which often lies beneath the surface of heroic tales. In particular, by listening attentively to Emer we can begin to hear echoes of a female discourse, a sense of women 'talking down the authority of patriarchal voices by which they are framed.'[5]

The representation of Emer in these narratives is, therefore, of considerable interest to students of other medieval vernacular literatures, and to feminist medievalists in particular. Emer constitutes, in fact, a compelling example of a heroic *secular* woman – married and fully integrated into the fabric of her aristocratic society, and yet capable of speaking and acting independently as an agent of moral order. She is neither the chaste female 'hero' of Old English literature,[6] nor the ideal mistress of Old French romance, nor the garrulous wife of the *fabliaux*. Her depiction in the Irish tales discussed here suggests that she was employed (or at least refashioned) by medieval Irish authors and redactors to express a more fair and compassionate (indeed, a more 'Christian') alternative to traditional customs and concerns. This is all the more remarkable in light of the anti-feminist discourse rampant throughout Europe in the Middle Ages. Emer's identification with the ideals of the Christian church seems to imply a greater fluidity (at least in medieval Ireland) of ecclesiastical views concerning women and their speech than has been hitherto acknowledged.

Emer constitutes an intriguing example of a female speaking subject whose words shape both her own fictional world and the reactions of her extra-textual audience. She is a complex and compelling figure who deserves to take her place among the other memorable women of medieval literature.

Appendix: Sources and Manuscripts

The Ulster Cycle is comprised of more than eighty heroic tales, poems and shorter pieces, although its centrepiece is undoubtedly the *Táin Bó Cúailnge*.[1] The *Táin* is a narrative on an epic scale, and many shorter tales either derive from it or depend on it for their existence and meaning. Some of these may have been originally independent stories which, over time, were drawn into the *Táin*'s orbit. Although the dating of these texts remains in many cases problematic, the ways in which the tales cross-reference each other, and the extent of audience familiarity assumed by the texts, suggest that already by the eighth century there existed a group of Ulster tales (in oral or perhaps even in written form) which were closely related to one another.[2]

Three of the four tales discussed in this study are found in the manuscript Lebor na Huidre (LU). This codex contains a large number of secular tales as well as religious texts. In the introduction to their edition, Best and Bergin identify three hands in the manuscript, two earlier ones and that of a later interpolator (whom they call H).[3] More recently, Tomás Ó Concheanainn has argued that this interpolator H, whom he calls the Reviser, should in fact be identified with Mael Muire (a scribe who died in 1106 and identified by Bergin and Best as M) rather than a later nameless scholar.[4] This view, which would necessitate a back-dating of the original scribes into the eleventh century, had found favour among some scholars.[5] However, in a very recent study Gearóid Mac Eoin has carefully examined the local references in the Reviser's alterations in LU and has concluded that this scribe could not have been Mael Muire, but was working later. Mac Eoin argues convincingly that the Reviser was a member of the learned Ua Maol Chonaire family, and that he carried out his revisions of LU some time in the mid- to late twelfth century.[6] This theory would affirm Mael Muire as one of the original scribes, working in the late eleventh or early twelfth century, and place the Reviser's work some fifty or more years later.

The other manuscript important for this study is the Yellow Book of Lecan (YBL), now Trinity College Dublin H.2.16. This is a huge manuscript containing a variety of texts from all branches of Irish learning, and consisting of several sections written at different times. The fourteenth-century section which forms the earliest nucleus of the book was apparently written at Leacán, Co. Sligo, by the famous scribe Gilla Ísa mac Fir Bhisigh.[7] This part of the manuscript contains many of the Ulster Cycle tales including the *Táin* and *Bricriu's Feast*, as well as a number of death tales, all of which were clearly composed much earlier.[8] *The Death of Aífe's Only Son* (discussed in chapter 3) is one of these tales from the fourteenth-century section of the manuscript.

For readers interested in further details, I offer the following brief discussions of the manuscript tradition of each text discussed in the preceeding chapters.

The Wooing of Emer (Tochmarc Emire)

This text is found in a number of manuscripts. The tale seems to have been a very popular one and obviously underwent considerable development throughout the medieval period. Rudolph Thurneysen posited three separate versions of the tale.[9] Version 1 survives only in fragmentary form; the beginning seems to have been lost. The middle and end of the tale, beginning with Forgall's plot to rid himself of his daughter's young suitor, is preserved in the Oxford manuscript Rawlinson B. 512.[10] This text is deemed by its editor, Kuno Meyer, to be the earliest, despite its appearance in a fifteenth-century manuscript.[11]

Thurneysen argued that Version 3, which is represented by several manuscripts, developed from the combination of Version I with a hypothetical Version 2, which is now lost.[12] The necessity of positing a Version 2 at all has since been questioned by several scholars, including Doris Edel and Séamus Mac Mathúna.[13] Version 3 is found complete in three manuscript texts: Stowe (R.I.A. D.iv.2), R.I.A. 23.N.10, and British Library Harleian 5280. There are also fragments in the Book of Fermoy and the British Library manuscript Egerton 92.[14] The Stowe text is the earliest complete example of Version 3; the fragment in LU, which is missing four leaves, is possibly earlier but incomplete. Thurneysen dated the Stowe manuscript to 1300; however, Van Hamel points out that this date is based solely on the fact that '1300' appears in a late hand on the cover of the manuscript; he posits a slightly later date.[15] The Royal Irish Academy catalogue of manuscripts lists the date as '15th cent. (?).'[16] Despite the lateness of this manuscript, Version 3 certainly existed earlier, when the Reviser of LU erased a portion of the earlier recension in that manuscript (from folio 123 on) and inserted a text of the Version 3 type instead.[17]

Some of the differences between Versions 1 and 3 are worth noting. Version 1 as we have it is incomplete, beginning after Cú Chulainn has already departed following his wooing dialogue with Emer. The text makes it clear, however, that a dialogue between the pair *has* occurred, and that Emer has made demands that must be fulfilled by the hero. Version 1 also omits the *dinnshenchas* material and its explanation to Lóeg the charioteer by the hero. The latter part of the tale is essentially intact, except for the prophecy of Scáthach; here the Version 1 text gives one line of her verse and points to another place in the same manuscript where the whole prophecy is recorded.[18]

The present study of this tale focuses on Thurneysen's Version 3, and citations are taken from Van Hamel's edition of the Stowe version.[19] As a literary study, it is not concerned with recovering an 'original' version of the tale.

Bricriu's Feast (Fled Bricrend)

This text survives in varying states of completeness in several manuscripts. Thurneysen identified three separate versions of the tale, the earliest of which is found in LU. Here, the text of *Fled Bricrend* is found on folios 99b–112b, but unfortunately breaks off before the end.[20] Thurneysen dated the earliest layer of this version to the eighth century.[21] However, Gearóid Mac Eoin has disputed this date, maintaining that nothing in the earliest portions need be older than 900.[22]

Later redactions of the tale, dating from the fifteenth and sixteenth centuries, survive in the British Library manuscript Egerton 93 and the Codex Vossianus lat. quart. 7; these two represent Thurneysen's 'Version B.' A third version (Thurneysen's 'Version C') appears in the Trinity College Dublin manuscript H.3.17, also dated to the sixteenth century.[23] In all four of these manuscripts the end of the tale is either missing or unreadable; fortunately, the ending survives in the Edinburgh manuscript Advocates' Library XL, another sixteenth-century codex.[24]

The various versions differ in the number of episodes included and in the degree of skill with which their respective redactors have woven them together into some sort of unity. Thurneysen concludes that although the Lebor na Huidre text (the earliest surviving version) contains interpolated material, the Reviser who introduced these additions was not their ultimate source, but rather worked from an earlier compilation.[25] *Fled Bricrend* is one of the LU texts which the Reviser has reshaped to some extent. Although his contributions to the tale as a whole are not overwhelming, he has erased and replaced the existing text starting from the last two lines of Emer's speech in the *bríatharcath* to the beginning of the heroes' journey to the house of Ailill and Medb.[26] This is the section which includes Sencha's misogynistic reaction to the women's resumption of their verbal contest, Emer's response to him, and Cú Chulainn's refusal to dispute further until he has had a chance to eat and rest – all of which constitute some of the most ambiguous sections of the tale. Although it is impossible to determine at this stage what the Reviser replaced, and whether or not he deliberately introduced ambiguous elements, this must remain a possibility.

One reason for the scarcity of critical attention paid to *Bricriu's Feast* may be the lack of a recent critical edition of the text. Although a new edition has been in preparation for some years now, it has not yet been published.[27] The existing editions are old and no truly satisfactory translation is available; most of them omit the *bríatharcath* section altogether.[28] Since chapter 2 of the present study is concerned chiefly with the first part of the tale, quotations are taken from the LU version.[29]

The Death of Aífe's Only Son (Aided Óenfir Aífe)

Aided Óenfir Aífe is not found in the Lebor na Huidre. The earliest version of the story survives only in the fourteenth-century section of the Yellow Book of Lecan, now Trinity College Dublin H.2.16, col. 955 (fol.214a–15a). Thurneysen dated the language of the tale to the ninth century,[30] while Van Hamel posits a late ninth or tenth century date.[31] Most scholars who have commented on *Aided Óenfir Aífe* agree that this tale is later in origin than the original nucleus of the *Táin*. Thurneysen speculates that the body of story around Cú Chulainn attracted the motif of the father who kills his son into its orbit sometime in the eighth century, after the main features of the *Táin* had coalesced.[32] Thurneysen's observation that even the oldest version of *Tochmarc Emire* implies an acquaintance with this tale is interesting but inconclusive, as is his suggestion that the implied knowledge could have been of an oral rather than a written version of the tale.[33]

Tomás Ó Concheanainn has recently discussed the close relationship between the LU and YBL versions of several tales, and contends that Gilla Ísa redacted both the *Táin* and *Togail Bruidne Da Derga* directly from LU.[34] In an even more recent article, he has extended this discussion to the relationship between YBL and the Book of Leinster, which he contends may also have been available to the Lecan scribes.[35] In light of this, and in light of Van Hamel's assertion that the language of the tale 'belongs to the later Old-Irish period,'[36] one might speculate on the possible existence of an earlier version of *Aided Óenfir Aífe* amongst the pages of LU now lost to us.

At any rate, although *Aided Óenfir Aífe* does not appear in either of the medieval tale lists, the tale certainly had taken shape before the twelfth century.[37] Cú Chulainn's battle with his son is mentioned twice in the Book of Leinster, in Cinaed úa hArtacáin's verses on the deaths of heroes,[38] and in the verses spoken by Cú Chulainn to Fer Diad in the *Táin* in which he indicates that his battle with Connla has already taken place:

> Ní tharla rumm sund co se
> á bacear Óenfer Aífe,
> da mac samla – galaib gliad –
> ní fuaras sund, a Fir Diad.'

> I have never met such as you until now
> since the only son of Aífe fell;
> your peer in deeds of battle
> I found not here, O Fer Diad.[39]

Thus the tale cannot have made its first appearance in YBL. We must therefore posit its origin in an earlier period, perhaps the ninth or tenth century as Van Hamel suggests.

The Wasting Sickness of Cú Chulainn (Serglige Con Culainn)

This tale is found in two manuscripts. The early version appears in LU, while the later version is found in the Trinity College manuscript H.4.22. These two texts are very similar, and Myles Dillon has concluded that the Trinity College version derives from that in LU.[40] The present discussion focuses on Dillon's edition of the LU text, with variants supplied from the Trinity College manuscript.[41]

The text as it stands appears to be a composite of two different recensions which have been woven together. Zimmer was the first to attempt to isolate the two recensions.[42] Thurneysen later attempted to improve on this analysis, and dated the earlier recension to the ninth century[43] and the later recension to the eleventh.[44] However, some points in his analysis are problematic. Dillon's detailed discussion of the relationship between the two recensions has become the standard one; he concludes that these two recensions were first combined in the Lebor Bude Sláne, the book which the Reviser cites as his source for his version of the story.[45] The most recent reassessment is that of Salberg, who essentially confirms Dillon's conclusions.[46]

As mentioned above, LU was substantially revised and expanded by the scribe known as the Reviser. The tale *Serglige Con Culainn* was drastically altered by the Reviser, who erased many leaves and copied a large amount of alternative text onto the old ones. The entire first portion of the tale – including the title, the description of the assembly, the coming of the birds, Cú Chulainn's sickness, his instructions to his fosterson Lugaid Réoderg, up to the beginning of Emer's lament to Lóeg – is in the hand of the Reviser.[47] The original text resumes until the Reviser intervenes again in portions of Lí Ban's speech to Cú Chulainn.[48] Lóeg's descriptions of the Otherworld are, with the exception of a few short interventions, in the original hand. The Reviser resumes at the end of Lóeg's description and carries on through the scenes of Cú Chulainn's battles on Lugaid's behalf up to the point where Cú Chulainn concludes his dubious assessment of his own performance in the Otherworld.[49] The original text then takes over at the point of Cú Chulainn's tryst with Fand and continues to the end.

Without knowing the exact nature of the material erased and replaced by the Reviser, it is difficult to draw wide-ranging conclusions. Moreover, it is not clear if it was the Reviser who joined the two recensions together, or if they were already blended in his source.[50] The Reviser certainly found the existing text unsatisfactory in some way and sought to improve it. As Tomás Ó Concheanainn has pointed out,

The reviser overhauled the manuscript in quite a drastic manner (adding to it in several ways) and left it a finished edition from his own hand. He certainly did not regard the original manuscript as an object of veneration, for it was yet no such thing ... The reviser's role was clearly that of a redactor doing exactly what other scholars had done before ...[51]

Whether the Reviser was merely combining existing elements as a redactor (inserting 'better' versions of what was already there) or adding his own inventions, he apparently left it as he wanted it.[52] Whatever his intentions, it is this version which has come down to us. It is with this version, not a hypothetical 'original' which can never be recovered, that the discussion presented here concerns itself.

Notes

Introduction

1 This term refers to a group of linked tales about a group of warriors clustered around Conchobar, king of Ulster. The 'Ulster Cycle' consists of a number of loosely linked heroic tales, poems, and shorter pieces, although the centrepiece is the epic *Táin Bó Cúailgne* (*The Cattle Raid of Cooley*).

2 The scholarship on these two authors is now vast. For Chaucer, of particular note are Carolyn Dinshaw's *Chaucer's Sexual Poetics* (Madison: University of Wisconsin Press, 1989) and the special issue of *Exemplaria* (vol. 2, no. 1, 1990) on the theme 'Reconceiving Chaucer: Literary Theory and Historical Interpretation.' For Chrétien de Troyes, see Joan Ferrante, *Woman as Image in Medieval Literature* (New York: Columbia University Press, 1975); Laurie Finke, 'Towards a Cultural Poetics of Romance,' *Genre* 22 (Summer 1989): 109–27; E. Jane Burns, *Bodytalk: When Women Speak in Old French Literature* (Philadelphia: University of Pennsylvania Press, 1993): 151–202; Matilda Tomaryn Bruckner, *Shaping Romance: Interpretation, Truth, and Closure in Twelfth-Century French Fictions* (Philadelphia: University of Pennsylvania Press, 1993); Michel-André Bossy, 'The Elaboration of Female Narrative Functions in *Erec et Enide*,' in Keith Busby and Eric Cooper, eds., *Courtly Literature: Culture and Context* (Amsterdam/Philadelphia: John Benjamins, 1990): 23–38; and Kathryn Gravdal, *Ravishing Maidens: Writing Rape in Medieval French Literature and Law* (Philadelphia: University of Pennsylvania Press, 1991).

3 Useful studies include Michelle Freeman's 'Marie de France's Poetics of Silence: The Implications for a Feminine *Translatio*,' *PMLA* 99 (1984): 860–83; Lynne Huffer's 'Christine de Pisan: Speaking Like a Woman/Speaking Like a Man,' in Edelgard DuBruck, ed., *New Images of Medieval Women: Toward a Cultural Anthropology* (Lewiston, NY: Mellen Press, 1989): 61–71; Barbara

Newman, *Sister of Wisdom: St. Hildegard's Theology of the Feminine* (Berkeley: University of California Press, 1987); and Karma Lochrie's *Margery Kempe and the Translations of the Flesh* (Philadelphia: University of Pennsylvania Press, 1991).

4 For the classic discussion of this problem, see Luce Irigaray, *Speculum of the Other Woman*, trans. Gillian C. Gill (Ithaca: Cornell UP, 1985): 22. For discussion and critique of Irigaray's views see Toril Moi, *Sexual/Textual Politics* (London: Methuen, 1985): 127–49; and Elizabeth Grosz, *Jacques Lacan: A Feminist Introduction* (London/New York: Routledge, 1990): 167–87.

5 Joan Ferrante, 'Male Fantasy and Female Reality,' *Women's Studies* 11 (1984): 67–97.

6 For a helpful discussion which is much indebted to Irigaray and Hélène Cixous, see Burns, *Bodytalk*, 86–7.

7 'Fearing for Chaucer's Good Name,' *Exemplaria* 2.1 (March 1990): 33. For a similarly devastating critique of Chaucer's representation of Criseyde, see Gretchen Mieszkowski's 'Chaucer's Much Loved Criseyde,' *Chaucer Review* 26 (1991): 109–32.

8 Edith Joyce Benkov, 'Language and Women: From Silence to Speech,' in Julian N. Wasserman and Lois Roney, *Sign, Sentence, Discourse: Language in Medieval Thought and Literature* (Syracuse: Syracuse University Press, 1989): 264.

9 Howard Bloch's exhaustive (and controversial) book *Medieval Misogyny and the Invention of Western Romantic Love* (Chicago: University of Chicago Press, 1991) discusses example after example. The heated responses to Bloch's original article, which he then expanded into this book, are printed in the *Medieval Feminist Newsletter*, 6 (Fall 1988), and shed more light on the many issues implied in a study of misogyny. For a handy guide to misogynistic texts, see the collection edited by Alcuin Blamires, *Woman Defamed and Woman Defended: An Anthology of Medieval Texts* (Oxford: Clarendon Press, 1992).

10 Ferrante, 'Male Fantasy,' 84–95.

11 'Enid the Disobedient: The *Mabinogion's Gereint and Enid*,' in Carol Levin and Jeanie Watson, eds., *Ambiguous Realities: Women in the Middle Ages and Renaissance* (Detroit: Wayne State University Press, 1987): 114–32; Patrick McConeghy, 'Women's Speech and Silence in Hartmann von Aue's *Erec*,' *PMLA* 102, no. 5 (1987): 772–83.

12 'Knowing Women: Female Orifices in Old French Farce and Fabliau,' *Exemplaria*, vol. 4, no. 1 (Spring 1992): 103.

13 Barthes, 'The Death of the Author,' in Stephen Heath, ed., *Image Music Text* (London: Fontana, 1977): 147; Toril Moi takes this position in *Sexual/Textual Politics*, 63–5.

14 My comments here are indebted to Moi's discussion, *Sexual/Textual Politics*, 63.

15 Helen Damico and Alexandra Hennessey Olsen, eds., *New Readings on Women in Old English Literature* (Bloomington: Indiana University Press, 1990).

16 Gillian Overing, *Language, Sign and Gender in Beowulf* (Carbondale: Southern Illinois University Press, 1990). See especially chapter 3, 'Gender and Interpretation in *Beowulf*.'

17 *Woman as Hero in Old English Literature* (Syracuse: Syracuse University Press, 1986).

18 'Women's Words as Weapons: Speech as Action in "The Wife's Lament",' *Texas Studies in Literature and Language* 23 (1981): 268–85.

19 'Gwydion and Aranrhod: Crossing the Borders of Gender in *Math*,' *Bulletin of the Board of Celtic Studies* 35 (1988): 1–9.

20 See especially Clover's article 'Hildigunnr's Lament,' in John Lindow et al., eds., *Structure and Meaning in Old Norse Literature* (Odense: Odense University Press, 1986): 141–83. Among Jochens' many contributions is '*Voluspá*: Matrix of Norse Womanhood,' *Journal of English and Germanic Philology* 88 (July 1989): 344–62.

21 Judith Jesch, *Women in the Viking Age* (Woodbridge: The Boydell Press, 1991).

22 Margaret Clunies Ross, *Prolonged Echoes: Old Norse Myths in Medieval Northern Society* (Viborg: Odense University Press, 1994).

23 Thomas Kinsella, trans., *The Táin* (Dublin: Dolmen Press, 1969): xiv–xv.

24 For this interpretation, see especially Patricia Kelly, 'The *Táin* as Literature,' in *Aspects of the Táin*, ed. J.P. Mallory (Belfast: December Publications, 1992): 69–102; for a wider discussion of 'troublesome' women, see Muireann Ní Bhrolcháin, '*Re Tóin Mná*: In Pursuit of Troublesome Women,' in *Ulidia: Proceedings of the First International Conference on the Ulster Cycle of Tales*, ed. J.P. Mallory and G. Stockman (Belfast: December Publications, 1994): 115–21.

25 The first of these two approaches sought to correlate characters in the narratives with actual pre-Christian Celtic or Indo-European deities. To this group belong T.F. O'Rahilly's *Early Irish History and Mythology* (Dublin: DIAS, 1946) and Anne Ross's *Pagan Celtic Britain* (London: Routledge & Kegan Paul, 1967). This earlier approach has been largely superseded by a second, related methodology which is deeply influenced by the structural anthropologists such as Durkheim, Dumézil, and Lévi-Strauss. This method seeks to discern in the narratives patterns of functionality which might hint at early Indo-European social organization. For an accessible guide to Dumézil's theories, see C. Scott Littleton, *The New Comparative Mythology*

(Berkeley: University of California Press, 1966). One of Lévi-Strauss's most influential works is *The Raw and the Cooked*, trans. J. and D. Weightman (London: Cape, 1970). Marie-Louise Sjoestedt (who was a student of Durkheim's) and Proinsias Mac Cana are influenced by both approaches; see Sjoestedt's *Gods and Heroes of the Celts*, trans. Myles Dillon (London: Methuen, 1949) and Mac Cana's *Celtic Mythology* (London: Hamlyn, 1970).

26 Among the Celticists influenced by the ideas of Lévi-Strauss is Patrick Ford; see his readings of medieval Welsh tales in the introduction to *The Mabinogi and Other Medieval Welsh Tales* (Berkeley: University of California Press, 1977): 1–30; and 'Prolegomena to a Reading of the *Mabinogi*: "Pwyll" and "Manawydan",' *Studia Celtica* 16/17 (1981–2): 110–25. For Dumézilian readings, see Elizabeth A. Gray, ed., *Cath Maige Tuired: The Second Battle of Mag Tuired*, Irish Texts Society, vol. 52 (1982); and Alwyn and Brinley Rees, *Celtic Heritage* (London: Thames & Hudson, 1961, repr. 1969). The Rees brothers' reading of myth also shows Jungian influences.

27 For a concise comment on the limitations of this approach, see Máire Herbert, 'The World, the Text, and the Critic of Early Irish Heroic Narrative,' *Text & Context* 3 (Autumn 1988): 2–6.

28 Kim McCone has recently pointed out that the anthropological studies of myth (such as those of Lévi-Strauss) are based upon *oral* tales from non-literate cultures, and thus cannot be unproblematically applied to early Irish narrative, which survives only in written form and which was transmitted within a literary tradition. See his discussion in *Pagan Past and Christian Present* (Maynooth: An Sagart, 1990): 62–6.

29 'Medb Chrúachna,' *ZCP* 17 (1928): 129–46. An elaboration of this theme is found in Proinsias Mac Cana's article, 'Aspects of the Theme of King and Goddess in Irish Literature,' *Études celtiques* 7, no. 1–2 (1955–6): 76–114, 346–413, 859–65.

30 The lasting effects of this foreclosure can be seen in the fact that to date virtually nothing has been written about Medb as a literary figure. Doris Edel does consider Medb in a 1986 article published in Dutch, 'Koningin Medb van Connacht en haar beoordelaars, vroeger en nu,' in the collection *'t Is kwaad gerucht, als zij niet binnen blijft* (Utrecht: Hes Uitgevers, 1986): 61–94. Edel contends that Medb is a reflection of actual female Celtic rulers of pre-Christian times. She does not, however, consider her as a literary figure. One of the very few articles which does this is the recent essay by Patricia Kelly, 'The Táin as Literature,' in J.P. Mallory, ed., *Aspects of the Táin* (Belfast: The Universities Press, 1992): 69–102.

31 'Merched Y Mabinogi: Women and the Thematic Structure of the Four Branches,' PhD dissertation, Cornell University, 1986, 1–3. Although

Valente's work focuses on the Middle Welsh tales of the *Mabinogi*, her introduction also considers the Irish material and constitutes a valuable assessment of the state of literary methodology in Celtic Studies.

32 Overing, *Language, Sign and Gender in Beowulf*, 78–81. See her extended discussion in chapter 3.

33 Toni O'Brien Johnson and David Cairns, in their introduction to *Gender in Irish Writing* (Philadelphia: Open University Press, 1991): 4.

34 Lévi-Strauss, *The Elementary Structures of Kinship*, trans. J.H. Bell and J.R. von Sturmer, ed. R. Needham (Boston: Beacon Press, 1969).

35 For the classic discussion, see Sherry B. Ortner, 'Is Female to Male as Nature is to Culture?' in Michelle Zimbalist Rosaldo and Louise Lamphere, eds., *Woman, Culture and Society* (Stanford: Stanford University Press: 1974): 67–87.

36 Sjoestedt, *Gods and Heroes*, 93.

37 Mac Cana, 'Women in Irish Mythology,' *The Crane Bag*, vol. 4, no. 1 (1980): 7–11.

38 Máire Herbert, 'Celtic Heroine? The Archaeology of the Deirdre Story,' in Toni O'Brien Johnson and David Cairns, eds., *Gender in Irish Writing* (Philadelphia: Open University Press, 1991): 13–22.

39 See especially the collection of essays called *Nature, Culture and Gender*, ed. Carol P. MacCormack and Marilyn Strathern (Cambridge: Cambridge University Press, 1980), especially 1–24.

40 'Nature, Culture and Gender: A Critique,' in *Nature, Culture and Gender*, 6–21.

41 As Jenny Jochens comments in a recent study, 'In the Old Norse context ... men's looks partook both of nature and of culture because their features and bodies were enhanced by fine clothing, but female beauty was most likely to be perceived primarily through the cultural optic of clothing, but – it should be added – a culture of women's own making'; see 'Before the Male Gaze: The Absence of the Female Body in Old Norse,' in Joyce Salisbury, ed., *Sex in the Middle Ages* (New York/London: Garland, 1991): 8.

42 *Speaking of the Middle Ages*, trans. Sarah White (Lincoln/London: University of Nebraska Press, 1986): 47.

43 The scribe known as the 'Reviser' of the manuscript Lebor na Huidre (LU) is one of the most well known of these interventionist redactors. For a more detailed discussion of his activities, see the appendix.

44 As Edgar Slotkin has pointed out, 'Given the attitude of scribes towards their work, we can think of each one of their productions as a kind of multiform of their original ... Surely, the "interpolation" of a late scribe may be traditional, meaningful, and necessary to the tale or that particular

152   Notes to pages 11–12

scribal performance of the tale.' See 'Medieval Irish Scribes and Fixed Texts,'
Éigse 17, part 4 (1978–9): 50.

45 See Nagy, 'Compositional Concerns in the *Acallam na Senórach*,' in
Donnchadh Ó Corráin et al., eds., *Sages, Saints and Storytellers*, 149–58; and
Ó Cathasaigh, 'The Rhetoric of *Scéla Cano meic Gartnáin*' (same volume):
233–50.

46 Herbert, 'Celtic Heroine?' (see n. 38). See also her discussion of the literary
and political uses of the traditional 'sovereignty' motif in some of the later
tales; see especially her discussion of the eleventh-century tale *Baile in Scáil*
in 'Goddess and King: The Sacred Marriage in Early Ireland,' in Louise
Fradenberg, ed., *Women and Sovereignty*, Cosmos 7 (Edinburgh: Edinburgh
University Press, 1992): 269–72.

47 Jeanie Watson, 'Enid the Disobedient'; and Roberta Valente, 'Gwydion and
Aranrhod: Crossing the Borders of Gender in *Math*.'

48 *Pagan Past and Christian Present*, 138–60.

49 'The Táin as Literature,' in *Aspects of the Táin*, especially 84–9.

50 See 'The Invention of Women in the *Táin*,' in *Ulidia*, ed. J.P. Mallory and
G. Stockman (Belfast: December Publications, 1994): 123–33.

51 T.M. Charles-Edwards, 'Honour and Status in Some Irish and Welsh Prose
Tales,' *Ériu* 29 (1978): 123–41; Nerys Patterson, 'Honour and Shame in
Medieval Welsh Society,' *Studia Celtica* 16/17 (1981–2): 73–103; Philip
O'Leary, 'The Honour of Women in Early Irish Literature,' *Ériu* 38 (1987):
27–44.

52 Dooley has adverted to an intriguing ecclesiastical typology of women
which can be transposed to secular tales; see her comments in 'The Invention of Women,' 129–30.

53 I use this term in a similar sense to that popularized by Julia Kristeva, by
which she means that any text is regarded as constituted by other texts
surrounding it. These other texts may or may not have been known directly
by the author of the primary text under consideration, or by any of the
text's successive audiences. Elaborating on Bakhtin's idea of the 'dialogic'
word, Kristeva sees a text as an *'intersection of textual surfaces'* (her italics)
and as 'a dialogue among several writings: that of the writer, the addressee
(or the character) and the contemporary or earlier cultural context.' See
'Word, Dialogue and Novel' in Toril Moi, ed., *The Kristeva Reader* (Oxford:
Basil Blackwell, 1986): 34–61. Although this definition allows for non-textual
intertexts, in practice, Kristeva herself tends to concentrate on *literary* texts
in her discussions.

54 Scholars have long assumed that literacy in Ireland began with the coming
of Christianity but recent work has suggested that there was some degree of

literacy even in the days of the Roman occupation of Britain; see Jane
Stevenson, 'The Beginnings of Literacy in Ireland,' *Proceedings of the Royal
Irish Academy*, vol. 89C (1989): 127–65.

55 Stevenson, 'The Beginnings of Literacy,' 151–3.
56 Ann Dooley and James P. Carley, 'An Early Irish Fragment of Isidore of
Seville's *Etymologiae*, in Lesley Abrams and James P. Carley, eds., *The
Archaeology and History of Glastonbury Abbey* (Woodbridge: Boydell Press,
1991): 135–61. James Mallory has argued that the descriptions of chariots in
the *Táin* had their origins not in folk memories of an Irish Iron Age past, but
in the parallel descriptions in Ovid's *Metamorphoses* and in Sidonius – in
other words, in a *literary* context. See 'Silver in the Ulster Cycle of Tales,' in
D. Ellis Evans et al., eds., *Proceedings of the Seventh International Congress of
Celtic Studies, Oxford, 1983* (Oxford: Oxbow Books 1986): 31–78; and 'The
World of Cú Chulainn,' in J.P. Mallory, ed., *Aspects of the Táin* (Belfast:
December Publications, 1992): 146–53. James Carney argued years ago for
the deep influence of classical literature (including the works of Homer) on
vernacular Irish texts and went so far as to declare 'Irish literature has, in
my opinion, approximately the same relationship to the European literature
that preceded it – whether Christian or classical – as has Latin to Greek';
Studies in Irish Literature and History (Dublin: DIAS, 1979): 312.
57 The scholars dubbed 'nativists' by these reformers stress the isolation and
self-referential character of the early Irish tradition. As Kim McCone puts it
in *Pagan Past and Christian Present*, 'The main objection to nativist attitudes
towards early Irish literature is that they preclude the appreciation of this
vast material in its own terms by treating it as a more or less haphazard,
imperfect and unthinkingly antiquarian inky precipitation out of an
infinitely richer and more extensive oral solution' (5).
58 Kuno Meyer, ed. and trans., 'The Instructions of King Cormac mac Airt,'
RIA Todd Lecture Series 15 (1909): 28–37.
59 The text is from Roland M. Smith's 'The *Senbriathra Fithail* and Related
Texts,' *Révue celtique* 45 (1928): 54, 55; my translation is based on his. Smith
suggests that parts of this text may have influenced the wooing dialogue in
Tochmarc Emire; see discussion in chapter 1 below.
60 See Elizabeth Gray's discussion in '*Cath Maige Tuired: Myth and Structure,*'
Éigse 18 (1980–1): 200–1.
61 Cecile O'Rahilly, ed., *Táin Bó Cúalnge from the Book of Leinster* (Dublin: DIAS,
1967): 134, ll. 4849–51; trans. 270. Although Recension 1 (in Lebor na
Huidre) also contains similar sentiments, critics have noted the Book of
Leinster version's sustained critique of Medb's behaviour. See, for instance,
Áine de Paor, 'The Common Authorship of some Book of Leinster Texts,'

Ériu 9, no. 2 (1923): 124. For a brief review of some other negative portrayals of women in medieval Irish tales, see Philip O'Leary, 'The Honour of Women in Early Irish Literature,' *Eriu* 38 (1987): 43.

62 This misogynistic clerical discourse is particularly evident when the texts are set against the writings of the Church Fathers (Jerome, Augustine, Origen), all of whom warn of the dangers of women's speech. See Bloch's *Medieval Misogyny*, 17–22.

63 The most recent edition of the prose version is an unpublished PhD dissertation by Muirenn Ní Bhrolcháin, 'The Prose Banshenchas' (University College, Galway, 1980).

64 For an edition (without translation) see Pádraig Ó Riain, *Corpus Genealogiarum Sanctorum Hiberniae* (Dublin: DIAS, 1985): 169–181.

65 James Carney, 'The Deeper Level of Early Irish Literature,' *Capuchin Annual* (1969): 162–5.

66 Máire Breathnach, 'A New Edition of *Tochmarc Becfhola*,' *Ériu* 35 (1984): 59–91. However, John Carey views this tale as disapproving of Becfola; see 'Otherworlds and Verbal Worlds in Middle Irish Narrative,' *Proceedings of the Harvard Celtic Colloquium* 9 (1989): 31–42.

67 Brian O. Murdoch, ed. and trans., *The Irish Adam and Eve Story from Saltair na Rann*, 2 vols. (Dublin: DIAS, 1976): ll. 1689–92; see Murdoch's comments on the passage in vol. 2, 117.

68 See F.X. Martin, *A New History of Ireland: Volume 2: Medieval Ireland*, ed. Art Cosgrove, chap. 2 (Oxford: Clarendon Press, 1987): 43–66.

69 Paul Zumthor, *Speaking of the Middle Ages*, 23.

70 Kelly, *A Guide to Early Irish Law*, 1.

71 See Donncha Ó Corráin, 'Women in Early Irish Society,' in Ó Corráin and Margaret MacCurtain, eds., *Women in Irish Society: The Historical Dimension* (Westport: Greenwood Press, 1979): 7.

72 These grounds included the husband's taking of a second wife (which was permissible under Irish law), impotence, and neglect. For a full discussion of divorce in early Irish law, see Fergus Kelly, *A Guide to Early Irish Law* (Dublin: DIAS, 1988): 73–5. See also the more detailed discussions of marriage laws in chapters 1 and 4 below.

73 For a general discussion of marriage laws in early medieval Ireland see Donncha Ó Corráin, 'Women in Early Irish Society,' 1–13.

74 A concern for women's well-being in other areas is reflected in the early law tract *Cáin Adamnáin*, most recently edited and analyzed by Máirín Ní Dhonnchadha, forthcoming.

75 This story appears in Kuno Meyer, ed., *Betha Colmáin maic Luacháin* (Dublin: Hodges, Figgis, 1911): 52–3.

76 Ó Corráin, 'Women in Early Irish Society,' 9–10.

77 Kelly, *A Guide to Early Irish Law*, 68–79. For a more detailed analysis of the issues, see R. Thurneysen et al., eds., *Studies in Early Irish Law* (Dublin: Royal Irish Academy, 1936), hereafter cited as *SEIL*.

78 Kelly, *A Guide to Early Irish Law*, 207.

79 Katherine Simms, in 'The Legal Position of Irishwomen in the Later Middle Ages,' *The Irish Jurist* (1975): 96–111, especially 108ff. Simms notes that 'Almost without exception the actions moved before the archbishop were initiated by wives who had already been cast off, often after many years of wedded life, and now sought to have their husbands compelled to return to them under threat of excommunication. The husbands invariably defended their behaviour by questioning the original validity of the marriage on conventional canonical grounds' (100).

80 For example, Gormflaith, daughter of Ua Focarta, wife of Toirdelbach Ua Briain, the king of Munster and high-king of Ireland, bequeathed a great deal of wealth to the church before her death in 1077; see the *Annals of Clonmacnoise*, ed. D. Murphy (Dublin: The University Press, 1896) for the year 1077.

81 For a thorough discussion of this incident, see Marie Therese Flanagan, *Irish Society, Anglo-Norman Settlers, Angevin Kingship: Interactions in Ireland in the Late Twelfth Century* (Oxford: Clarendon Press, 1989): 80–95.

82 See, for instance, Proinsias Mac Cana's discussion of Mór Muman in 'Aspects of the Theme of King and Goddess in Irish Literature,' *Études celtiques* 7 (1955–6): 76–114; 8 (1958–9): 59–65.

83 Simms notes the later examples of Tadhg O Conor abducting his mother from her husband's house and giving her to O Reilly 'as a ransom for himself' in 1243, and of Somhairle MacDonnell forcing MacMahon to divorce his wife and marry his (Somhairle's) daughter in 1365; see Simms, 'The Legal Position of Irishwomen,' 110 and notes. She observes that the kin-group's 'power to protect seems to have included the power to control, in some cases to the point of tyranny.'

84 Robin Flower, *The Irish Tradition* (Oxford: Clarendon Press, 1947): 72–80; Proinsias Mac Cana, 'The Rise of the Later Schools of *filidheacht*,' *Ériu* 25 (1974): 126–46. Tomás Ó Cathasaigh calls the eleventh and twelfth centuries 'a watershed in the history of Irish literature' and a 'great age of compilation'; he says, 'Following upon the reform of the Church in this period, custody of the manuscript tradition passed from the monasteries to the newly established lay schools which were to be conducted by hereditary learned families, and it was the members of these families who continued the manuscript transmission of the literature up to the seventeenth century.'

See 'Pagan Survivals: The Evidence of Early Irish Narrative,' in *Irland und Europa: Ireland and Europe* (Stuttgart: Klett-Cotta, 1984): 295, n. 22.

85 Rudolf Thurneysen, *Die irische Helden- und Königsage bis zum 17. Jahrhundert* (Halle: Niemeyer, 1921), hereafter cited simply as *Heldensage*, 89ff; Cecile O'Rahilly, *Táin Bó Cúalnge from the Book of Leinster* (Dublin: DIAS, 1967): ix–xxv.

86 For examples of these attributions in the Lebor na Huidre, see Tomás Ó Concheanainn, 'A Connacht Medieval Literary Heritage: Texts Derived from Cín Dromma Snechtai through Leabhar na hUidhre,' *Cambridge Medieval Celtic Studies* 16 (Winter 1988): 1–40.

87 For a recent reevaluation of the early date see Séamus Mac Mathúna's discussion in *Immram Brain: Bran's Voyage to the Land of Women* (Tübingen: Niemeyer, 1985): 421–69. He suggests that the Cín Dromma Snechta may have been a tenth-century manuscript. James Carney has argued for the existence of an early alternate tradition of the *Táin* as represented by the poem *Conailla Medb míchuru*; Carney dates this poem to 600 A.D. at the latest and suggests that the poet's information dates back even earlier. This would move the tradition of the *Táin* in some form 'almost to the brink of the pagan period.' See Carney, 'Early Irish Literature: The State of Research,' in *Proceedings of the Sixth International Congress of Celtic Studies, Galway 1979* (Dublin: DIAS, 1983): 122.

88 See P.L. Henry's recent edition and discussion, 'Verba Scáthaige,' *Celtica* 21 (1990): 191–207.

89 See Thurneysen, *Heldensage*, 377–95 for *Tochmarc Emire*, and 447–50 for *Fled Bricrend*. In the dating of the former he agrees with Kuno Meyer, who argued decades before that the earliest version of *Tochmarc Emire* (in the manuscript Rawlinson B 512) represented a pre-Norse version of the tale; see 'The Oldest Version of the Tochmarc Emire,' *Révue celtique* 11 (1890): 453–7. In the case of *Fled Bricrend*, Gearóid Mac Eoin questions Thurneysen's dating of the earliest layer of the text to the eighth century and sees no reason to judge it any earlier than about 900; see 'The Dating of Middle Irish Texts,' *Proceedings of the British Academy* 68 (1982): 121.

90 Thurneysen, *Heldensage*, 404, dates the language of *Aided Óenfir Aífe* to the ninth century, while Van Hamel posits a late ninth or tenth century date; see Van Hamel's edition of the tale, *Compert Con Culainn and Other Stories* (Dublin: DIAS, 1933, rep. 1978): 9. In fact, it is possible that a version of this tale may have been included in LU, in one of the portions now lost; such a theory is, of course, unprovable. Thurneysen dates the earliest version of *Serglige Con Culainn* to the ninth century (*Heldensage*, 415).

91 Proinsias Mac Cana, 'The Influence of the Vikings on Celtic Literature,' in

The Impact of the Scandinavian Invasions on the Celtic-speaking Peoples, ed. Brian O Cuív (Dublin: DIAS, 1983): 103–4.

92 This codex contains a large number of secular tales as well as some religious material. For a more detailed discussion of this manuscript, see the Appendix.

93 Tomás Ó Concheanainn, 'Gilla Ísa Mac Fir Bhisigh and a Scribe of his School,' *Ériu* 25 (1974): 168–9.

94 For a complete list of the contents, see T.K. Abbott and E.J. Gwynn, *Catalogue of Irish Manuscripts in the Library of Trinity College Dublin* (Dublin: Hodges, Figgis, 1921): 94–110.

95 The Irish word 'scél' means both 'story' and 'knowledge, information, tidings' – a conjunction which, as Proinsias Mac Cana has pointed out, is particularly apt in light of the common fusion of both 'learning and entertainment' so often found in medieval Irish tales; see his discussion of the taxonomy of the tales in *The Learned Tales of Medieval Ireland* (Dublin: DIAS, 1980): 24–5.

96 For the complete tale lists, see Mac Cana, *Learned Tales,* 41–65.

97 Mac Cana, *Learned Tales,* 128–31, notes the omission from both lists of several tales which were clearly well known in the period, and speculates that the tale lists as they survive represent a 'propagandist literature' developed during the ninth to eleventh centuries by a learned class which felt its authority over traditional material increasingly threatened.

98 Mac Cana, *Learned Tales,* 25; Alwyn and Brinley Rees, *Celtic Heritage,* 271.

99 Some motifs turn up again and again; for instance, the episode of Cú Chulainn being dunked in three vats of cold water to cool his heroic ardour (ll. 594–9 in *Serglige Con Culainn*) also appears in the Boyhood Deeds section of the *Táin.*

100 For recent and extended discussions of these issues, see Tomás Ó Concheanainn, 'The Source of the YBL Text of TBC,' *Ériu* 34 (1983): 175–84; 'Notes on *Togail Bruidne Da Derga,'* *Celtica* 17 (1985): 73–90; 'The Manuscript Tradition of Two Middle Irish Leinster Tales,' *Celtica* 18 (1986): 13–33; and 'Aided Nath Í and Uí Fhiachrach Genealogies,' *Éigse* 25 (1991): 1–27.

101 I use this term in a slightly different sense than Tomás Ó Cathasaigh does in his book *The Heroic Biography of Cormac mac Airt* (Dublin: DIAS, 1977). Cú Chulainn's biography consists of his birth tale, his initiation and boyhood deeds, his courtship of Emer, various adventures, his involvement in the *Táin,* his slaying of his only son, his love-sickness, and the tale of his death.

102 There are references in the early texts to *banfili* or women poets, the most

notable being Líadan in the tale *Líadan and Cuirithir*; see Kuno Meyer's edition (London: D. Nutt, 1902). Yet no texts survive which are definitely attributed to women before the Early Modern period.

103 See Proinsias Mac Cana, 'The Poet as Spouse of His Patron,' *Ériu* 39 (1988): 79–85; and Katharine Simms, 'The Poet as Chieftain's Widow: Bardic Elegies,' in *Sages, Saints and Storytellers*, 400–11.

104 *Bodytalk*, 11–12, and notes 44 and 45.

105 See Jane Chance, *Woman as Hero in Old English Literature*. Syracuse: Syracuse University Press, 1986.

1: *The Wooing of Emer*: The Sweet Speech of Courtship

1 'Es gibt wohl keine andere irische Sage, in die so viel fremde Sagenbestandteile ... aufgenommen worden sind,' *Die irische Helden- und Königsage bis zum 17. Jahrhundert* (Halle: Niemeyer, 1921), 381.

2 A.C.L. Brown, 'The Knight of the Lion,' *PMLA* New Series, vol. 13. 4 (1905): 673–706.

3 'On *Tochmarc Emere*,' *Ériu* 9 (1923): 98–108.

4 Rees and Rees, *Celtic Heritage*, 271. This is one of many passages in their study which shows the influence of Jungian ideas on their analysis of medieval Celtic texts.

5 'The Christian Revision of *Eachtra Airt Meic Cuind ocus Tochmarc Delbchaime Ingine Morgain*,' in Patrick Ford, ed., *Celtic Folklore and Christianity* (Santa Barbara: McNally & Loftin, 1983): 159–79.

6 Vincent Dunn, *Cattle-Raids and Courtships*, (New York: London Garland Publishing, 1989), especially chap. 4, 'The *Tochmarca*,' 69–96. Dunn (12–13) borrows the terms 'syntagmatic' and 'paradigmatic' from Roman Jakobson and M. Halle, *Fundamentals of Language* (The Hague: Mouton, 1956) and F. de Saussure, *Course in General Linguistics*, ed. C. Bally and A. Sechehaye, trans. A. Reidlinger (New York: McGraw-Hill, 1959, repr. 1966), and stresses that the paradigmatic courtship story is 'pointedly distanced from the world of the audience, usually by means of explicitly mythic content' and therefore does not, unlike the cattle-raid story, offer 'specific models of behaviour' (*Cattle-Raids and Courtships*, 12).

7 Dunn devotes one of his chapters to Old French narrative, and sees the Arthurian romances as the French version of the 'paradigmatic' courtship story. His views contrast in intriguing ways with Kathryn Gravdal's treatment of the same material in *Ravishing Maidens: Writing Rape in Medieval French Literature and Law* (Philadelphia: University of Pennsylvania Press, 1991), especially chapter 2.

8 See, for example, T.F. O'Rahilly, *Early Irish History and Mythology*; Marie-Louise Sjoestedt, *Gods and Heroes of the Celts*, especially chapter 3, 'The Mother-Goddesses of Ireland' and chapter 6, 'The Hero of the Tribe'; and more recently, Proinsias Mac Cana, 'Mythology in Early Irish Literature' in *The Celtic Consciousness* (Toronto: McClelland and Stewart, 1981): 143–54.

9 *Cattle-Raids and Courtships*, 73.

10 'Cú Chulainn and Yvain: The Love Hero in Early Irish and Old French Literature,' *Studies in Philology* 72.2 (April 1975): 115–39.

11 'Concepts of Eloquence in "Tochmarc Emire",' *Studia Celtica* 26/27 (1991–2): 125–54.

12 Doris Edel, *Helden auf Freiersfüssen. 'Tochmarc Emire' und 'Mal y kavas Kulhwch Olwen': Studien zur frühen inselkeltischen Erzähltradition*. Verhandelingen der Koninklijke Nederlandse Akademie van Wetenschappen, Afdeling Letterkunde, Nieuwe Reeks, Deel 107. Amsterdam: North Holland Publishing, 1980. Edel's study is a valuable one, yet is hampered by a determined quest for 'original' elements in the tale which causes her to devalue elements which she considers to be textual accretions.

13 Cormier, 'Cú Chulainn and Yvain,' 122. Cormier's credibility is undermined somewhat by his lack of attentiveness to some of the details of the tale. For example, he states that once in Scáthach's realm Cú Chulainn 'calmly seduces her daughter'; on the contrary, it is clear in the tale that it is the daughter who seduces *him*, and her pursuit of the hero is prefaced by one of the most striking portrayals of female desire in medieval literature.

14 A fourth recent article by John Carey, 'Otherworlds and Verbal Worlds in Middle Irish Narrative,' contains a brief discussion of *Tochmarc Emire*. Carey makes the intriguing suggestion that '*Tochmarc Emire* is a story looking at itself, a narrative concerned with narrative' and states, 'In the world of *Tochmarc Emire*, verbal and spatial journeys overlap and supplement each other'; see *Proceedings of the Harvard Celtic Colloquium* 9 (1989): 33, 35. As interesting as it is, Carey's article is of little relevance to the study of Emer's speech in the narrative.

15 Muireann Ní Bhrolcháin's recent statement that, like Étaín, Emer 'wait[s] for [her] proper prince to come like the docile Cinderella, Snow White and Sleeping Beauty of the fairy tales' seems to me to be a misreading of the text as a whole; see '*Re Tóin Mná*: In Pursuit of Troublesome Women,' *Ulidia*, ed. J.P. Mallory and G. Stockman (Belfast: December Publications, 1994): 117.

16 I use the terminology of speech act theorists J.L. Austin and John R. Searle. See Austin, *How to Do Things with Words* (Cambridge: Harvard University Press, 1962) and Searle, *Speech Acts: An Essay on the Philosophy of Language* (Oxford: Oxford University Press, 1971).

17 The agonistic level mirrors the paradigm established by the heroic warrior society itself: every person is a potential combatant until he or she has proven personal worth.

18 Mac Cana, *Learned Tales*, 41ff. 'List A,' which is found in the twelfth-century Book of Leinster as well as the later Trinity College MS H.3.17, is the fuller of the two, listing thirteen *tochmarca* in all: *Tochmarc Meidbe/Neime, Tochmarc Emire, Tochmarc Ailbe/Aillme, Tochmarc Etaine, Tochmarc Faefe/Fea, Tochmarc Feirbe, Tochmarc Finnine, Tochmarc Greine Finne, Tochmarc Greine Duinne, Tochmarc Saidbe, Tochmarc Fithirne 7 Darine, Tochmarc mna Cruinn,* and *Tochmarc Eithne Uathaige.* Not all of these tales survive today.

19 Vincent Dunn's introduction to *Cattle-Raids and Courtships* provides one definition of the boundaries between these two sub-genres. I use the term 'mythical' here to designate narratives with overt and sustained supernatural elements which seem central to their structure.

20 The text has been edited and translated by Osborn Bergin and R.I. Best in *Ériu* 12 (1937): 137–96.

21 Edited and translated into German by Rudolph Thurneysen, *ZCP* 13 (1921): 251–82.

22 Edited by Wolfgang Meid, (Dublin: DIAS, 1967). All quotations are from this edition.

23 Edited and translated by R. Best, *Ériu* 3 (1907): 149–73.

24 *Fidchell* features frequently in medieval Irish tales as a board game with human figures that was popular among the upper classes (especially royalty).

25 The depiction of Findabair in this tale is sharply at odds with the portrait of her in the *Táin*, where she is the beautiful but passive daughter used by Medb and Ailill as a bribe to induce young men to fight against the enemy Cú Chulainn in single combat.

26 The *Táin Bó Fraích* consists of two sections, one (the portion discussed here) a 'wooing,' the other a 'cattle-raid' in which Froech must go in search of his stolen cattle. In the latter section he already has a wife and children, and Findabair is not mentioned. See Carney's discussion, *Studies in Irish Literature and History*, 27–65.

27 'This is what Findabair used to say afterwards when she saw any beautiful thing: that it was more beautiful for her to see Froech coming across the [river] Dublind, the body for shining whiteness and the hair for loveliness, the face for shapeliness, the eye so blue-grey, and he a gentle youth without fault or blemish, face broad above, narrow below, and he straight and perfect, the branch with the red berries between the throat and the white face. This is what Findabair used to say: that she had never seen anything

half or a third as beautiful as he.' Translation is by Carney, *Studies in Irish Literature and History*, 7–8. This passage is briefly discussed by Ann Dooley, in 'The Invention of Women in the *Táin*,' *Ulidia*, ed. J.P. Mallory and G. Stockman (Belfast: December Publications, 1994): 129.

28 Meid, *Táin Bó Fraích*, 36, ll. 129–33. The English translation is Carney's, 6.

29 Meid, *Táin Bó Fraích*, 39, ll. 258–60; translation by Carney, 10.

30 See R. Thurneysen's edition, 'Tochmarc Ailbe "Das Werben um Ailbe",' *ZCP* 13 (1921): 251–82. Although the tale is probably later in its original composition than *Tochmarc Emire*, Ailbe is mentioned in several twelfth-century sources including the Book of Leinster.

31 O Hehir, 'The Christian Revision of *Eachtra Airt Meic Cuind*,' 159.

32 Bécuma is clearly subject to clerical censure in this text, which shows many signs of having undergone a thorough Christian reworking.

33 R.I. Best, ed. and trans., 'The Adventures of Art Son of Conn, and the Courtship of Delbchaem,' *Ériu* 3 (1907): 168, par. 24; trans. 169.

34 Best, 'The Adventures of Art Son of Conn', 168, par. 25; trans. 169. It is interesting to compare the wording of *Tochmarc Emire*'s enumeration of Emer's qualities:

... is sí congab na sé búada fuirri .i. búaid crotha, búaid ngotha, búaid mbindiusa, búaid ndruine, búaid ngaíse, búaid ngensa [Van Hamel, ed, *Compert Con Culainn and Other Stories*, 23, par. 10].

... it is she who possessed the six gifts, that is the gift of lovely shape, the gift of voice, the gift of sweet speech, the gift of embroidery, the gift of intelligence, the gift of chastity [my translation].

35 Doris Edel, *Helden auf Freiersfüssen*, 98.

36 Fergus Kelly, *A Guide to Early Irish Law*, 1. All of the surviving early Irish legal texts have been edited (without translation) by Daniel Binchy in his monumental 6–volume *Corpus Iuris Hibernici*, hereafter cited as *CIH* (Dublin: DIAS, 1978).

37 The law-text *Cáin Lánamna* distinguishes nine or ten different unions; see Binchy, *CIH*, 502, l. 29–519, l. 35. It is also edited and translated (into German) by Thurneysen in *SEIL*, 1–75.

38 See Kelly's discussion of marriage laws in *A Guide to Early Irish Law*, 70–3.

39 There is a later story in which Emer elopes with another man, and which contains some interesting antifeminist statements; see Kuno Meyer's edition of *Aithed Emere le Tuir n-Glesta mac ríg Lochlann* in 'Anecdota from the Stowe Ms. No. 992,' *Révue celtique* 6 (1894): 184.

40 Alwyn & Brinley Rees, *Celtic Heritage*, 267.
41 In fact, the area where she dwells was part of the Viking settlement which included Dublin and its environs from A.D. 841 onward; this would also contribute to the sense that she is exempt from normal restraints. However, see discussion below.
42 See especially Alain Renoir, 'A Reading Context for "The Wife's Lament",' in *Anglo-Saxon Poetry: Essays in Appreciation*, ed. L.E. Nicholson and D.W. Frese (Notre Dame: University of Notre Dame Press, 1975): 114–41.
43 The most accessible discussion of the theory's application to literature is that of Mary Louise Pratt, *Toward a Speech Act Theory of Literary Discourse* (Bloomington: Indiana University Press, 1977), especially chapter 3. For a good discussion of the pitfalls of applying speech act theory to literature see Stanley Fish, 'How to Do Things with Austin and Searle: Speech Act Theory and Literary Criticism,' *Modern Language Notes* 91 (1976): 983–1025.
44 Sayers, 'Concepts of Eloquence in *Tochmarc Emire*,' 129.
45 Austin and Searle distinguish between 'perlocutionary acts' and 'perlocutionary effects'; see Austin, *How to Do Things with Words*, 101–3, Searle, *Speech Acts*, 25, 46. A perlocutionary act carries with it the intention to produce effects in the hearer beyond those of the illocutionary act itself. A perlocutionary effect is not necessarily the effect *intended* by the speaker. For a more thorough discussion of intention, see Searle, 'What is a Speech Act?' in Searle, ed., *The Philosophy of Language* (Oxford: Oxford University Press, 1971): 39–53.
46 Baudió, 'On Tochmarc Emere,' 105 and notes.
47 Sayers, 'Concepts of Eloquence,' 128.
48 Edel, *Helden auf Freiersfüssen*, 212–13. For gnomes, see H.M. and N.K. Chadwick, *The Growth of Literature*, vol. 1 (Cambridge: Cambridge University Press, 1932): 377ff.
49 Thurneysen's edition, *ZCP* 13 (1921): 270, l. 4, trans. by John Carey. I am grateful to Dr Carey for sending me a copy of his forthcoming English translation of the tale. Carey notes that Ailbe's answer here is a play on the homonyms *linn* (lake) and *linn* (liquid).
50 Here Thurneysen (270) lists variants in other manuscripts which give Ailbe's answer a more specific sense: 'Briathra carad im chuirm vel tochmairc' and 'Briathra tochmhuirce' ('Words of a friend around the cup, or of courtship' and 'words of courtship').
51 This is Thurneysen's emendation; his note reads: 'l. étrumu.' Carey's translation follows the original reading, not Thurneysen's.
52 Probably because his translation is intended for a general audience, Carey does not acknowledge the variant readings. However, they are an important indication of the specific concern with courtship here.

53 The sense of this line may be 'the mind of a woman wavering between two prospective mates.' The last two examples cited here seem to carry clear misogynist undertones, in identifying woman as an unstable creature. One might argue that Ailbe here is simply supplying Finn with the kind of patriarchal stereotyping he expects to hear, in order to win the riddling contest; her triumph over Finn in clever speech at the end of the tale suggests that Ailbe is able to manipulate discourse for her own purposes.

54 Thurneysen, 'Tochmarc Ailbe "Das Werben um Ailbe",' 280–1.

55 Citations (Irish and English) are from the most recent edition of these verses by Karin Olsen, 'The Cuckold's Revenge: Reconstructing Six Irish *Roscada* in *Táin Bó Cúailnge*,' *Cambrian Medieval Celtic Studies* 28 (Winter 1994): 51–69; for the passage cited here, see p. 55.

56 Olsen, 'The Cuckold's Revenge,' 61. Olsen discusses both the many textual problems and the interpersonal dynamics in this scene.

57 Olsen, 'The Cuckold's Revenge', 65–6. Although this passage is difficult, Olsen points out that it nevertheless shows Medb defending her actions masterfully; here she justifies her behaviour as political strategy.

58 Olsen, 'The Cuckold's Revenge,' 68.

59 Tomás Ó Cathasaig maintains that this pronoun refers to Mael Fothartaig, not to the fool Mac Glass; see 'Varia III: The Trial of Mael Fothartaig,' *Ériu* 36 (1985): 179. My discussion assumes that he is correct.

60 David Greene, ed., *Fingal Rónáin and Other Stories* (Dublin: DIAS, 1955): 6–7. My translation is based on that of T.M. Charles-Edwards, 'Honour and Status in Some Irish and Welsh Prose Tales,' *Ériu* 29 (1978):132, and the alternate suggestions made by Tomás Ó Cathasaigh, 'Varia III: The Trial of Mael Fothartaig,' 177–80. As Charles-Edwards points out, 'The Cows of Aífe may be, as the gloss says, rocks on the mountain-side, but probably ... they were a conventional meeting place for the purpose that the daughter of Echaid had in mind [a trysting place]' (135).

61 The text of LU reads: 'Doriacht Cu Chulaind co airm i mbátár in ingenrad foí sin. 7 bennachais dóib'; see Bergin and Best's edition, 310, ll. 10237–8.

62 In early Irish culture, driving left-hand-wise around someone or something signified a challenge or insult; moving right-hand-wise signified good will.

63 Literally, 'safety of eye-defect to you.' All citations are taken from A.G. Van Hamel's edition, *Compert Con Culainn and Other Stories* (Dublin: DIAS, 1956); this phrase is found on p. 26, par. 17. All translations are my own.

64 Among these is St Brigit, who drives around the countryside in her chariot with her female attendants; see Donncha Ó hAodha, ed. and trans., *Bethu Brigte* (Dublin: DIAS, 1978): 9, #29; trans. 27.

65 There may be an intentional *double entendre* here, since the word *feis(s)* / *fess*

is the verbal noun of *foaid*, 'spends the night' and has the primary meaning of 'spending the night, sleeping'; the word thus came to mean 'sleeping with another person, coition.' A secondary meaning was 'food, supper, feast'; see *DIL*, s.v.

66 Van Hamel, ed., *Compert Con Culainn and Other Stories*, 26, #17. Emer's questions are perhaps reminiscent of the questions asked of St Patrick by the daughters of King Loíguire in Tírechán's Latin life: 'Ubi vos sitis et unde uenistis? ...' ('Whence are you and whence have you come? ...'); see Ludwig Bieler, ed. and trans., *The Patrician Texts in the Book of Armagh*, Scriptores Latini Hiberniae, vol. 10 (Dublin: DIAS, 1970): 142, #26, trans. 143.

67 This meaning derives *forfóemthar* from *foeim, -foim -fóem*, 'accepts, receives.' Alternatively, this may be read as 'that does not fail,' deriving *forfóemthar* from *fo-émid*, 'fails'; *DIL*, s.v.

68 This phrase is often translated as 'a watchman who is not farseeing,' but there may be a cultural significance to this phrase, which seems to refer to an ideal of social decorum for chaste women. My translation here reflects this idea.

69 This phrase is difficult; my translation assumes it is a place-name, but this is extremely tentative.

70 Beds were often made of rushes in medieval Ireland; hence, the idea of 'rushes not broken' also refers to her chastity, and continues the sexual subtext in her words.

71 The remainder of this phrase is extremely obscure and cannot be translated.

72 Van Hamel, *Compert Con Culainn*, 27, #18. My translation of this passage must remain tentative. Van Hamel's text includes the glosses from the later manuscript 'H' which the LU text omits; compare Bergin and Best's edition of LU, *Lebor na hUidre*, 311, ll. 10254–60.

73 Sayers, 'Concepts of Eloquence,' 130.

74 For instance: Temair ḇan
              ḇaine i̱ngen
              i̱nching gensa
   As Doris Edel notes (*Helden aus freiersfüssen*, 236), the text is corrupt in places and the alliteration lost.

75 See below for a fuller discussion of Emer's reference to Tara.

76 Meyer, 'The Oldest Version of Tochmarc Emire,' 435, points out that *garta*, the genitive of *gart*, is often glossed by *enech*, the usual word for 'honour,' or *féile*, 'liberality, bounty, hospitality.'

77 O'Leary, 'The Honour of Women in Early Irish Literature,' 40.

78 It is perhaps important to note the contrast between Emer's controlled behaviour here and that of Scáthach's daughter Uathach, whose uncon-

trolled gaze of desire upon the hero leads her to seek permission from her mother to make him her lover. See discussion below.

79 Findabair's admiring gaze upon the physical beauty of her suitor Froech in *Táin Bó Fraích* (noted earlier) would be a contrasting example.

80 Mac Cana, *Learned Tales*, 24–5; Alwyn and Brinley Rees, *Celtic Heritage*, 271.

81 Sayers, 'Concepts of Eloquence,' 132.

82 Van Hamel, *Compert Con Culainn*, 28, #21.

83 John Searle, 'A Classification of Illocutionary Acts,' *Language in Society* 5 (1976): 10.

84 Van Hamel, *Compert Con Culainn*, 30, #26. My translation here incorporates that of Edel (*Helden aus Freiersfüssen*, 108, note 36). She points out that this description of Emer as a paradigm of beauty echoes that of Étaín: 'Cruth cach co hEtain. Caem cach co hEtain' ('Beautiful is every woman until compared with Étaín. Dear is every woman until compared with Étaín').

85 Van Hamel, *Compert Con Culainn*, 30, #26; my translation here incorporates that of Sayers, 'Concepts of Eloquence,' 134.

86 Van Hamel, *Compert Con Culainn*, 31, 26–7.

87 Kelly, *A Guide to Early Irish Law*, 70–1, 72–3. The emphasis on chastity for the *cétmuinter* may be a reflection of Christian influence.

88 Van Hamel, *Compert Con Culainn*, 31, #27. Most commentators have assumed that the 'alchuing' ('yoke') referred to here is the yoke of Emer's gown; but Sayers suggests that it refers to the double yoke of the war chariot. Thus the yoke would represent Emer's breasts and the plain beyond the yoke would be her abdomen; see Sayers, 'Concepts of Eloquence,' 135.

89 Emer's naming of this ford after the future death of her aunt highlights the self-reflexive nature of the tale.

90 Van Hamel, *Compert Con Culainn*, 31, #27. The translation of this passage is very tentative due to the complicated word-play here; Edel (*Helden aus Freiersfüssen* 230) translates it as 'zum silbernen Frauenjoch, auf welchem die schnellsprudelnde Brea Fedelm strömen lässt'(?) ('to the silver woman-yoke, on which the fast-gushing Brea has Fedelm run'?).

91 See Pratt's summary of the different kinds of speech acts in *Toward a Speech Act Theory of Literary Discourse*, 80–1.

92 Van Hamel, *Compert Con Culainn*, 32 #27. It is interesting to compare this declaration of intent with Cú Chulainn's much less structured promise of a tryst with Derbforgall, made not to the girl herself but to her father: 'ticed dia blíadnae co hÉrinn im degaidse mad áil dí, 7 fogéba messe and.' ('Let her come this day a year from now to Ireland after me if she desires, and she will find me there') (Van Hamel, *Compert Con Culainn*, 62, #82).

93 Searle, 'A Classification of Illocutionary Acts,' 11.

94 Van Hamel, *Compert Con Culainn*, 53, #73.
95 For a thorough discussion of this type of utterance see Charles-Edwards, 'Honour and Status in some Irish and Welsh Prose Tales,' 123–41.
96 It is perhaps interesting to compare Emer's *modus operandi* with that of Dornolla, the ugly daughter of Domnall in Alba who seeks revenge against Cú Chulainn for refusing to sleep with her. The text does not record a single word of Dornolla's, and her power against the hero is not verbal but magical. Dornolla clearly belongs to a sinister (non-verbal) aspect of womanhood. All of the helpful women in the tale use speech.
97 Van Hamel (*Compert Con Culainn*, 52) lists variants on this phrase: the Stowe manuscript has 'can ic tindscrae' ('without bride-price'), while two other manuscripts (Rawlinson B 512 and Harleian 5280) both read 'conicc tindscrae' ('with bride-price').
98 Van Hamel, *Compert Con Culainn*, 51–2, # 70.
99 Van Hamel, *Compert Con Culainn*, 54, #76.
100 P.L. Henry, '*Verba Scáthaige,*' *Celtica* 21 (1990): 191–207.
101 This seems to have been a chariot with blades protruding from the wheels.
102 Van Hamel, *Compert Con Culainn*, 63–4, # 86–7.
103 Van Hamel, *Compert Con Culainn*, 23, #10.
104 Kelly (*A Guide to Early Irish Law*, 78) notes that women who were skilled at embroidery had unusual legal status: 'The author of the text on pledge-interests (*Bretha im Fuillema Gell*) attaches more significance to the use of the articles pledged by women than to the rank of the donor. He points out that the interest on the needle of an embroideress extends up to an ounce of silver "because the woman who embroiders earns more profit even than queens".' The text cited here has been edited by Binchy, *CIH*, 464, ll. 2–3.
105 The Irish word is *gaes* (DIL, *s.v.*) which means 'sagacity, intelligence, acuteness.'
106 Van Hamel, *Compert Con Culainn*, 27 #18.
107 DIL, *s.v.*
108 Emer plays on both meanings of the word here.
109 By the twelfth century, Tara's image as 'prize' had shifted from political reality to literary motif.
110 Gray, *Cath Maige Tuired*, ll.230–93; trans. 39, 41. There may be a subtle yet intentional parallel between Lug's difficulty in obtaining entrance to Tara and the difficulty his mortal 'son' Cú Chulainn will have in gaining access (specifically, sexual access) to Emer, a human, female incarnation of Tara.
111 Whitley Stokes, ed. and trans., 'The Bodleian Dinnshenchas,' *Folk-Lore* 3 (1892): 470. The text offers an alternate explanation of the name, linking

it instead with another Tea, the wife of one of the sons of Míl of Spain, who was allegedly buried there. Both explanations link the place with women.

112 Sjoestedt, *Gods and Heroes of the Celts*, chap. 6.
113 Donncha Ó Corráin, 'Women in Early Irish Society,' 1–13.

2: *Bricriu's Feast*: Women's Words as Weapons

1 Each of the three noble women has, of course, her retinue of fifty (nameless, voiceless) women who accompany her at all times.
2 Medb's strategy of assuring each hero that he is her choice for the *curadmir* parallels that of Bricriu at the beginning of the tale; and although her motivation is clearly not that of pure mischief as it is for Bricriu, the strategic similarities between the two scenes inevitably highlights Medb's deceitfulness. Bláthnat's betrayal of her husband is very much a Samson and Delilah tale; see R.I. Best's edition and translation, 'The Tragic Death of Cúrói Mac Dári,' *Ériu* 2 (1905): 18–35.
3 The tragic subtext is hinted at through the presence of both Bláthnat and Cú Roí; the lonely testing of Cú Chulainn throughout the many episodes of the tale recalls his solitary defence of Ulster in the *Táin*.
4 For a thorough discussion of the repetitive phrases characteristic of misogynistic discourse see Bloch's *Medieval Misogyny*.
5 LU folio 99b, ll. 8038–40 in Bergin and Best, eds., *Lebor na hUidre*.
6 See D.A. Binchy, 'The Legal Capacity of Women,' in *SEIL*, 215.
7 See Nancy Power, 'The Classes of Women Described in *Senchas Már*,' *SEIL*, 99.
8 T.M. Charles-Edwards, 'Honour and Status' in 'Some Irish and Welsh Prose Tales,' *Ériu* 29 (1978): 123–4.
9 Charles-Edwards, 'Honour and Status,' 128–9.
10 Charles-Edwards, 'Honour and Status,' 131–40.
11 Feasts are almost always arenas of conflict in early Irish literature, partly because seating arrangements and protocol within the hall are intensely status-oriented. Other tales involving conflicts at feasts include *The Intoxication of the Ulstermen* (*Mesca Ulad*) and the later *Feast of the Fort of the Geese* (*Fled Dúin na nGéd*). See Philip O'Leary's article, 'Contention at Feasts in Early Irish Literature,' *Éigse* 20 (1984): 115–27.
12 See Rudolf Thurneysen, ed., *Scéla Mucce Meic Dathó* (Dublin: DIAS, 1935): 13, #14. The translation is my own.
13 Michael Herren, ed. and trans., *The Hisperica Famina I: The A-Text* (Toronto: Pontifical Institute for Mediaeval Studies, 1974): 64–5, ll. 20–31.

14 See Herren's discussion of these issues in his introduction to *Hisperica Famina*, 27–44.

15 Another example of a verbal contest between two men is *Immacallam in Dá Thuarad*, ed. Whitley Stokes, 'The Colloquy of the Two Sages,' *Révue celtique* 26 (1905): 4–64 which describes the verbal duel between an older poet and a younger poet.

16 Rudolf Thurneysen, ed., 'Tochmarc Ailbe "Das Werben um Ailbe",' *ZCP* 13 (1921): 270. I cite the recent translation by John Carey, forthcoming.

17 For an edition of the text see Bergin and Best, 'Tochmarc Étaíne,' *Ériu* 12 (1937): 137–96. A translation can be found in Jeffrey Gantz, *Early Irish Myths and Sagas*, 39–59.

18 'Is and sin friscócbat mná Connacht forsna buidne 7 fordringtís mná firu do déscin crotha Con Culaind' ('Then the women of Connacht climbed up on the hosts and the women of Munster climbed on men's shoulders that they might behold the appearance of Cú Chulainn'); Cecile O'Rahilly, ed. and trans., *Táin Bó Cúailnge: Recension I*, (Dublin: DIAS, 1976): 72, ll. 2367–8, trans. 190.

19 Myles Dillon, ed., *Serglige Con Culainn* (Dublin: 1975) ll. 25–31. The translation is my own.

20 Dillon, ed., *Serglige Con Cullainn*, ll. 52–6.

21 The first part of *Aided Lugdach ocus Derbforgaille* corresponds closely to an episode in *Serglige Con Culainn*, the tale discussed in chapter 4.

22 Carl Marstrander, 'The Deaths of Lugaid and Derbforgaill,' *Ériu* 5 (1911): 208–9, ll. 17–27; trans. 214–15.

23 Lisa Bitel discusses this tale in her article, '"Conceived in Sins, Born in Delights": Stories of Procreation from Early Ireland,' *Journal of the History of Sexuality*, vol. 3, no. 2 (1992): 181–202. Regarding the connection between sex and urination, she cites Charles Bowen's comments in 'Great-Bladdered Medb: Mythology and Invention in the *Táin Bó Cuailnge*,' (*Éire/Ireland* 10 [1975]: 26–33) that 'a woman's sexual power [is measured] by the capacity of her "inner space," with the bladder undoubtedly serving as an analogue for the vagina and uterus.' Bitel speculates that a woman's urination skills were further connected with sexuality because 'a woman who can control urination clearly has well-developed vaginal muscles' (Bitel 188, n. 23).

24 Arguments between women are depicted in the later lament poetry; see, for instance, the verbal jousting between the grieving wife Eibhlín Dubh and her dead husband's sister in 'The Lament for Art O'Leary,' in Seán Ó Tuama, ed. and Thomas Kinsella, trans., *An Duanaire 1600–1900: Poems of the Dispossessed* (Dublin: Dolmen Press, 1981): 200ff. See also Angela Bourke's analysis of the poem in 'Performing – Not Writing,' *Graph* 1 (Winter, 1991): 28–31.

25 All citations are taken from Best and Bergin's edition of *Lebor na hUidre* (LU) (Dublin: DIAS, 1929, repr. 1992); this passage is found in LU ll. 8225–30. I am grateful to Proinsias Mac Cana for supplying me with a provisional translation of the text; the translations presented here are based on his.

26 Bricriu is punning on the name 'Lendabair' here, which is etymologically connected to the noun *lennán*, (lover, sweetheart, beloved), by extension 'darling, favourite'; *DIL* s.v.

27 The word *aíne* literally means 'brightness,' and is often translated as 'fame'; but it can also imply physical brightness, and here may refer to Lendabair's beauty.

28 LU, ll. 8236–8239.

29 Literally, 'May you sit safely.'

30 LU, ll. 8242–7. The qualities enumerated by Bricriu here recall the *sé búada* (six gifts) of Emer listed in *The Wooing of Emer*, although most of the actual terms are different (for a comparison, see chapter 1). The similarities may be due to the familiarity of the redactors with traditions about Emer. Alternatively, they may be traditional phrases for ideal women.

31 Kuno Meyer, ed. and trans., *Hail Brigit: An Old-Irish Poem on the Hill of Alenn* (Halle/Dublin: Niemeyer/Hodges, Figgis, 1912).

32 See Myles Dillon, 'The Archaism of the Early Irish Tradition,' *Proceedings of the British Academy* 33 (1947): 253.

33 See for instance, Gerard Murphy, *Early Irish Metrics* (Dublin: DIAS, 1961): 2–7; Calvert Watkins, 'Indo-European Metrics and Archaic Irish Verse,' *Celtica* 6 (1965): 194–249; and Daniel Binchy, 'Varia Hibernica: The So-called "Rhetorics" of Irish Saga,' in *Indo-Celtica* (Munich: Hueber, 1972): 29–38.

34 Carney, *Studies in Irish Literature and History*, 298.

35 Mac Cana, 'On the Use of the Term *Retoiric*,' *Celtica* 7 (1966): 89. More recently, Daniel Melia has pointed out that the marginal '.r.' is used – at least in LU – to mark non-poetic passages such as lists of place-names, feats, and the victims of Cú Chulainn; see 'Further Speculation on Marginal .R.' *Celtica* 21 (1990): 362–7.

36 Breatnach, 'Canon Law and Secular Law in Early Ireland: The Significance of the *Bretha Nemed*,' *Peritia* 3 (1984): 439, 458.

37 Aitchison, N.B., 'The Ulster Cycle: Heroic Image and Historical Reality,' *Journal of Medieval History* 13 (1987): 98.

38 While Fedelm and Lendabair speak about twenty lines each, Emer develops her arguments over forty-six lines.

39 LU, ll. 8280–7.

40 For a fuller discussion of early Irish marriage laws see chapter 4 below.

41 LU, ll. 8291–5.

42 An example of this occurs later on in *Bricriu's Feast*, ll. 8590–604. Emer's

sister Fíal's description of Cú Chulainn and his charioteer in *The Wooing of Emer* (Van Hamel, ed., *Compert Con Cullainn and Other Stories*, 24–6, #12–16) is another example.

43 The fact that Bricriu has also avoided mentioning Lóegaire's family might imply that he is of lower status than his wife who is, after all, the daughter of the king, Conchobar.

44 LU, ll. 8302–17.

45 This Amorgin appears to be the same poet whom Cú Chulainn lists as one of his fosterers in *The Wooing of Emer* (Van Hamel, ed., *Compert Con Culainn*, 30, #24).

46 Presumably from *coibled* (activity, vigour); *DIL*, s.v. Mac Cana suggests 'sheer vivacity.'

47 From *sóer* (noble, free) (in a legal sense) + *lige* (lying down, sleeping); *DIL*, s.v. *saer*, *lige*. This may be another hint of the importance placed on the first marriage and the status of the *cétmuinter*. Mac Cana translates instead 'never has there been loving passion in a noble couch.'

48 Or, 'good sense,' s.v. *cíall*. Mac Cana translates 'quickness of mind.'

49 This translation assumes *fuither* is derived from *foídir* (to send). The passage is unclear.

50 This is Mac Cana's solution to a difficult reading. The *DIL* lists this occurrence of the word separately from *adarc*, *aiderc* (horn), and offers no translation. However, it may mean something like 'the horned ones.'

51 This is a very tentative translation of a difficult line. *Chutma* could be from *cutaim* (collapse).

52 This is tentative. Mac Cana suggests an alternative reading in which the subject is Cú Chulainn instead of the Ulstermen: 'He is likened to bright red blood.' This involves reading *samlaithir* for *samlaitir*.

53 *Crothle* could be from *crothal* (a rattle). The DIL makes no attempt to translate *garmilíne*.

54 LU, ll. 8323–68. The language of the passage is difficult and many phrases are unclear.

55 LU, ll. 8337–40.

56 Ann Dooley points out the extent to which Emer's use of blood imagery here echoes Fedelm's similar description of Cú Chulainn in the *Táin*, as well as that of Emer's own elegy in her husband's death tale; see 'The Invention of Women in the *Táin*,' *Ulidia*, ed, J.P. Mallory & G. Stockman, 129.

57 LU, ll. 8344–6.

58 Charles-Edwards, 'Honour and Status,' 138; he cites in support of this the law tract *Críth Gablach*, which deals in detail with rank in early Irish society.

59 Literally, the 'nine-days debility.' This strange condition, which reduced the

Ulstermen to weakness in times of battle need, was a result of the curse of the goddess Macha; see Bergin, Best, and O'Brien, eds., *Noínden Ulad 7 Emuin Machae*, in *The Book of Leinster*, vol. 2 (Dublin: DIAS, 1956): 467–8, folios 125b l. 2 – 126a l. 30.

60 LU, l. 8327.

61 LU, ll. 8330–1.

62 LU, ll. 8332–4.

63 Searle, 'A Classification of Illocutionary Acts,' 10–11.

64 The word *laíches* denotes a married laywoman, but its connections with the masculine form *laích, láech* (warrior) give it the extended meaning of 'wife of a warrior' or perhaps in some cases 'female warrior' (*DIL*, s.v.). It is possible that these secondary senses are present in Sencha's use of the word; certainly by engaging in the *bríatharcath* the women have shown themselves to be 'female warriors.'

65 LU, ll. 8423–38. The tentative translation here is my own.

66 The meaning of this phrase is obscure, and appears variously as *bruud gine* and *brud ngeme* in other sources. In his discussion of martial feats Sayers suggests that *brúd ngeme* is the correct reading and translates 'crushing (of) roar'; see his 'Martial Feats in the Old Irish Ulster Cycle,' *The Canadian Journal of Irish Studies* 9, no. 1 (1983): 58.

67 LU, ll. 8440–54. It is interesting to note the similarities between Emer's list of her husband's gifts here and the list of *her own* gifts given at the beginning of *Tochmarc Emire*: 'búaid crotha, búaid ngotha, búaid mbindiusa, búaid ndruine, búaid ngaíse, búaid ngensa ... bad chomacdais dó ar aís 7 cruth 7 cenél ...' ('the gift of shape, the gift of voice, the gift of sweet speech, the gift of embroidery, the gift of intelligence, the gift of chastity ... [he would not marry a woman of Erin unless] she was his match in people and form and race') (*The Wooing of Emer*, Van Hamel, ed., 23, #10).

68 LU, ll. 8467–8.

69 Thurneysen (*Heldensage*, 447–9) suggests that the various versions of *Fled Bricrend* were combined with greater or lesser skill by several redactors. Thus, apparently contradictory moments such as this may be due to an awkward joining of versions in the Reviser's source (the page in question was written by the Reviser of LU). For a more detailed discussion of the Reviser, see the Appendix.

3: The Death of Aífe's Only Son: 'Do not slay your only son'

1 Elizabeth A. Gray, ed. and trans., *Cath Maige Tuired: The Second Battle of Mag Tuired* (London: Irish Texts Society, vol. 52, 1982); Kuno Meyer, ed., 'The

Quarrel between Finn and Oisín,' in *Fianaigecht*, RIA Todd Lecture Series, vol. 16 (Dublin: Hodges, Figgis, 1910): 22–7; Richard J. O'Duffy, ed. and trans., *Oide Cloinne Tuireann: The Fate of the Children of Tuireann* (Dublin: M.H. Gill and Son, 1901).

2 Gray, *Cath Maige Tuired*, 34–7.
3 The other father-son conflict in *The Second Battle of Mag Tuired* – that between Dian Cécht and his son Míach – *does* end in the father's slaying of his son. The two disagree over the appropriate form of healing for Núadu's missing hand. Dian Cécht forges a new hand out of silver, but Míach has the power to restore a hand of flesh and bone. His father opposes this healing and strikes his son three times with a sword in an attempt to kill him, but each time the son heals himself with his power. The fourth blow kills him. Possibly Míach's healing power is considered too dangerous to be allowed to continue, since it seems to defy death itself. At any rate, the father-son conflict here seems to involve more than simple rivalry. See Gray, *Cath Maige Tuired*, 33.
4 Meyer, *Fianaigecht*, 22–7.
5 O'Duffy, *Oide Cloinne Tuireann*, 67–136. For a fuller discussion of the father-son conflict in these tales see Tom Peete Cross, '"Sohrab and Rustum" in Ireland,' *Journal of Celtic Studies* 1 (1950): 176–82.
6 Elizabeth A. Gray, 'Lug and Cú Chulainn: King and Warrior, God and Man,' *Studia Celtica* 24/25 (1989/90): 47.
7 Gray, *Cath Maige Tuired*, 49.
8 Cecile O'Rahilly, ed., *Táin Bó Cúalnge from the Book of Leinster* (Dublin: DIAS, 1967, repr. 1984): 96, ll. 3456–9, trans. 231.
9 See Cecile O'Rahilly, *Táin Bó Cúailnge: Recension 1* (Dublin: DIAS, 1976): ll. 399–824; trans. 136–48; and her edition *Táin Bó Cúalnge from the Book of Leinster*, ll. 739–1216, trans. 158–71.
10 O'Rahilly, *Recension 1*: ll. 799–802, 807–10; trans. 147.
11 In his edition of the tale, Van Hamel (*Compert Con Culainn*, 11) emends *na airberthe* to *na hairberta*, and glosses this plural form as 'intelligence, conscience' (137).
12 Kuno Meyer, 'The Death of Conla,' *Ériu* 1 (1904): 113–21. All references will be to this edition. Passage cited is 114; my translation is based on Meyer's (115).
13 The Irish text is from Van Hamel's edition of *Tochmarc Emire* in *Compert Con Culainn and Other Stories* (Dublin: DIAS, 1978), 55, #76. The translation is my own.
14 Van Hamel, *Compert Con Culainn*, 22, #7.

15 In her edition of the *Prose Banshenchas* (PhD dissertation, Galway, 1980, 84) Muirenn Ní Bhrolcháin notes the names of a son and a daughter supposedly born to Cú Chulainn's wife Eithne Inguba; but since the *Banshenchas* text is later and apparently dependent on *Tochmarc Emire* and *Serglige Con Culainn* for its information, this is likely a later addition and not an independent tradition.

16 Edward Gwynn, ed. and trans., *The Metrical Dindshenchas*, Part 4, *RIA Todd Lecture Series*, vol. 11 (Dublin: Hodges, Figgis, 1924): 132–3, and Whitley Stokes, 'The Rennes Dindsenchas,' *Révue celtique* 16 (1895): 46–7. Geoffrey Keating, writing much later, also summarizes the tale, giving a fair amount of detail about the circumstances of the boy's birth and travel to Ireland but then dispensing with the combat between father and son in a few lines. See Patrick S. Dineen, ed. & trans., *History of Ireland*, Irish Texts Society, vol. 8 (1908): 216–19.

17 Gwynn, *The Metrical Dindshenchas*, vol. 12, part 5 (1935): 95.

18 Gwynn, *The Metrical Dindshenchas*, vol 11, part 4 (1924): 132. All quotations are from this edition.

19 Gwynn, *The Metrical Dindshenchas*, 132, ll. 9–12; trans. 133.

20 See Edward Gwynn's introduction to his edition of the *Metrical Dindshenchas*, part 5, vol. 12, 111. See also Tomás Ó Concheanainn, 'The Three Forms of Dinnshenchas Érenn,' *The Journal of Celtic Studies* 3 (1981): 88–131, and 'A Pious Redactor of Dinnshenchas Érenn,' *Ériu* 33 (1982): 85–98.

21 This is a tentative translation.

22 This is the translation offered in the *DIL*, s.v. *atharda*.

23 Whitley Stokes, 'The Rennes Dindsenchas,' *Révue celtique* 16 (1895): 46–7, edited from an Irish manuscript in the library at Rennes. This portion of the manuscript was probably written in the fourteenth or fifteenth centuries but the text may date to the eleventh or twelfth centuries. The translation is my own, based on that offered by Stokes.

24 This is the Trinity College manuscript H.3.17, a miscellaneous vellum codex copied in the sixteenth century. An edition and translation of this text was published by J.G. O'Keeffe 'Cuchulinn and Conlaech,' in *Ériu* 1 (1904): 123–7. A more recent edition is found in Daniel Binchy's *Corpus Iuris Hibernici* (1978): 2127 l. 191 – 2128 l. 17. Citations are from the latter, and translations are my own.

25 Binchy's edition has 'aenfer aibe'; see *CIH*, 2127, l. 23. 842.23.

26 Fergus Kelly, *A Guide to Early Irish Law* (Dublin: DIAS, 1988): 127–8. Early Ireland, like early Germanic societies, assigned a price (analogous to

wergild), based on social status, to each person. If a person were killed, a payment in this amount had to be paid to the victim's kin-group to prevent them from taking revenge on the perpetrator. Theoretically, any crime could be paid for in this way, and blood feuds could thereby be avoided.

27 Binchy, *CIH*, 14, l. 16.
28 *CIH*, 15, l. 4.
29 *CIH*, 1301, l. 39 – 1302, l. 1; Kelly, *A Guide to Early Irish Law*, 220.
30 See Seán Mac Airt and Gearóid Mac Niocaill, eds. and trans., *The Annals of Ulster* (Dublin: DIAS, 1983). The period of increase is A.D. 803–1123. The period between 1102–96 is similarly filled with incidents of *fingal* in *The Annals of Inisfallen*; see Seán Mac Airt's edition (Dublin: DIAS, 1951).
31 The phrase 'é mád roba hi sídaib do-sein' is difficult, chiefly because of the possible meanings of the word 'síd,' which can mean both 'peace' and 'fairy mound, Otherworld dwelling.' O'Keeffe, 'Cuchulinn and Conlaech,' translates 'though he belonged to them' and places a question mark after this. 'Sídaib' could mean 'peace-contracts,' but this seems hardly applicable to Connla's warlike entrance on the scene.
32 That is, a native, a 'law-abiding freeman'; see Kelly, *A Guide to Early Irish Law*, 304.
33 *CIH*, 2128, ll. 4–15. The translation is mine, based on O'Keeffe's.
34 Kelly, *A Guide to Early Irish Law*, 151, cites an example regarding illegal distraint in *CIH*, 1726, l. 29 – 1737, l. 28, and goes on to note that the penalties for some crimes were waived altogether if the perpetrator acted in ignorance.
35 See T.M Charles-Edwards' discussion in 'The Social Background to Irish *Peregrinatio*,' *Celtica* 11 (1976): 46–50.
36 Kelly, *Guide to Early Irish Law*, 5–6.
37 Kelly, *Guide to Early Irish Law*, 6.
38 *CIH*, 2128, ll. 9–10. It is interesting to compare the insistence of this legal text on the boy's alien status with the contrasting view implied in the prose *dinnshenchas* cited earlier, in which the verse calls Ulster Connla's *atharda* ('patrimony').
39 Kelly, *Guide to Early Irish Law*, 75 cites as an example *CIH*, 45 l. 3.
40 See Kelly's discussion, *Guide to Early Irish Law*, 207. The most common sexual context seems to be determining whether or not a husband is impotent. The testimony of a female witness is also accepted in a case where a husband claims his wife has an incurable defect which prevents her from having sexual relations with him; a woman can examine the wife to determine the truth of his claim, and this woman's word is considered legally valid. See David Greene, 'Varia I,' *Ériu* 33 (1982): 161–3.

41 *CIH*, 45, l. 11; Kelly, *Guide to Early Irish Law*, 207.
42 *CIH*, 351, l. 26, 443, l. 30 – 444, l. 6. Binchy ('The Legal Capacity of Women in Regard to Contracts,' *SEIL*, 207–34) notes an apparent development in the rights of women throughout the surviving texts, and suggests that by the time the *Cáin Lánamna* (The Law of Couples) was written down, 'the archaic incapacity of women had begun to break down' (210) and women were increasingly able to make contracts independently of their husbands. He does not mention a corresponding increase in women's ability to act as witnesses.
43 For example, a woman's full honour-price was payable if she were kissed against her will (*CIH*, 2229, l. 15). See Kelly, *Guide to Early Irish Law*, 136–7.
44 Philip O'Leary points out that in the medieval tales the 'sacrifice of life – that of others or one's own – is far easier for the Irish warrior than the sacrifice of ego'; 'Magnanimous Conduct in Irish Heroic Literature,' *Éigse* 25 (1991): 38–9.
45 O'Leary, '*Fír fer*: An Internalized Ethical Concept in Early Irish Literature?' *Éigse* 22 (1987): 1.
46 Meyer, 'The Death of Conla,' 116, #5; Harry Roe, in a personal communication with me, suggests that *nimardraic* may derive from *arthraigid(ir)* (appears to), but even so the meaning of the phrase is unclear.
47 Meyer, 'The Death of Conla,' 116, #7.
48 Meyer, 'The Death of Conla,' 118, #9.
49 Cecile O'Rahilly, ed., *Táin Bó Cúalnge from the Book of Leinster*, 71–100, ll. 2606–3596.
50 This strange ordeal entails finishing the half-quatrain spoken by another person with a second half-quatrain of one's own. For a fuller discussion of how this verbal gaming might be perceived as a legitimate ordeal, see Charles-Edwards, 'Honour and Status,' 133–9, and Ó Cathasaigh, 'The Rhetoric of *Fingal Rónáin*,' *Celtica* 17 (1985): 139–43.
51 Charles-Edwards, 'Honour and Status,' 140.
52 Joan Radner, 'Fury Destroys the World,' *Mankind Quarterly* 23, no. 1 (fall 1982): 41–60; Donnchadh Ó Corráin, 'Historical Need and Literary Narrative,' *Proceedings of the Seventh International Congress of Celtic Studies* (Oxford: 1983): 141–58; and John Carey, 'Myth and Mythography in *Cath Maige Tuired*,' 53–69.
53 N.B. Aitchison, 'The Ulster Cycle: Heroic Image and Historical Reality,' *Journal of Medieval History* 13 (1987): 105.
54 The 'Poem of Prophecies,' edited and translated by Eleanor Knott (*Ériu* 18, 1958: 55–75) perhaps provides some context for this. Amidst a litany of (allegedly prophesied) woes is this stanza:

61. Mairfidh in mac in t-athir
    uma n-orba aenachaigh,
    7 bráthir araile,
    biaidh máthir gan míngaire.

'The son will slay the father over a heritage of a single field, and one brother another, the mother will be without tender (filial) care' (70, trans. 71). Knott dates the poem's composition to some time between 1036 and 1150, and observes that its tone fits the context of rampant war and pestilence in eleventh- and twelfth-century Ireland.

55 See Aubrey Gwynn, *The Irish Church in the Eleventh and Twelfth Centuries* (Dublin: Four Courts Press, 1992).

56 Deriving *taidbecht* from *ábacht*, which has the primary meaning of 'joke, pleasantry, humour, drollery' (*DIL*, s.v.); Ann Dooley, in a personal communication, suggests 'play-acting' as an alternative to 'bombast' in this context.

57 This translation is based on Van Hamel's emendation of *sug set* to *súgfet* in his edition of the tale in *Compert Con Culainn and Other Stories*, 14. Connla's little javelin recalls the toy javelin of Cú Chulainn in the 'Boyhood Deeds' section of the *Táin*.

58 Meyer, 'The Death of Conla,' 118, #8–9.

59 *Cluiche* is a loaded word in many of the Ulster tales. In his childhood, Cú Chulainn is presented as being at his deadliest when he is 'playing games'; and in the Book of Leinster *Táin* he laments after killing Fer Diad:

'Cluchi cách, gaíne cách
    co roich Fer Diad issin n-áth. (O'Rahilly, *Táin Bó Cúalgne from the Book of Leinster*, 99, ll. 3574–5).

'Game was all and sport was all until it came to my meeting with Fer Diad on the ford' (trans. 234).

60 Gantz (*Early Irish Myths and Sagas*, 150) translates 'round his neck,' and Meyer has 'over his neck.' But *brágaid* can also mean 'throat, gullet' (*DIL*, s.v. *brága*).

61 Dillon, ed., *Serglige Con Culainn*, ll. 179–222.

62 The relevant passages are paragraphs 5 and 6, and paragraphs 8 and 9 (references are to Meyer's edition).

63 Because of this alignment with a male hero and his warning speech, Emer, it seems to me, only partially resembles the 'hysteric' figure discussed by Hélène Cixous and Catherine Clément in *The Newly Born Woman*

(Minneapolis: University of Minnesota Press, 1986), a work which has influenced Gillian Overing and other feminist critics. Emer's challenging speech certainly introduces a dissenting voice, but her position echoes that of a male (read 'legitimate') voice within the heroic society.

64 This impulse is discussed by Carney, *Studies in Irish Literature and History*, Dublin: DIAS, 1955): 298.

65 Searle, 'A Classification of Illocutionary Acts,' 10.

66 In Searle's terminology, a directive is an attempt 'by the speaker to get the hearer to do something'; see 'A Classification of Illocutionary Acts,' 11.

67 Meyer, 'The Death of Conla,' 118, #9.

68 I cannot agree with Philip O'Leary when he states that 'Cú Chulainn rejects her rational and humane intervention brusquely but entirely logically from the point of view of his society' ('The Honour of Women,' 34). This view ignores the legal sanctions against *fingal*.

69 Meyer, 'The Death of Conla,' 120, #11.

70 Meyer, 'The Death of Conla,' 120, #12.

71 Meyer, 'The Death of Conla,' 118, #9.

72 P.L. Henry, ed., 'Verba Scáthaige,' *Celtica* 21 (1990): 191–207.

73 For a discussion of this and other examples, see Philip O'Leary, 'Magnanimous Conduct in Irish Heroic Literature,' *Éigse* 25 (1991): 28–44.

74 See Kelly's discussion of women and the marriage laws, *Guide to Early Irish Law*, 70–5.

75 There is certainly no indication that Emer is jealous of Aífe here; Philip O'Leary is likely correct in speculating that the affair with Aífe poses little threat to Emer's honour because it took place long ago and far away; see 'The Honour of Women,' 34, n.40.

76 O Hehir assumes that all women (or at least the important ones) are goddesses in disguise: 'It was in the course of wooing Émer that Cú Chulaind encountered Aífe, and Émer knows all about Aífe because Aífe is an aspect of herself. The Earth is tomb as well as womb. Cú Chulaind's acceptance – indeed his mastery – of the goddess in her terrible aspect makes him the supereminent hero'; see 'The Christian Revision of *Eachtra Airt meic Cuind*,' 176.

77 Derek S. Thomson, ed., *Branwen verch Lyr* (Dublin: DIAS, 1976): 14, ll. 365–9.

78 Despite his warning speech I would include Condere in this realm of action, since he is part of the heroic Ulster warrior band which Connla challenges.

79 Meyer, 'The Death of Conla,' 120, #13.

80 In the prose *dinnshenchas*, Cú Chulainn does raise a lament; the text states, 'Ros-fuc leis Cu cul*ainn* iarsin *coro*[n]adnacht oc [Oenach] Airrbe Rofir, 7 coro cachoin a guba' ('Thereafter Cúchulainn took him away and buried

him at Oenach Airbi Rofir, and sang his dirge'). See Whitley Stokes' edition and translation, 'The Rennes Dindsenchas,' *Révue celtique* 16 (1895): 47.

4: *The Wasting Sickness of Cú Chulainn*: The Language of Desire

1 The component *serg* in *serglige* means 'decline, wasting sickness' (*DIL*, s.v.); but a contemporary audience would have likely recognized the play on the similar word *serc* (love) since Cú Chulainn's illness is really a 'love-sickness.'
2 The definition by H.M. and Nora Chadwick of an actual, historical heroic age in *The Growth of Literature* (Cambridge: Cambridge University Press, 1932: 13–18) may seem a little outmoded now; I use the term (in quotation marks) simply because it conveniently encapsulates a number of concepts which seem important to the operation of the society depicted in the text such as the warrior ethos and the importance of honour and status.
3 This is a more correct term than 'polygamy' for the legal situation that obtained in early Ireland, for although in rare cases it seems that a woman could separate from an infertile husband to 'seek a child' with another man, it was usually the men who had multiple wives. See Binchy, *CIH*, 48, ll. 27–32, 294, l. 13; and Kelly's discussion, *A Guide to Early Irish Law*, 68–75.
4 See Mac Cana, *Learned Tales*, 20–65.
5 See Vincent Dunn, *Cattle-Raids and Courtships*, 19–96.
6 The characteristics of this type of tale are discussed by the Rees brothers in *Celtic Heritage*, 279–96.
7 Osborn Bergin and R.I. Best, ed. & trans., in 'Tochmarc Étaíne,' *Ériu* 12 (1937): 137–93. For a full summary of this tale, see chapter 1.
8 In a further structural parallel between the two tales, *The Wooing of Étaín* pits the mortal husband against the immortal in a battle for the love of Étaíne. In *The Wasting Sickness of Cú Culainn*, a mortal woman battles the immortal for Cú Chulainn's love.
9 This version is found in the Yellow Book of Lecan (YBL) and in Egerton 1782; see Eleanor Knott ed., *Togail Bruidne Da Derga* (Dublin: DIAS, 1963): 1–3. In LU, both *The Wooing of Étaín* and *The Destruction of Da Derga's Hostel* are acephalous; thus, we must rely on other manuscripts to supply the missing beginnings. But since Thurneysen (*Heldensage*, 24–5) has dated the versions of *The Destruction of Da Derga's Hostel* joined in YBL to the ninth century, it seems reasonable to assume that this version with the fairy mistress motif was well known in the tradition.
10 R.I. Best, ed. and trans., 'The Adventures of Art Son of Conn, and the Courtship of Delbchaem, *Ériu* 3 (1907): 149–73.

11 See Hans P.A. Oskamp, ed. and trans., 'Echtra Condla,' *Études celtiques* 14 (1974–5): 207–28.

12 See, for instance, Brendan O Hehir's discussion in 'The Christian Revision of *Eachtra Airt meic Cuind*,' 159–79.

13 The law tracts *Cáin Lánamna* and the *Senchas Már*, and the Heptads, all refer to several grades of wife and the possibility of having more than one wife (probably each of a different grade) at a time. See Kelly, *A Guide to Early Irish Law*, 70–5, and Donnchadh Ó Corráin, 'Marriage in Early Ireland,' 5–24. *Cáin Lánamna* has been edited and translated (into German) by Thurneysen in *SEIL*, 1–80. See also Nancy Power's discussion in the same volume, 'The Classes of Women Described in the *Senchas Már*,' 81–108.

14 This law tract is edited by Binchy in *CIH*, 2301, ll. 35–8, as well as in 'Bretha Crólige,' *Ériu* 12 (1938): 44, #57.

15 See Aubrey Gwynn, *The Twelfth Century Reform* (Dublin: Gill, 1968): 4, who translates the letter. Clearly Irish marriage laws clashed with canon law much earlier; see Ó Corráin's discussion of marriage within kindred and the marriage of heiresses in 'Irish Law and Canon Law,' in *Irland und Europa: Die Kirche im Frühmittelalter*, ed. Proinseas Ní Chathain and Michael Richter (Stuttgart: Klett-Cotta 1984): 157–61. It is likely that tensions between church law and Irish marriage law continued through the intervening centuries.

16 See the appendix for a fuller account of the Reviser's activities.

17 Nancy Power ('Classes of Women Described in the *Senchas Már*,' *SEIL*, 86–7) refers to the commentary in the Heptads and commentaries on *Lebor Aicle*. The first wife is not allowed to kill her rival, but if she does she pays reduced penalties. It seems that second wives were commonly taken in the case of the first wife's failure to bear sons. This appears to be Emer's situation, at least according to the Ulster Cycle tales.

18 Heptad 6 states that a jealous wife is exempt from fines or payment of sick-maintenance in the event that she injures her rival; see Binchy, *CIH*, 7, ll. 29–8, l. 20. Flanagan (*Irish Society, Anglo-Norman Settlers, Angevin Kingship*, 92, n. 31) suggests that serial monogamy rather than polygyny was the rule, at least among kings. However, in *Serglige Con Culainn* Cú Chulainn's confusion over Emer's objections to Fand suggests that the practice of taking a second wife while still married to the first is the custom referred to in this tale.

19 This colophon is discussed in more detail below.

20 Cecile O'Rahilly, ed. & trans., *Táin Bó Cualnge from the Book of Leinster*, 136, trans. 272.

21 Ó Corráin, 'Irish Origin Legends and Genealogy: Recurrent Aetiologies,' in

History and Heroic Tale: A Symposium, ed. T. Nyberg (Odense: Odense
University Press, 1985): 51–96.

22 For a fuller discussion of this scribe and his activities in LU, see the appendix.

23 See her introduction to *Táin Bó Cúailnge: Recension I*, xii, and xv, where she
states, 'In a text which must have been frequently handled and which had
such a large stock of stereotyped expressions and commonplaces one might
well suspect that some of the additions of the Reviser (or of his predecessor)
were not borrowings from a variant version but rather his own original
work.' In a footnote she adds, 'That some of the H-interpolations in, for
example, TBDD were inventions of H [the Reviser] himself or of his predecessor seems probable. On a leaf of smaller dimensions 93–94 intercalated
by H there are added fourteen descriptions of members of Conaire's
household' (xv, n. 3).

24 For a contrasting opinion see Myles Dillon's introduction to his edition of
the tale (*Serglige Con Culainn*, xii), where he draws attention to Thurneysen's remarks that 'we know from other texts on which the same Interpolator has worked that he was not himself the compiler, but drew his material
from compilations already made (*Heldensage* 414).' Gearóid Mac Eoin
appears to agree with this view, at least to some extent; see his recent study
'The Interpolator H in Lebor na Huidre,' *Ulidia*, 40.

25 Most scholars who have commented at all on this tale have dismissed this
episode as foreign to the original story; see Dillon's comments, *Serglige Con
Culainn*, x–xiii. He views the Lugaid Réoderg episode as having been added
by whoever compiled the two versions of the tale. More recently, Tomás Ó
Cathasaigh has suggested that the passage is included for its relevance to
kingship ideology; see 'Reflections on *Compert Con Culainn* and *Serglige Con
Culainn*,' *Ulidia*, 87–8. Translators (such as Jeffrey Gantz and Cross and
Slover) omit this episode altogether.

26 See John Carey's recent analysis in 'The Uses of Tradition in *Serglige Con
Culainn*,' *Ulidia*, 77–84.

27 See Best and Bergin, eds., *Lebor na hUidre*, 126, ll. 4034–9.

28 The question of possible irony in this text demands further attention, and is
the subject of a future study. For the purposes of this discussion, it is
sufficient to note that the *literati* of medieval Ireland were aware of notions
of *ironia*, particularly as defined by Isidore of Seville.

29 I include here Catherine McKenna's article, 'The Theme of Sovereignty in
Pwyll,' *Bulletin of the Board of Celtic Studies* 29 (1982): 35–52; Joan Radner,
'Interpreting Irony in Medieval Celtic Narrative: The Case of *Culhwch ac*

Olwen,' *CMCS* 16 (Winter 1988): 41–5; and Margaret Sinex, 'Irony in Walter Map's De Nugis Curialium' (PhD dissertation, University of Toronto, 1993).

30 Siân Echard, 'Expectation and Experimentation in Medieval Arthurian Narrative: A Study of Anglo-Latin, Middle English and Middle Welsh Texts' (PhD dissertation, University of Toronto, 1990).

31 Northrop Frye, *Anatomy of Criticism* (Princeton: Princeton University Press, 1957): 40. This is also called 'discrepant awareness' by D. Muecke in *Irony and the Ironic* (London: Methuen, 1982).

32 See Ó Corráin's comments about *Scéla Muicce meic Dáthó* cited above, p. 114. Máire Herbert has recently discussed *Fled Dúin na nGéd* as a tale which plays with audience expectations in *'Fled Dúin na nGéd*: A Reappraisal,' *CMCS* 18 (Winter 1989): 75–87. Joseph Nagy's discussion of the ironic interplay of opposing perspectives in the *Acallamh na Senórach* is also valuable, but relates to a text later than ours; see 'Compositional Concerns in the *Acallam na Senórach*,' in *Sages, Saints and Storytellers*, 150–7.

33 The two most recent discussions of the tale, by John Carey and Tomás Ó Cathasaigh, both read it 'straight'; see Carey, 'The Uses of Tradition in *Serglige Con Culainn*,' *Ulidia*, 77–84, and Ó Cathasaigh, 'Reflections on *Compert Con Culainn* and *Serglige Con Culainn*,' *Ulidia*, 85–9.

34 See especially Linda Hutcheon's recent study *Irony's Edge: The Theory and Politics of Irony* (London & New York: Routledge, 1994).

35 See Joan Radner's discussion, 'Interpreting Irony in Medieval Celtic Narrative: The Case of *Culhwch ac Olwen*,' *CMCS* 16 (winter 1988): 41–59.

36 A good example is Radner's discussion of the endless tasks described by the giant.

37 The only similar episode is found in *Bricriu's Feast* (see chapter 2 above) when Cú Chulainn claims to be too tired to dispute at the feast despite his wife's lavish praise of him.

38 In fact, Cú Chulainn's career is full of similar situations. On the one hand he seems to have an affinity for the female world (perhaps because he retains so many of the attributes of a child even as an adult). On the other hand, he is almost always the victor over women, whether through the aid of a helper or through his own strength and ingenuity.

39 Van Hamel, *Compert Con Culainn and Other Stories*, 52, #71.

40 Dillon, *Serglige Con Culainn*, l. 35.

41 Obviously, servants don't count; a few lines later he kills two of Medb's handmaidens.

42 Dillon, *Serglige*, ll. 37–8.

43 Thomson, *Pwyll Pendeuic Dyuet* (Dublin: DIAS, 1980): 1–2.

44 Birds chained together also appear in *The Dream of Oengus* (*Aislinge Oengusso*) and *The Conception of Cú Chulainn* (*Compert Con Culainn*), and seem to be a consistent marker of the Otherworld in Irish tradition.

45 Or 'charged/blamed'; Dillon, *Serglige Con Culainn*, l. 63.

46 Mary Wack offers a radically different interpretation of this scene. Of Cú Chulainn's anger here, she says, 'His emotion is compounded of humiliation, anger, and knowledge of his wife's own anger, shame, and accurate prediction regarding the birds. The Otherworldly vision thus arrives at a moment of great emotional turmoil. The women who beat him nearly to death and cause his long wasting may be seen as doubles for his wife: they punish him as he fears or imagines she would, should she give vent to her wrath ... If we accept that Fand may function psychologically as a double for Cú Chulainn's wife, then his passionate affair with Fand in the Otherworld can be seen as a fantasy of reconciliation with his wife.' See *Lovesickness in the Middle Ages* (Philadelphia: University of Pennsylvania Press, 1990): 28–9. Although this is an intriguing psychological interpretation, Wack's reading does not take into account the legal context of the tale.

47 Dillon, *Serglige Con Culainn*, ll. 262–302.

48 Edited by Kuno Meyer, RIA Todd Lecture Series, vol. 15 (Dublin: Hodges, Figgis, 1909). Meyer dates the text to the ninth century; its earliest appearance is in the twelfth-century Book of Leinster.

49 This is the earliest example of this group; Fergus Kelly states in the introduction to his edition that 'orthography and syntax point to a date c. 700 A.D.'; *Audacht Moraind* (Dublin: DIAS, 1976): xiv.

50 Dillon, *Serglige Con Culainn*, ll. 261–5.

51 In fact, one of the further ironies in the tale is that the 'cure' for Cú Chulainn's love-sickness (which seems to symbolize sexual desire) only replaces one set of troubles with another. Cú Chulainn may have regained his physical strength, but he has not recovered his good sense, and he certainly seems unprepared for the storm of jealousy which his affair with Fand has unleashed in Emer.

52 It should be noted that this passage is an interweaving of versions A and B (generally dated to the eleventh and ninth centuries respectively). Thurneysen (*Heldensage*, 423), Dillon ('On the Text of Serglige Con Culainn,' 42, nn. 15, 16), and Windisch (*Irische Texte* I, 203) all agree that this passage consists of two parts, and that Cú Chulainn's poem describing the battle differs considerably from the description of it earlier in the prose text (ll. 588–94). Thus, the contradictions may be simply a consequence of the awkward blending of the two versions. See the appendix for a more detailed discussion of versions A and B.

53 This is Dillon's emendation, following Gerard Murphy. LU reads 'i soc-raidi'; the later, seventeenth-century manuscript TCD H.4.22 (often dubbed 'H' by editors) reads 'isocraiti.'

54 Without the emendation of 'i socraidi' to 'ó chraidi' the phrase might trans-late as 'in [the midst of] the host lips speak.'

55 Dillon, *Serglige Con Culainn*, ll. 662–9, 678–81. This is a difficult passage, and parts of the translation are tentative.

56 O'Rahilly, *Táin Bó Cúailnge: Recension I*, 60 (ll. 1951–6), trans. 179.

57 Dillon, *Serglige Con Culainn*, ll. 702–5; 'do scor ó nirt mná' could also be 'from the strength of a woman.'

58 See, for instance, Jack Goody and Ian Watt, 'The Consequences of Literacy,' *Comparative Studies in Society and History* 5 (1962–3): 304–45. For more recent discussions of literacy, see Walter Ong, *Orality and Literacy: The Technologiz-ing of the Word* (London: Methuen, 1982, repr. 1984) and Brian Stock, *The Implications of Literacy* (Princeton: Princeton University Press, 1983).

59 See, for instance, the tentative suggestion made by Patrick Sims-Williams about Gildas's use of native and Latin imagery in 'Gildas and Vernacular Poetry,' in *Gildas: New Approaches*, ed. Michael Lapidge and David Dumville, Studies in Celtic History 5 (Woodbridge: Boydell Press, 1984): 169–92.

60 The most important recent work is Kim McCone's *Pagan Past and Christian Present*, (Maynooth: An Sagart, 1990).

61 The violent act of horse-whipping has a parallel in *Fingal Rónáin*, in Congal's whipping of Rónán's young wife, who has been soliciting Mael Fothartaig. In both instances of whipping, a sexual transgression is in-volved.

62 There is irony here, whether intentional or not; Lóeg *has* in fact returned with a cure for his master – the plan that Cú Chulainn should sleep with Fand. This is not the kind of cure that Emer has in mind, although her doubts about whether or not she is able to help him may draw attention to the ambiguities here.

63 Or, perhaps, 'image'; *DIL*, s.v. *delb*.

64 Dillon, *Serglige Con Culainn*, ll. 371–86.

65 The passage in question (ll. 81–5 in Dillon's edition) is problematic, and seems to be a conflation of two versions; in one of these, Cú Chulainn is unable to speak, while in the other he clearly gives spoken directions as to where he is to be taken. Because of this confusion, it is perhaps unwise to attribute undue significance to his adamant rejection of Dún Delca as a place of convalescence. See Dillon's discussion of the two versions, 'On the Text of *Serglige Con Culainn*,' *Éigse* 3, part 2 (1941): 120–9.

66 Searle, 'A Classification of Illocutionary Acts,' 10–11.

67 Dillon, *Serglige Con Culainn*, ll. 351–4.

68 That is, upright in a physical sense; standing straight and tall; *DIL*, s.v. *cóir*.

69 Dillon translates 'like warriors storming over battle-chariots' in 'The Wasting Sickness of Cú Chulainn,' *Scottish Gaelic Studies* 7 (1953): 70.

70 Dillon, *Serglige Con Culainn*, ll. 692–5. The manuscript LU indicates that Emer speaks this passage, but the phrase just before this speech implies that the speaker is Fand. Clearly there was some confusion on the part of the scribes. If the speech is to be taken as Emer's, it only adds weight to her challenging stance, as words and actual weapons join in a double threat.

71 For an illuminating discussion of a female character as a link between violence and signification, see Gillian Overing's analysis of Modthryth in *Language, Sign and Gender in Beowulf*, 101–7.

72 Dillon, *Serglige Con Culainn*, ll. 706–8.

73 See O'Leary's discussion in 'The Honour of Women,' 27–44.

74 Dillon, *Serglige Con Culainn*, ll. 720–1.

75 Dillon, *Serglige Con Culainn*, ll. 722–6.

76 Dillon, *Serglige Con Culainn*, ll. 727–8.

77 Dillon, *Serglige Con Culainn*, ll. 748–51.

78 An emendation; LU and H read 'tara.'

79 Emended from *tairsem*, LU; *tairisium*, H.

80 Literally, 'I shall yield it to your control'; see Dillon's note, p. 43.

81 Dillon, *Serglige Con Culainn*, ll. 732–43.

82 Dillon, *Serglige Con Culainn*, ll. 771–4. The last phrase is difficult. The sense seems to be that love goes 'out of mind.' The *DIL* suggests for *a heol* 'knowledge of it' or 'out of knowledge,' or 'into oblivion; astray'; *eól, s.v.*

83 Dillon, *Serglige Con Culainn*, ll. 775–8. Fand's remarks on the nature of love and its implications for women seem so authentic that it is tempting to speculate that her poems were originally composed by a female poet. Such an idea is, of course, unprovable. However, the possibility is suggested by the few references to female poets scattered throughout medieval Irish literature, the most notable of which is Líadan in *Líadan and Cuirithir*, ed. Kuno Meyer (London: D. Nutt, 1902).

84 Or 'distress.' Dillon, *Serglige Con Culainn*, ll. 803–6.

85 Dillon, *Serglige Con Culainn*, ll. 820–5.

86 Dillon, *Serglige Con Culainn*, ll. 132–3.

87 It is interesting to note that Manannán is always present in the background; in fact, he appears among the Otherworld enemies fighting Cú Chulainn (ll. 670–3). Whether one sees this as the debris of an older myth, or a

sparsely interwoven sub-theme of an enmity between Cú Chulainn the mortal and Manannán the immortal, has little effect on this reading of the tale.

88 This poem is found on folio 50a of LU, and is written by the first scribe and glossed by the Reviser.

Mac Lonan dixit:
> Mían mná Tethrach (.i. badb) a tenid (.i. gae 7 arm)
> slaide sethnach (.i. táeb) iar sodain
> suba (.i. fuil) luba (.i. corp) fo lubaib (.i. foferaib)
> ugail (.i. súli) troga (.i. cend) dúr drogain (.i. fiac)

Mac Lonan said:
> The desire of a woman of Tethra (that is, a goddess) from fire (that is, spear and weapon)
> Destroying of a thin body (that is, side) after that
> Joyful (that is, blood) the body (that is, body) under bodies (that is, under men)
> eyes (that is, eyes) head (that is, head) belonging to a raven (that is, raven).

This translation is extremely tentative. For an anecdote concerning a Flann mac Lonáin (who may be the figure referred to here) see Osborn Bergin, ed., 'A Story of Flann mac Lonáin,' *Anecdota from Irish Manuscripts*, vol. 1, 45–50.

89 Dillon, *Serglige Con Culainn*, ll. 827–9.

90 Compare Cú Chulainn's enumeration of Fand's attractions with his reasons for choosing Emer in *The Wooing of Emer* (Van Hamel, ed., *Compert Con Culainn*, 30, #26) where he states that he has chosen her because no other woman could debate with him as she has done. See chapter 1 above.

91 *Aided Muirchertach meic Erca*, ed. Lil Nic Dhonnchada (Dublin: DIAS, 1964).

92 A preliminary discussion of the 'Otherworld as literary device' can be found in John Carey's article, 'Otherworlds and Verbal Worlds in Middle Irish Narrative,' *Proceedings of the Harvard Celtic Colloquium* 9 (1989): 31–42.

93 Or, perhaps, 'ghosts.'

94 Dillon, *Serglige Con Culainn*, ll. 844–9.

95 Tomás Ó Cathasaigh, 'Reflections on *Compert Conchobuir* and *Serglige Con Culainn*,' *Ulidia*, 89. John Carey's comments on the representation of the Otherworld in this tale, and on this colophon in particular, are also pertinent; he says 'I wonder whether it may be significant that [version] A's two references to demons come at the very beginning and the very end of its

version of the *Serglige*: they may have been placed there to disarm criticism of the keen interest in the Otherworld evinced in the body of the text, or perhaps even to atone for it.' See 'The Uses of Tradition in *Serglige Con Culainn,' Ulidia*, 83.

96 Dillon, *Serglige Con Culainn*, ll. 748–9.

Conclusion

1 Julia Kristeva, 'Word, Dialogue and Novel,' in Toril Moi, ed., *The Kristeva Reader* (Oxford: Basil Blackwell, 1986): 34–61.
2 Patricia Kelly, 'The Táin as Literature,' in J.P. Mallory, ed., *Aspects of The Táin* (Belfast: December Publications, 1992): 85–5.
3 Dooley, 'The Invention of Women in the *Táin,' Ulidia*, 129–30.
4 Muirenn Ní Bhrolcháin, *'Re Tóin Mná*: In Pursuit of Troublesome Women,' *Ulidia*, 115.
5 Dooley, 'The Invention of Women,' 123.
6 Jane Chance, *Woman as Hero in Old English Literature* (Syracuse: Syracuse University Press, 1986).

Appendix

1 Gerard Murphy and Eleanor Knott, *Early Irish Literature* (New York: Barnes & Noble, 1966): 114–31. The medieval writers of these tales clearly envisioned them as having taken place around the time of Christ, in early pre-Christian Ireland, although the tales as they have come down to us appear to have been composed in the Christian period. Conchobar, Cú Chulainn, and the other recurrent characters are not historical persons.
2 Tomás Ó Cathasaigh, 'Reflections on *Compert Con Culainn* and *Serglige Con Culainn,' Ulidia*, ed. J.P. Mallory & G. Stockman, 85–9.
3 R.I. Best and Osborn Bergin, eds., *Lebor na hUidre* (Dublin: RIA, 1929): xiii.
4 'The Reviser of Leabhar na Huidhre,' *Éigse* 15, pt 4 (1974): 277–88. See also his article 'LL and the Date of the Reviser of LU,' *Éigse* 20 (1984): 212–25.
5 David N. Dumville, '"Scéla Laí Brátha" and the Collation of Leabhar na Huidhre,' *Éigse* 16 (1975–6): 24–8.
6 Gearóid Mac Eoin, 'The Interpolator H in Lebor na hUidre,' *Ulidia*, 39–46; see especially pp. 45–6 for his conclusions on dating.
7 Tomás Ó Concheanainn, 'Gilla Ísa Mac Fir Bhisigh and a Scribe of his School,' *Ériu* 25 (1974): 168–9.
8 For a complete list of the contents, see T.K. Abbott and E.J. Gwynn, *Catalogue of Irish Manuscripts in the Library of Trinity College Dublin* (Dublin: Hodges, Figgis, 1921): 94–110.

9 Thurneysen, *Heldensage*, 377ff.
10 For a discussion of this manuscript see R.I. Best, 'Notes on Rawlinson B 512,' *ZCP* 17 (1924): 389ff; he notes that there is a scribal heading to the gathering which contains *Tochmarc Emire* to the effect that materials are being taken from the Book of Dub Da Lethe (1049–64). Séamus Mac Mathúna observes that *Tochmarc Emire* is found in a portion of the manuscript which also includes *Verba Scáthaige, Forfess Fer Falgae, Immram Brain, Baile in Scáil,* and *Echtra Condlai*; see his remarks in *Immram Brain*, 3.
11 See Meyer's discussion in 'The Oldest Version of the Tochmarc Emire,' *Révue celtique* 11 (1890): 437–9. He notes the much simpler style, the omission of several episodes (including Cú Chulainn's encounters with Derbforgall), and the absence of glosses, and contends that this text represents a pre-Norse version of the tale, probably dating back to the eighth century. However, a recent article by William Sayers linking a character mentioned even in this early version of *Tochmarc Emire* to Wulfstan of Winchester (who lived in the tenth century) implies a questioning of this early date; see 'Irish Evidence for the *De Harmonia Tonorum* of Wulfstan of Winchester,' *Mediaevalia* 14 (1991 for 1988): 23–38.
12 Thurneysen, *Heldensage*, 377ff. See also Van Hamel's introduction to the tale in *Compert Con Culainn and Other Stories* (Dublin: DIAS, 1978): 16.
13 See Edel's comments in *Helden auf Freiersfüssen*, Appendix 1, 265. Mac Mathúna calls Thurneysen's remarks 'misleading' and stresses that the 'Rawlinson text represents what remains of Recension I. The first part of this recension is not extant. The Rawlinson text is not to be combined with the opening of *TEm*. in *U* [Lebor na Huidre], as Thurneysen suggests, although he is probably correct in stating that the *R* [Rawlinson] text constitutes the latter part of an eleventh century version of a text originally composed in the eighth or ninth century'; see Mac Mathúna, *Immram Brain: Bran's Journey to the Land of the Women* (Tübingen: Niemeyer, 1985): 465.
14 Van Hamel, ed., *Compert Con Culainn*, 16.
15 Van Hamel, ed., *Compert Con Culainn*, 17.
16 T.F. O'Rahilly, *Catalogue of Manuscripts in the Royal Irish Academy* (Dublin: Hodges, Figgis, 1926), MS. 1223, p. 3297.
17 Van Hamel, *Compert Con Culainn*, 16.
18 Meyer, 'The Oldest Version,' 452–3.
19 In Van Hamel, ed, *Compert Con Culainn*.
20 See Bergin and Best, eds., *Lebor na hUidre*, 246–77. Their note at the bottom of page 277 reads, 'breaks off, five leaves missing.'
21 Thurneysen, *Heldensage*, 449, 667.
22 Gearóid Mac Eoin, 'The Dating of Middle Irish Texts,' *Proceedings of the British Academy* 69 (1982): 109–37, especially 121.

23 Thurneysen, *Heldensage*, 447–67.
24 Thurneysen, *Heldensage*, 447–8; George Henderson, ed. and trans., *Bricriu's Feast*, Irish Texts Society, vol. 2 (London: 1899): xxiv–xlvi. The Edinburgh manuscript also contains a number of other Ulster Cycle tales; for a complete description, see Donald MacKinnon, *A Descriptive Catalogue of Gaelic Manuscripts in the Advocates' Library Edinburgh* (Edinburgh: Constable, 1912): 153–7.
25 Thurneysen, *Heldensage*, 448–9.
26 Lines 8367–8561 in Bergin and Best, eds., *Lebor na hUidre*, pp. 255–60. The Reviser has also made other interpolations in the manuscript and has glossed some difficult passages; see, for instance, ll. 8828–9045.
27 The editors are Proinsias Mac Cana and Edgar Slotkin.
28 See, for instance, the translations by Jeffrey Gantz in *Early Irish Myths and Sagas*, 228, and by Cross and Slover in *Ancient Irish Tales*, 260. These translations both omit the *bríatharcath* section.
29 Citations are taken from Bergin and Best, eds., *Lebor na hUidre*, 246–77. There is also an earlier edition by Windisch with comparative readings from Egerton 93 and H.3.17, in *Irische Texte*, vol. 1 (Leipzig: Verlag von S. Hirzel, 1880): 235–311. George Henderson's edition, based mostly on LU, includes a rather old-fashioned English translation.
30 Thurneysen, *Heldensage*, 404.
31 Van Hamel, ed., *Compert Con Culainn*, 9.
32 Thurneysen, *Heldensage*, 403.
33 Thurneysen, *Heldensage*, 404.
34 See Tomás Ó Concheanainn, 'The Source of the YBL Text of TBC,' *Ériu* 34 (1983): 175–84, and 'Notes on *Togail Bruidne Da Derga*,' *Celtica* 17 (1985): 73–90.
35 '*Aided Nath Í* and Uí Fhiachrach Genealogies,' *Éigse* 25 (1991): 1–27.
36 Van Hamel, ed., *Compert Con Culainn*, 9.
37 See Proinsias Mac Cana, *Learned Tales*, 41–65. Mac Cana points out that exclusion from both lists does not mean a given tale did not exist at the time; he notes that 'one could compile a respectable collection of early tales which are not included in either' and mentions *Aided Óenfir Aífe* among his examples of these (p. 66).
38 'For Tráig Baile, bressim ngle, dorochair Oinfer Aife,' 'On Traig Baile – clear noise – Aife's only son has fallen'; see Whitley Stokes's edition and translation in *Révue celtique* 23 (1902): 307. Thurneysen (*Heldensage*, 20–1) rejects the attribution of the verses on the deaths of heroes to Cináed úa hArtacáin. However, Gerard Murphy has pointed out the shakiness of Thurneysen's grounds for this rejection and affirms the value of the verses for proving the

existence in the tenth century of traditions about these heroes; see 'Two Sources in Thurneysen's *Heldensage,' Ériu* 16 (1952): 151–6.

39 Cecile O'Rahilly, ed., *Táin Bó Cúalnge From the Book of Leinster*, 96, ll. 3456–9 (folio 88a), trans. p. 231.

The Fer Diad episode was likely an independent tale which was at some point incorporated into the *Táin*. Thurneysen judged the language of the tale and the metres of its poems to be consistent with an eleventh-century composition, but since the episode is also referred to by Cinaed úa hArtacáin some version of the story must have been circulating in the tenth century. See O'Rahilly's discussion of the Fer Diad episode in her introduction to *The Stowe Version of Táin Bó Cúailnge* (Dublin: DIAS, 1961): xxiv–xxix.

40 Despite Heinrich Zimmer's conclusion in 'Keltische Studien 5. Über den compilatorischen character der irischen sagentexte im sogenannten Lebor na hUidre,' *Zeitschrift für vergleichende Sprachforschung* 28 (1887): 617 that LU and H derive from a common source, Dillon believes that H is likely a copy of LU with some corrections and changes; see his discussion in 'The Trinity College Text of *Serglige Con Culainn,' Scottish Gaelic Studies* 6 (1949): 139–146. In a review of Dillon's edition of *Serglige Con Culainn*, Howard Meroney criticizes this opinion as an 'unconvincing argument' but neglects to substantiate this claim or offer an alternative; see *The Journal of Celtic Studies* 2 (1958): 243.

41 Dillon, *Serglige Con Culainn* (DIAS).

42 Zimmer, 'Keltische studien 5,' *Zeitschrift für vergleichende Sprachforschung* 28 (1887): 594.

43 Thurneysen, *Heldensage*, 415.

44 Thurneysen, *Heldensage*, 414, n 3.

45 Myles Dillon, 'On the Text of Serglige Con Culainn,' *Éigse* 3 (1941–2): 120–9; see also his discussion in the introduction to his edition *Serglige Con Culainn*, xii–xvi. But compare Howard Meroney's comments in his review, *The Journal of Celtic Studies* 2 (1958): 243–6.

46 Trond Kruke Salberg, 'The Question of the Main Interpolation of H into M's Part of the *Serglige Con Culainn* in the *Book of the Dun Cow* and Some Related Problems,' *ZCP* 45 (1992): 161–81.

47 See Bergin and Best, eds., *Lebor na hUidre*, 104–12; this corresponds to ll. 1–338 of Dillon's edition.

48 Bergin and Best, eds., *Lebor na hUidre*, 114–15; Dillon, *Serglige Con Culainn*, ll. 418–52.

49 Bergin and Best, eds., *Lebor na hUidre*, 121; Dillon, *Serglige Con Culainn*, l. 681.

50 See Salberg, 'The Question of the Main Interpolation,' 161–79.

51 Tomás Ó Concheanainn, 'The Reviser of Leabhar na hUidhre,' 288.

52 For a contrasting opinion see Myles Dillon's introduction to his edition of
   the tale (*Serglige Con Culainn*, xii), where he draws attention to
   Thurneysen's remarks that 'we know from other texts on which the same
   Interpolator has worked that he was not himself the compiler, but drew his
   material from compilations already made (*Heldensage* 414).'

References

Abbott, T.K., and E.J. Gwynn, eds. *Catalogue of Irish Manuscripts in the Library of Trinity College, Dublin*. Dublin: Hodges, Figgis, 1921.

Aitchison, N.B., 'The Ulster Cycle: Heroic Image and Historical Reality. *Journal of Medieval History* 13 (1987): 87–116.

Austin, J.L. *How to Do Things with Words*. Cambridge: Harvard University Press, 1962.

Barthes, Roland. 'The Death of the Author.' In *Image Music Text*. Ed. Stephen Heath. London: Fontana, 1977. 142–8.

Baudiš, Joseph. 'On *Tochmarc Emere.*' *Ériu* 9 (1923): 98–108.

Benkov, Edith Joyce. 'Language and Women: From Silence to Speech.' In *Sign, Sentence, Discourse: Language in Medieval Thought and Literature*. Ed. Julian N. Wasserman and Lois Roney. Syracuse: Syracuse University Press, 1989. 245–65.

Bergin, Osborn, and R.I. Best, eds. & trans. '*Tochmarc Étaíne.*' *Ériu* 12 (1937): 137–93.

– 'A Story of Flann mac Lonáin.' In *Anecdota from Irish Manuscripts*. Vol. 1. Ed. Osborn Bergin et al. Halle: Niemeyer, 1912. 45–50.

– , and M.A. O'Brien, eds. *The Book of Leinster*. 6 vols. DIAS, 1954–67.

Best, R.I., ed. and trans. 'The Adventures of Art Son of Conn, and the Courtship of Delbchaem.' *Ériu* 3 (1907): 149–73.

– 'The Tragic Death of Cúrói Mac Dári.' *Ériu* 2 (1905): 18–35.

– 'Notes on Rawlinson B.512.' *ZCP* 17 (1928): 389–91.

– , and Osborn Bergin, eds. *Lebor na hUidre*. Dublin: Royal Irish Academy, 1929, rept. 1992.

Bhreathnach, Máire. 'A New Edition of *Tochmarc Becfhola.*' *Ériu* 35 (1984): 59–91.

Bieler, Ludwig, ed. and trans. *The Patrician Texts in the Book of Armagh*. Scriptores Latini Hiberniae, vol. 10. Dublin: DIAS, 1970.

Binchy, D.A. 'Varia Hibernica: The So-Called "Rhetorics" of Irish Saga.' In *Indo-Celtica*. Munich: Hueber, 1972. 29–38.

– ed. *Corpus Iuris Hibernici*. 6 vols. Dublin: DIAS, 1978.

Bitel, Lisa. '"Conceived in Sins, Born in Delights": Stories of Procreation from Early Ireland.' *Journal of the History of Sexuality*, 3, no. 2 (1992): 181–202.

Blamires, Alcuin, ed. *Woman Defamed and Woman Defended: An Anthology of Medieval Texts*. Oxford: The Clarendon Press, 1992.

Bloch, R. Howard. *Medieval Misogyny and the Invention of Western Romantic Love*. Chicago: University of Chicago Press, 1991.

Bollard, J.K. 'The Thematic Structure of the Four Branches of the Mabinogi.' *Transactions of the Honourable Society of Cymmrodorion* (1974–5): 250–76.

Booker, Keith. '"Nothing that is so is so': Dialogic Discourse and the Voice of the Woman in the Clerk's Tale and Twelfth Night.' *Exemplaria* 3, no. 2 (Fall 1991): 519–37.

Bossy, Michel-André. 'The Elaboration of Female Narrative Functions in *Erec et Enide*.' In *Courtly Literature: Culture and Context*. Ed. Keith Busby and Eric Cooper. Amsterdam/Philadelphia: John Benjamins, 1990. 23–38.

Bourke, Angela. 'Performing – Not Writing.' *Graph* 1 (Winter, 1991): 28–31.

Bowen, Charles. 'Great-Bladdered Medb: Mythology and Invention in the *Táin Bó Cuailnge*.' *Éire/Ireland* 10 (1975): 26–33.

Breatnach, Liam. 'Canon Law and Secular Law in Early Ireland; The Significance of the *Bretha Nemed*.' *Peritia* 3 (1984): 439–59.

Brown, A.C.L. 'The Knight of the Lion.' *PMLA* new series 13, no. 4 (1905): 673–706.

Bruckner, Matilda Tomaryn. *Shaping Romance: Interpretation, Truth, and Closure in Twelfth-Century French Fictions*. Philadelphia: University of Pennsylvania Press, 1993.

Burns, E. Jane. 'Knowing Women: Female Orifices in Old French Farce and Fabliau.' *Exemplaria* 4, no. 1 (Spring 1992): 81–104.

– *Bodytalk: When Women Speak in Old French Literature*. Philadelphia: University of Pennsylvania Press, 1993.

Carey, John. 'Myth and Mythography in *Cath Maige Tuired*.' *Studia Celtica* 24/25 (1989–90): 53–69.

– 'Otherworlds and Verbal Worlds in Middle Irish Narrative.' *Proceedings of the Harvard Celtic Colloquium* 9 (1989): 31–42.

– 'The Uses of Tradition in *Serglige Con Culainn*.' In *Ulidia: Proceedings of the First International Conference on the Ulster Cycle of Tales, Belfast and Emain Macha, 8–12 April, 1994*. Ed. J.P. Mallory and G. Stockman. Belfast: December Publications, 1994. 77–84.

Carney, James. *Studies in Irish Literature and History*. Dublin: DIAS, 1955.

– 'The Deeper Level of Early Irish Literature.' *Capuchin Annual* (1969): 160–71.

– 'Early Irish Literature: The State of Research.' In *Proceedings of the Sixth International Congress of Celtic Studies, 1979.* Ed. G. Mac Eoin. Dublin: DIAS, 1983. 113–30.

Chadwick, H.M., and Nora K. Chadwick. *The Growth of Literature*. Vol. 1. Cambridge: Cambridge University Press, 1932.

Chance, Jane. *Woman as Hero in Old English Literature*. Syracuse: Syracuse University Press, 1986.

Charles-Edwards, T.M. 'The Social Background to Irish *Peregrinatio*.' *Celtica* 11 (1976): 43–59.

– 'Honour and Status in Some Irish and Welsh Prose Tales.' *Ériu* 29 (1978): 123–41.

Cixous, Hélène, and Catherine Clément. *The Newly Born Woman*. Trans. Betsy Wing. Minneapolis: University of Minnesota Press, 1986.

Clover, Carol. 'Hildigunnr's Lament.' In *Structure and Meaning in Old Norse Literature*. Ed. John Lindow et al. Odense: Odense University Press, 1986.

Cormier, Raymond. 'Cú Chulainn and Yvain: The Love Hero in Early Irish and Old French Literature.' *Studies in Philology* 72, no. 2 (April, 1975): 115–39.

Cross, Tom Peete. 'A Note on "Sohrab and Rustum" in Ireland.' *Journal of Celtic Studies* 1 (1950): 176–82.

– , and C.H. Slover, trans. *Ancient Irish Tales*. Totowa, N.J.: Barnes & Noble, 1936.

Damico, Helen, and Alexandra Hennessey Olsen, eds. *New Readings on Women in Old English Literature*. Bloomington: Indiana University Press, 1990.

de Paor, Aíne. 'The Common Authorship of Some Book of Leinster Texts.' *Ériu* 9 (1923): 118–46.

Dictionary of the Irish Language. Compact edition. Dublin: Royal Irish Academy, 1983.

Dillon, Myles. 'On the Text of *Serglige Con Culainn*.' *Éigse* 3, 2 (1941): 120–9.

– 'The Archaism of the Early Irish Tradition.' *Proceedings of the British Academy* 33 (1947): 245–64.

– 'The Trinity College Text of *Serglige Con Culainn*.' *Scottish Gaelic Studies* 6 (1949): 139–46.

– ed., *Serglige Con Culainn*. Dublin: DIAS, 1975.

Dineen, Patrick S., ed. & trans. *Foras Feasa ar Éirinn: A History of Ireland by Geoffrey Keating*. Irish Texts Society, vol. 8, London 1908.

Dinshaw, Carolyn. *Chaucer's Sexual Poetics*. Madison: University of Wisconsin Press, 1989.

Dooley, Ann. 'The Invention of Women in the *Táin.*' In *Ulidia: Proceedings of the First International Conference on the Ulster Cycle of Tales, Belfast and Emain Macha, 8–12 April, 1994.* Ed. J.P. Mallory and G. Stockman. Belfast: December Publications, 1994. 123–33.

– , and James P. Carley. 'An Early Irish Fragment of Isidore of Seville's *Etymologiae.*' In *The Archaeology and History of Glastonbury Abbey.* Ed. Lesley Abrams and James P. Carley. Woodbridge: Boydell Press, 1991. 135–61.

Dumville, David N. '"Scéla Lái Brátha" and the Collation of Leabhar na Huidhre.' *Éigse* 16 (1975–6): 24–8.

Dunn, Vincent. *Cattle-Raids and Courtships: Medieval Narrative Genres in a Traditional Context.* New York: Garland, 1989.

Echard, Siân. 'Expectation and Experimentation in Medieval Arthurian Narrative: A Study of Anglo-Latin, Middle English and Middle Welsh Texts.' PhD dissertation, University of Toronto, 1990.

Edel, Doris. *Helden auf Freiersfüssen. 'Tochmarc Emire' und 'Mal y kavas Kulhwch Olwen': Studien zur frühen inselkeltischen Erzähltradition.* Verhandelingen der Koninklijke Nederlandse Akademie van Wetenschappen, Afdeling Letterkunde, Nieuwe Reeks, Deel 107. Amsterdam: North Holland Publishing, 1980.

– 'Koningin Medb van Connacht en haar beoordelaars, vroeger en nu.' In the collection *'T Is kwaad gerucht, als zij niet binnen blijft.* UC Utrecht: Hes Uitgevers, 1986. 61–94.

Ferrante, Joan. *Woman as Image in Medieval Literature.* New York: Columbia University Press, 1975.

– 'Male Fantasy and Female Reality in Courtly Literature.' *Women's Studies* II (1984). 67–97.

Finke, Laurie. 'Towards a Cultural Poetics of Romance.' *Genre* 22 (Summer 1989): 109–27.

Fish, Stanley. 'How to Do Things with Austin and Searle: Speech Act Theory and Literary Criticism.' *Modern Language Notes* 91 (1976): 983–1025.

Flanagan, Marie Therese. *Irish Society, Anglo-Norman Settlers, Angevin Kingship: Interactions in Ireland in the Late Twelfth Century.* Oxford: Clarendon Press, 1989.

Flower, Robin. *The Irish Tradition.* Oxford: The Clarendon Press, 1947.

Ford, Patrick K., trans. *The Mabinogi and Other Medieval Welsh Tales.* Berkeley: University of California Press, 1977.

– 'Prolegomena to a Reading of the *Mabinogi*: "Pwyll" and "Manawydan".' *Studia Celtica* 16/17 (1981–2): 110–25.

Freeman, Michelle. 'Marie de France's Poetics of Silence: The Implications for a Feminine *Translatio.*' *PMLA* 99 (1984): 860–83.

Frye, Northrop. *Anatomy of Criticism*. Princeton: Princeton University Press, 1957.

Gantz, Jeffrey, trans. *Early Irish Myths and Sagas*. London: Penguin, 1981.

Goody, Jack, and Ian Watt. 'The Consequences of Literacy.' *Comparative Studies in Society and History* 5 (1962–3): 304–45.

Gravdal, Kathryn. *Ravishing Maidens. Writing Rape in Medieval French Literature and Law*. Philadelphia: University of Pennsylvania Press, 1991.

Gray, Elizabeth A., ed. and trans. *Cath Maige Tuired: The Second Battle of Mag Tuired*. Irish Texts Society, vol. 52. London 1982.

– 'Cath Maige Tuired: Myth and Structure.' *Éigse* 18 (1980–1): 183–209, vol. 19, pt 1 (1982): 1–35, vol. 19, pt 2 (1983): 230–62.

– 'Lug and Cú Chulainn: King and Warrior, God and Man.' *Studia Celtica* 24/25 (1989/90): 38–52.

Greene, David, ed. *Fingal Rónáin and Other Stories*. Dublin: DIAS, 1955.

– 'Varia I.' *Ériu* 33 (1982): 161–3.

Grosz, Elizabeth. *Jacques Lacan: A Feminist Introduction*. London/New York: Routledge, 1990.

Gwynn, Aubrey. *The Twelfth Century Reform*. Dublin: Gill, 1968.

– *The Irish Church in the Eleventh and Twelfth Centuries*. Dublin: Four Courts Press, 1992.

Gwynn, Edward. *The Metrical Dindshenchas*. RIA Todd Lecture Series, vols 8–12. Dublin: Hodges, Figgis, 1903–35.

Hansen, Elaine Tuttle. 'Fearing for Chaucer's Good Name.' *Exemplaria* 2, no. 1 (Spring 1990): 23–36.

Henderson, George, ed. and trans. *Fled Bricrend: Bricriu's Feast*. Irish Texts Society, vol. 2, London 1899.

Henry, P.L., ed. 'Verba Scáthaige.' *Celtica* 21 (1990): 191–207.

– 'The World, the Text, and the Critic of Early Irish Heroic Narrative.' *Text and Context* 3 (Autumn 1988): 1–9

Herbert, Máire. 'Fled Dúin na nGéd: A Reappraisal.' *CMCS* 18 (Winter 1989): 75–87.

– 'Celtic Heroine? The Archaeology of the Deirdre Story.' In *Gender in Irish Writing*. Ed. Toni O'Brien Johnson and David Cairns. Philadelphia: Open University Press, 1991. 13–39.

– 'Goddess and King: The Sacred Marriage in Early Ireland.' In *Women and Sovereignty*. Ed. Louise Fradenberg. Cosmos 7. Edinburgh: Edinburgh University Press, 1992. 264–74.

Herren, Michael, ed. and trans. *The Hisperica Famina I: The A- Text*. Toronto: Pontifical Institute for Mediaeval Studies, 1974.

– 'Classical and Secular Learning among the Irish.' *Florilegium* 3 (1981): 118–57.

Huffer, Lynne. 'Christine de Pisan: Speaking Like a Woman/Speaking Like a Man.' In *New Images of Medieval Women: Toward a Cultural Anthropology*. Ed. Edelgard DuBruck. Lewiston, NY: Mellen Press: 1989.

Hutcheon, Linda. *Irony's Edge: The Theory and Politics of Irony*. London/New York: Routledge, 1994.

Irigaray, Luce. *Speculum of the Other Woman*. Trans. Gillian C. Gill, Ithaca: Cornell University Press, 1985.

Jesch, Judith. *Women in the Viking Age*. Woodbridge: The Boydell Press, 1991.

Jochens, Jenny. '*Voluspá*: Matrix of Norse Womanhood.' *Journal of English and Germanic Philology* 88 (July 1989): 344–62.

– 'Before the Male Gaze: The Absence of the Female Body in Old Norse.' In *Sex in the Middle Ages*. Ed. Joyce Salisbury. New York/London: Garland, 1991. 3–29.

Johnson, Toni O'Brien, and David Cairns, eds. *Gender in Irish Writing*. Milton Keynes/Philadelphia: Open University Press, 1991.

Kelly, Fergus, ed. *Audacht Morainn*. Dublin: DIAS, 1976.

– *A Guide to Early Irish Law*. Dublin: DIAS, 1988.

Kelly, Patricia. 'The Táin as Literature.' In *Aspects of the Táin*. Ed. J.P. Mallory. Belfast: December Publications, 1992. 69–102.

Kinsella, Thomas, trans. *The Táin*. Dublin: The Dolmen Press, 1969.

Knott, Eleanor, ed. and trans. 'A Poem of Prophecies.' *Ériu* 18 (1958): 55–75.

– , ed. *Togail Bruidne Da Derga*. Dublin: DIAS, 1963.

– , and Gerard Murphy. *Early Irish Literature*. New York: Barnes & Noble, 1966.

Kristeva, Julia. 'Word, Dialogue and Novel.' In *The Kristeva Reader*. Ed. Toril Moi. Oxford: Basil Blackwell, 1986. 34–61.

Lévi-Strauss, Claude. *The Raw and the Cooked*. Trans. J. and D. Weightman. London: Cape, 1970.

– *The Elementary Structures of Kinship*. Trans. J.H. Bell and J.R. von Sturmer, ed. R. Needham. Boston: Beacon Press, 1969.

Littleton, C. Scott. *The New Comparative Mythology: An Anthropological Assessment of the Theories of Georges Dumézil*. Berkeley: University of California Press, 1966.

Lochrie, Karma. *Margery Kempe and the Translations of the Flesh*. Philadelphia: University of Pennsylvania Press, 1991.

Mac Airt, Seán, and Gearóid Mac Niocaill, eds. and trans. *The Annals of Inisfallen*. DIAS, 1951.

– *The Annals of Ulster*. Dublin: DIAS, 1983.

Mac Cana, Proinsias. 'Aspects of the Theme of King and Goddess in Irish Literature.' *Études celtiques* 7 (1955–6): 76–114; 8 (1958–9): 59–65, 859–65.

– 'On the Use of the Term *Retoiric*.' *Celtica* 7 (1966): 65–90.

- *Celtic Mythology*. London: Hamlyn, 1970.
- 'The Rise of the Later Schools of *filidheacht*.' *Ériu* 25 (1974): 126–46.
- 'The Sinless Otherworld of *Immram Brain*.' *Ériu* 27 (1976): 95–115.
- *The Learned Tales of Medieval Ireland*. DIAS, 1980.
- 'Women in Irish Mythology.' *The Crane Bag* 4, no. 1 (1980): 7–11.
- 'Mythology in Early Irish Literature.' In *The Celtic Consciousness*. Ed. R. O'Driscoll. Toronto: McClelland and Stewart, 1981. 143–54.
- 'The Influence of the Vikings on Celtic Literature.' In *The Impact of the Scandinavian Invasions on the Celtic-speaking Peoples*. Ed. Brian O'Cuiv. Dublin: DIAS, 1983. 78–118.
- 'The Poet as Spouse of His Patron.' *Ériu* 39 (1988): 79–85.
MacCormack, Carol P., and Marilyn Strathern, eds. *Nature, Culture and Gender*. Cambridge: Cambridge University Press, 1980.
Mac Eoin, Gearóid. 'The Dating of Middle Irish Texts.' *Proceedings of the British Academy* 68 (1982): 109–37.
- , ed. *Proceedings of the Sixth International Congress of Celtic Studies, Galway 1979*. DIAS, 1983.
- 'The Interpolator H in Lebor na hUidre.' In *Ulidia: Proceedings of the First International Conference on the Ulster Cycle of Tales, Belfast and Emain Macha, 8–12 April, 1994*. Ed. J.P. Mallory and G. Stockman. Belfast: December Publications, 1994. 39–46.
MacKinnon, Donald. *A Descriptive Catalogue of Gaelic Manuscripts in the Advocates' Library Edinburgh*. Edinburgh: Constable, 1912.
Mac Mathúna, Séamus. *Immram Brain: Bran's Journey to the Land of Women*. Tübingen: Max Niemeyer, 1985.
Mallory, J.P. 'Silver in the Ulster Cycle of Tales.' In *Proceedings of the Seventh International Congress of Celtic Studies, Oxford, 1983*. Ed. D. Ellis Evans. Oxford: Oxbow Books 1986. 31–78.
- 'The World of Cú Chulainn: The Archaeology of the *Táin Bó Cúailgne*.' In *Aspects of the Táin*. Ed. J.P. Mallory. Belfast: December Publications, 1992. 146–53.
Marstrander, Carl, ed. and trans. 'The Deaths of Lugaid and Derbforgaill.' *Ériu* 5 (1911): 201–18.
Martin, B.K. 'Medieval Irish *Aitheda* and Todorov's "Narratologie".' *Studia Celtica* 10–11 (1975–6): 138–51.
McCone, Kim. Review of *History and Heroic Tale*. Ed. Tore Nyberg et al. *CMCS* 13 (Summer 1987): 106–9.
- *Pagan Past and Christian Present*. Maynooth: An Sagart, 1990.
McKenna, Catherine. 'The Theme of Sovereignty in *Pwyll*.' *Bulletin of the Board of Celtic Studies* 29 (1982): 35–52.

Meid, Wolfgang, ed. *Táin Bó Fraích*. Dublin: DIAS, 1974.

Melia, Daniel. 'Remarks on the Structure and Composition of the Ulster Death Tales.' *Studia Hibernica* 17/18 (1977–8): 36–57.

– 'Further Speculation on Marginal .R.' *Celtica* 21 (1990): 362–7.

Meroney, Howard, Review of *Serglige Con Culainn*, ed. Myles Dillon. *The Journal of Celtic Studies* 2 (1958): 243–6.

Meyer, Kuno, ed. and trans. 'The Oldest Version of the Tochmarc Emire.' *Révue celtique* 11 (1890): 433–57.

– 'Anecdota from the Stowe Ms. No. 992.' *Révue celtique* 6 (1894): 173–87.

– *Líadan and Cuirithir*. London: D. Nutt, 1902.

– 'The Death of Conla.' *Ériu* 1 (1904): 114–21.

– *The Instructions of King Cormac mac Airt*. RIA Todd Lecture Series 15. Dublin: Hodges, Figgis, 1909. 28–37.

– 'The Quarrel between Finn and Oisín.' In *Fianaigecht*. RIA Todd Lecture Series 16. Dublin: Hodges Figgis, 1910.

– *Betha Colmáin maic Luacháin*. Dublin: Hodges, Figgis, 1911.

– *Hail Brigit: An Old-Irish Poem on the Hill of Alenn*. Halle: Niemeyer, 1912.

– *Sanais Cormaic: An Old-Irish Glossary. Anecdota from Irish Manuscripts*. Vol. 4. Ed. Osborn Bergin et al. Halle: Niemeyer, 1912.

Mieszkowski, Gretchen. 'Chaucer's Much Loved Criseyde.' *Chaucer Review* 26 (1991): 109–32.

Moi, Toril. *Sexual/Textual Politics*. London: Methuen, 1985.

Muecke, D. *Irony and the Ironic*. London: Methuen, 1970.

Murdoch, Brian O., ed. and trans. *The Irish Adam and Eve Story from Saltair na Rann*. 2 vols. Dublin: DIAS, 1976.

Murphy, D., ed. *The Annals of Clonmacnoise*. Dublin: The University Press, 1896.

Murphy, Gerard. 'Two Sources in Thurneysen's *Heldensage*.' *Ériu* 16 (1952): 145–56.

– *Early Irish Metrics*. Dublin: DIAS, 1961.

Nagy, Joseph Falaky. 'Close Encounters of the Traditional Kind in Medieval Irish Literature.' In *Celtic Folklore and Christianity*. Ed. Patrick Ford. Santa Barbara: McNally & Loftin, 1983.

– 'Heroic Destinies in the *Macgnímrada* of Finn and Cú Chulainn.' *ZCP* 40 (1984): 23–39.

– *The Wisdom of the Outlaw*. Berkeley: University of California Press, 1985

– 'Compositional Concerns in the *Acallam na Senórach*.' In *Sages, Saints and Storytellers: Celtic Studies in Honour of Professor James Carney*. Ed. Donnchadh Ó Corráin et al. Maynooth: An Sagart, 1989. 149–58.

Ní Bhrolcháin, Muirenn. 'The Prose Banshenchas.' PhD diss., University College, Galway, 1980.

– 'Re Tóin Mná: In Pursuit of Troublesome Women.' In *Ulidia: Proceedings of the*

First International Conference on the Ulster Cycle of Tales, Belfast and Emain Macha, 8–12 April, 1994. Ed. J.P. Mallory and G. Stockman. Belfast: December Publications, 1994. 115–21.

Newman, Barbara. *Sister of Wisdom: St. Hildegard's Theology of the Feminine.* Berkeley: University of California Press, 1987.

Nic Dhonnchadha, Lil. *Aided Muirchertaig Meic Erca.* Dublin: DIAS, 1964.

Ó Cathasaigh, Tomás. *The Heroic Biography of Cormac mac Airt.* Dublin: DIAS, 1977.

– 'Cath Maige Tuired as Exemplary Myth.' In *Folia Gadelica: Essays Presented to R.A. Breatnach.* Ed. P. de Brún et al. Cork: Cork University Press, 1983. 1–19.

– 'Pagan Survivals: The Evidence of Early Irish Narrative.' In *Irland und Europa: Die Kirche im Frühmittelalter. Ireland and Europe: The Early Church.* Ed. Proinseas Níchathain and Michael Richter. Stuttgart: Klett-Cotta, 1984. 291–307

– 'The Rhetoric of *Fingal Rónáin.*' *Celtica* 17 (1985): 123–44.

– 'Varia III: The Trial of Mael Fothartaig.' *Ériu* 36 (1985): 177–80.

– 'The Rhetoric of *Scéla Cano meic Gartnáin.*' In *Sages, Saints and Storytellers: Celtic Studies in Honour of Professor James Carney.* Ed. Donnchadh Ó Corráin et al. Maynooth: An Sagart, 1989. 233–50.

– 'Reflections on *Compert Con Culainn* and *Serglige Con Culainn.*' In *Ulidia: Proceedings of the First International Conference on the Ulster Cycle of Tales, Belfast and Emain Macha, 8–12 April, 1994.* Ed. J.P. Mallory and G. Stockman. Belfast: December Publications, 1994. 85–9.

Ó Coileáin, Sean. 'The Structure of a Literary Cycle.' *Ériu* 25 (1974): 88–125.

– 'Oral or Literary: Some Strands of the Argument.' *Studia Hibernica* 17–18 (1977–8): 1–35.

– 'Echtrae Nerai and its Analogues.' *Celtica* 21 (1990): 427–40.

Ó Concheanainn, Tomás. 'The Reviser of Leabhar na Huidhre.' *Éigse* 15, pt 4 (1974): 277–88.

– 'Gilla Ísa Mac Fir Bhisigh and a Scribe of his School.' *Ériu* 25 (1974): 157–71.

– 'The Three Forms of Dinnshenchas Érenn.' *The Journal of Celtic Studies* 3 (1981): 88–131.

– 'A Pious Redactor of Dinnshenchas Érenn.' *Ériu* 33 (1982): 85–98.

– 'The Source of the YBL Text of TBC.' *Ériu* 34 (1983): 175–84.

– 'LL and the Date of the Reviser of LU.' *Éigse* 20 (1984): 212–25.

– 'Notes on *Togail Bruidne Da Derga.*' *Celtica* 17 (1985): 73–90.

– 'The Manuscript Tradition of Two Middle Irish Leinster Tales.' *Celtica* 18 (1986): 13–33.

– 'A Connacht Medieval Literary Heritage: Texts Derived from Cín Dromma Snechtai through Leabhar na hUidhre.' *CMCS* 16 (Winter 1988): 1–40.

– 'Aided Nath Í and Uí Fhiachrach Genealogies.' *Éigse* 25 (1991): 1–27.

Ó Corráin, Donnchadh. 'Women in Early Irish Society.' In *Women in Irish Society: The Historical Dimension.* Ed. D. Ó Corráin and Margaret MacCurtain. Westport: Greenwood Press, 1979. 1–13.

– 'Irish Law and Canon Law.' In *Irland und Europa: Die Kirche im Frühmittelalter. Ireland and Europe: The Early Church.* Ed. Proinseas Ní Chathain and Michael Richter. Stuttgart: Klett-Cotta, 1984. 157–61.

– 'Marriage in Early Ireland.' In *Marriage in Ireland.* Ed. Art Cosgrove. Dublin: College Press, 1985. 5–24.

– 'Irish Origin Legends and Genealogy: Recurrent Aetiologies.' In *History and Heroic Tale: A Symposium.* Ed. T. Nyberg et al. Odense: University Press, 1985. 51–96.

– 'Historical Need and Literary Narrative.' In *Proceedings of the Seventh International Congress of Celtic Studies Oxford, 1983.* Ed. D. Ellis Evans. Oxford: Oxbow Books, 1986. 141–58.

Ó Cróinín, Dáibhí. 'Donatus. Finit Amen.' Review of *Donat et la tradition de l'enseignement grammatical. Peritia* 2 (1983): 307–11.

O'Duffy, Richard J., ed. and trans. *Oide Cloinne Tuireann: The Fate of the Children of Tuireann.* Dublin: M.H. Gill and Son, 1901.

Ó hAodha, Donncha, ed. and trans. *Bethu Brigte.* Dublin: DIAS, 1978.

O Hehir, Brendan. 'The Christian Revision of *Eachtra Airt meic Cuind ocus Tochmarc Delbchaime Ingine Morgain.*' In *Celtic Folklore and Christianity.* Ed. Patrick Ford. Santa Barbara: McNally & Loftin, 1983. 159–79.

O'Keeffe, J.G., ed. and trans. 'Cuchulinn and Conlaech.' *Ériu* 1 (1904): 123–7.

O'Leary, Philip. 'Contention at Feasts in Early Irish Literature.' *Éigse* 20 (1984): 115–27.

– 'Fír Fer: An Internalized Ethical Concept in Early Irish Literature?' *Éigse* 22 (1987): 1–14.

– 'The Honour of Women in Early Irish Literature.' *Ériu* 38 (1987): 27–44.

– 'Magnanimous Conduct in Irish Heroic Literature.' *Éigse* 25 (1991): 28–44.

Ó Máille, Tomás. 'Medb Chrúachna.' *ZCP* 17 (1928): 129–46.

O'Rahilly, Cecile, ed. & trans. *The Stowe Version of Táin Bó Cuailnge.* Dublin: DIAS, 1961.

– *Táin Bó Cúalnge from the Book of Leinster.* Dublin: DIAS, 1967, repr. 1984.

– *Táin Bó Cúalnge: Recension I.* Dublin: DIAS, 1976.

O'Rahilly, T.F. *Catalogue of Irish Manuscripts in the Royal Irish Academy.* Dublin: Hodges, Figgis, 1926.

– *Early Irish History and Mythology.* Dublin: DIAS, 1946.

Ó Riain, Pádraig. *Corpus Genealogiarum Sanctorum Hiberniae.* Dublin: DIAS, 1985.

Ó Tuama, Seán, ed. and Thomas Kinsella, trans., *An Duanaire 1600–1900: Poems of the Dispossessed*. Philadelphia: University of Pennsylvania Press, 1981.

Olsen, Karin. 'The Cuckold's Revenge: Reconstructing Six Irish *Roscada* in *Táin Bó Cúailgne*.' *Cambrian Medieval Celtic Studies* 28 (Winter 1994): 51–69.

Ong, Walter. *Orality and Literacy: The Technologizing of the Word*. London: Methuen, 1982; rept. 1984.

Ortner, Sherry B. 'Is Female to Male as Nature is to Culture?' In *Woman, Culture and Society*. Ed. Michelle Zimbalist Rosaldo and Louise Lamphere. Stanford: Stanford University Press: 1974. 67–87.

Oskamp, Hans P.A. 'Echtra Condla.' *Études celtiques* 14 (1974–5): 207–28.

Overing, Gillian. *Language, Sign and Gender in Beowulf*. Carbondale: Southern Illinois University Press, 1990.

Plummer, Charles. *Vitae Sanctorum Hiberniae*. 2 vols. Oxford: The Clarendon Press, 1910.

Pratt, Mary Louise. *Toward a Speech Act Theory of Literary Discourse*. Bloomington: Indiana University Press, 1977.

Radner, Joan. 'Fury Destroys the World: Historical Strategy in Ireland's Ulster Epic.' *Mankind Quarterly* 23, no. 1 (Fall 1982): 41–60

– 'Interpreting Irony in Medieval Celtic Narrative: The Case of *Culhwch ac Olwen*.' *CMCS* 16 (Winter 1988): 41–59.

Rees, Alwyn and Brinley. *Celtic Heritage*. London: Thames & Hudson, 1961.

Renoir, Alain. 'A Reading Context for "The Wife's Lament".' In *Anglo-Saxon Poetry: Essays in Appreciation*. Ed. L.E. Nicholson and D.W. Frese. Notre Dame: University of Notre Dame Press, 1975. 114–41.

Ross, Anne. *Pagan Celtic Britain: Studies in Iconography and Tradition*. London: Routledge & Kegan Paul, 1967.

Ross, Margaret Clunies. *Prolonged Echoes: Old Norse Myths in Medieval Northern Society*. Viborg: Odense University Press, 1994.

Salberg, Trond Kruke. 'The Question of the Main Interpolation of H into M's Part of the *Serglige Con Culainn* in the *Book of the Dun Cow* and Some Related Problems.' *ZCP* 45 (1992): 161–81.

Sayers, William. 'Martial Feats in the Old Irish Ulster Cycle.' *Canadian Journal of Irish Studies* 9, no. 1 (1983): 45–80.

– 'Irish Evidence for the *De Harmonia Tonorum* of Wulfstan of Winchester.' *Mediaevalia* 14 (1991): 23–38.

– 'Concepts of Eloquence in "Tochmarc Emire".' *Studia Celtica* 26/27 (1991–2): 125–54.

Searle, John R. *Speech Acts: An Essay on the Philosophy of Language*. Oxford: Oxford University Press, 1971.

– 'What is a Speech Act?' In *The Philosophy of Language*. Ed. John R. Searle. Oxford: Oxford University Press, 1971. 39–53.

– 'A Classification of Illocutionary Acts.' *Language in Society* 5 (1976): 1–23.

Simms, Katharine. 'The Legal Position of Irishwomen in the Later Middle Ages.' *The Irish Jurist* (1975). 96–111.

– *From Kings to Warlords*. Dover, N.H.: Boydell Press, 1987.

– 'The Poet as Chieftain's Widow: Bardic Elegies.' In *Sages, Saints and Storytellers: Celtic Studies in Honour of Professor James Carney*. Ed. Donnchadh Ó Corráin et al. Maynooth: An Sagart, 1989. 400–11.

Sims-Williams, Patrick. 'Gildas and Vernacular Poetry.' In *Gildas: New Approaches*. Eds. Michael Lapidge and David Dumville. London: Boydell Press, 1984.

Sinex, Margaret Ann. 'Irony in Walter Map's *De Nugis Curialium*.' PhD. Dissertation, University of Toronto, 1993.

Sjoestedt, Marie-Louise. *Gods and Heroes of the Celts*. Trans. Myles Dillon. 1940. London: Methuen, 1949.

Slotkin, Edgar. 'Medieval Irish Scribes and Fixed Texts.' *Éigse* 17, pt 4 (1978–9): 437–50.

– 'Folkloristics and Medieval Celtic Philology: A Theoretical Model.' In *Celtic Folklore and Christianity*. Ed. Patrick Ford. Santa Barbara: McNally & Loftin, 1983. 213–25.

Smith, Roland M. 'The *Senbriathra Fithail* and Related Texts.' *Révue celtique* 45 (1928): 1–61.

Stevenson, Jane. 'The Beginnings of Literacy in Ireland.' *PRIA* 89C (1989): 127–65.

Stock, Brian. *The Implications of Literacy*. Princeton: Princeton University Press, 1983.

Stokes, Whitley, ed. and trans. 'The Bodleian Dinnshenchas.' *Folk-Lore* 3 (1892): 467–516.

– 'The Rennes Dindsenchas.' *Révue celtique* 16 (1895): 46–7.

– 'On the Deaths of Some Irish Heroes.' *Révue celtique* 23 (1902): 303–48.

– 'The Colloquy of the Two Sages.' *Révue celtique* 26 (1905): 4–64

– , and John Strachan, eds. *Thesaurus Paleohibernicus*. Vol. 1. Cambridge: Cambridge University Press, 1901.

Straus, Barrie Ruth. 'Women's Words as Weapons: Speech as Action in "The Wife's Lament".' *Texas Studies in Literature and Language* 23, no. 2 (Summer 1981): 268–85.

Thomson, Derek S., ed. *Branwen verch Lyr*. Dublin: DIAS, 1976.

Thomson, R.L., ed. *Pwyll Pendeuic Dyuet*. Dublin: DIAS, 1980.

Thurneysen, Rudolf. *Die irische Helden- und Königsage bis zum 17. Jahrhundert.* Halle: Niemeyer, 1921.

– 'Tochmarc Ailbe "Das Werben um Ailbe".' *ZCP* 13 (1921): 251–82.

– *Scéla Mucce Meic Dathó.* Dublin: DIAS, 1935.

– , et al., eds. *Studies in Early Irish Law.* Dublin: RIA, 1936.

Valente, Roberta. 'Merched Y Mabinogi: Women and the Thematic Structure of the Four Branches.' PhD dissertation, Cornell University, 1986.

– 'Gwydion and Aranrhod: Crossing the Borders of Gender in *Math.*' *Bulletin of the Board of Celtic Studies* 35 (1988): 1–9.

Van Hamel, A.G., ed. *Compert Con Culainn and Other Stories.* Dublin: DIAS, 1956.

Wack, Mary. *Lovesickness in the Middle Ages.* Philadelphia: University of Pennsylvania Press, 1990.

Watkins, Calvert. 'Indo-European Metrics and Archaic Irish Verse.' *Celtica* 6 (1965): 194–249.

Watson, Jeanie. 'Enid the Disobedient: The *Mabinogion*'s *Gereint and Enid.*' In *Ambiguous Realities: Women in the Middle Ages and Renaissance.* Ed. Carol Levin and Jeanie Watson. Detroit: Wayne State University Press, 1987. 114–32.

Windisch, Ernst, ed. *Irische Texte* Vol. I. Leipzig: Verlag Von S. Hirzel, 1880.

Zimmer, Heinrich. 'Keltische studien 5. Über den compilatorischen character der irischen sagentexte im sogenannten Lebor na hUidre.' *Zeitschrift für vergleichende Sprachforschung* 28 (1887). 417–689.

Zumthor, Paul. *Speaking of the Middle Ages.* Trans. Sarah White. Lincoln: University of Nebraska Press, 1986.

Index